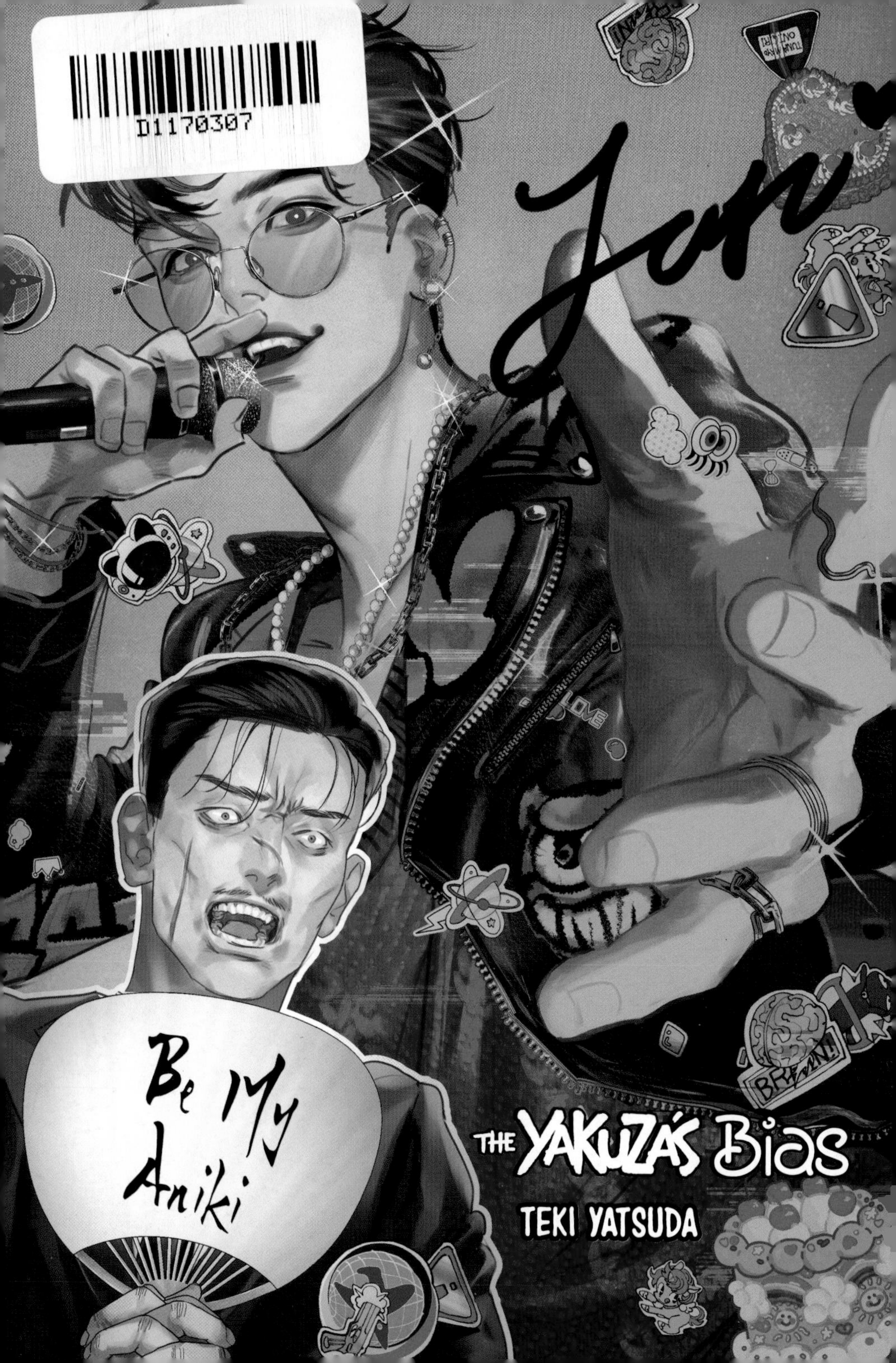
Jun
Be My Aniki
LOVE

THE YAKUZA'S Bias

TEKI YATSUDA

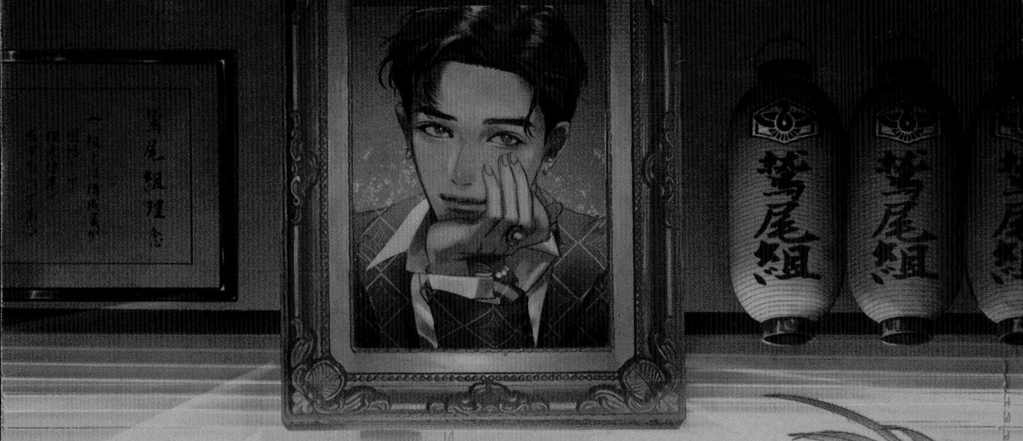
鷲尾組
鷲尾組

CONTENTS

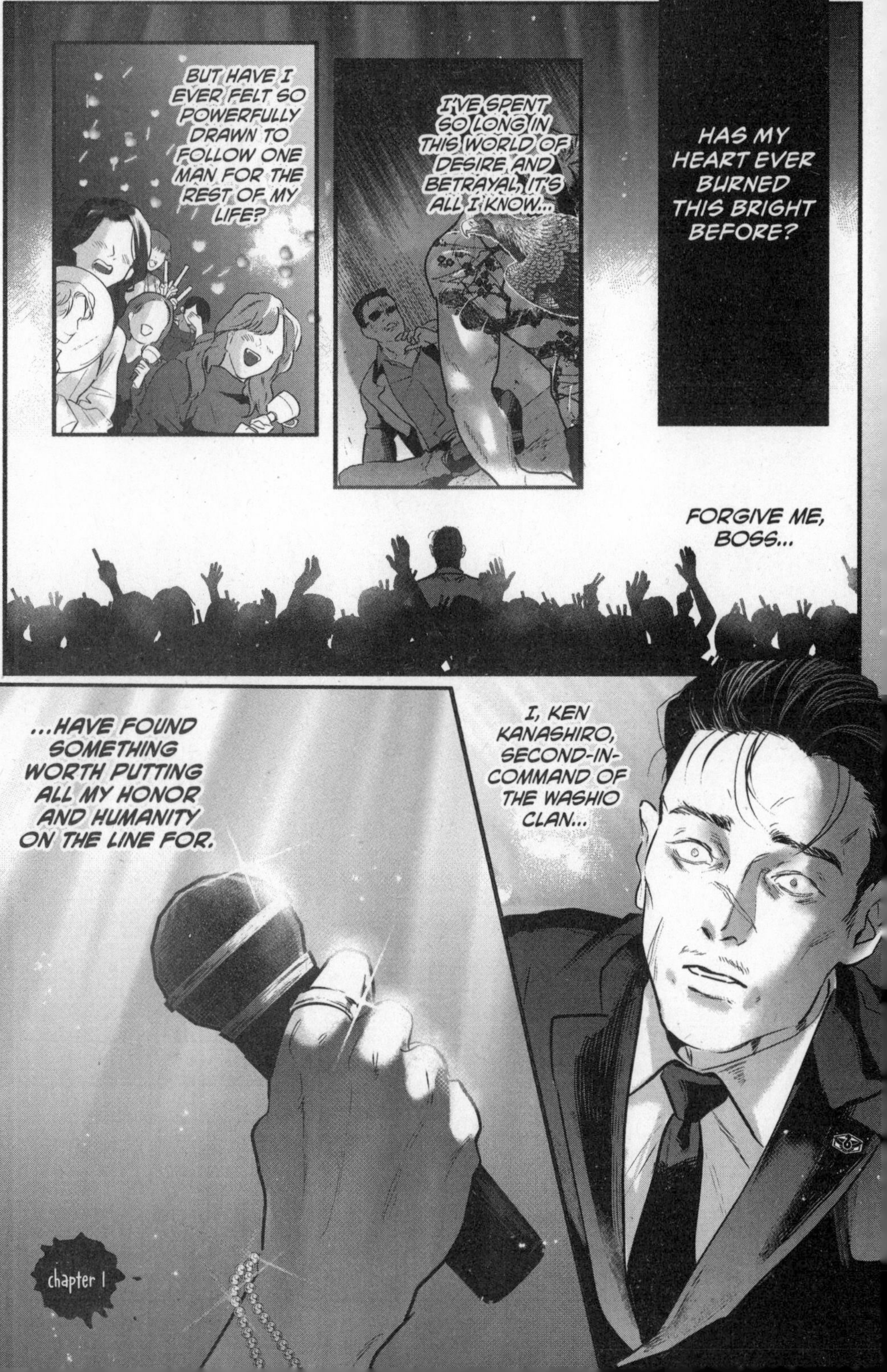
HAS MY HEART EVER BURNED THIS BRIGHT BEFORE?
I'VE SPENT SO LONG IN THIS WORLD OF DESIRE AND BETRAYAL, IT'S ALL I KNOW...
BUT HAVE I EVER FELT SO POWERFULLY DRAWN TO FOLLOW ONE MAN FOR THE REST OF MY LIFE?
FORGIVE ME, BOSS...
I, KEN KANASHIRO, SECOND-IN-COMMAND OF THE WASHIO CLAN...
...HAVE FOUND SOMETHING WORTH PUTTING ALL MY HONOR AND HUMANITY ON THE LINE FOR.
chapter 1

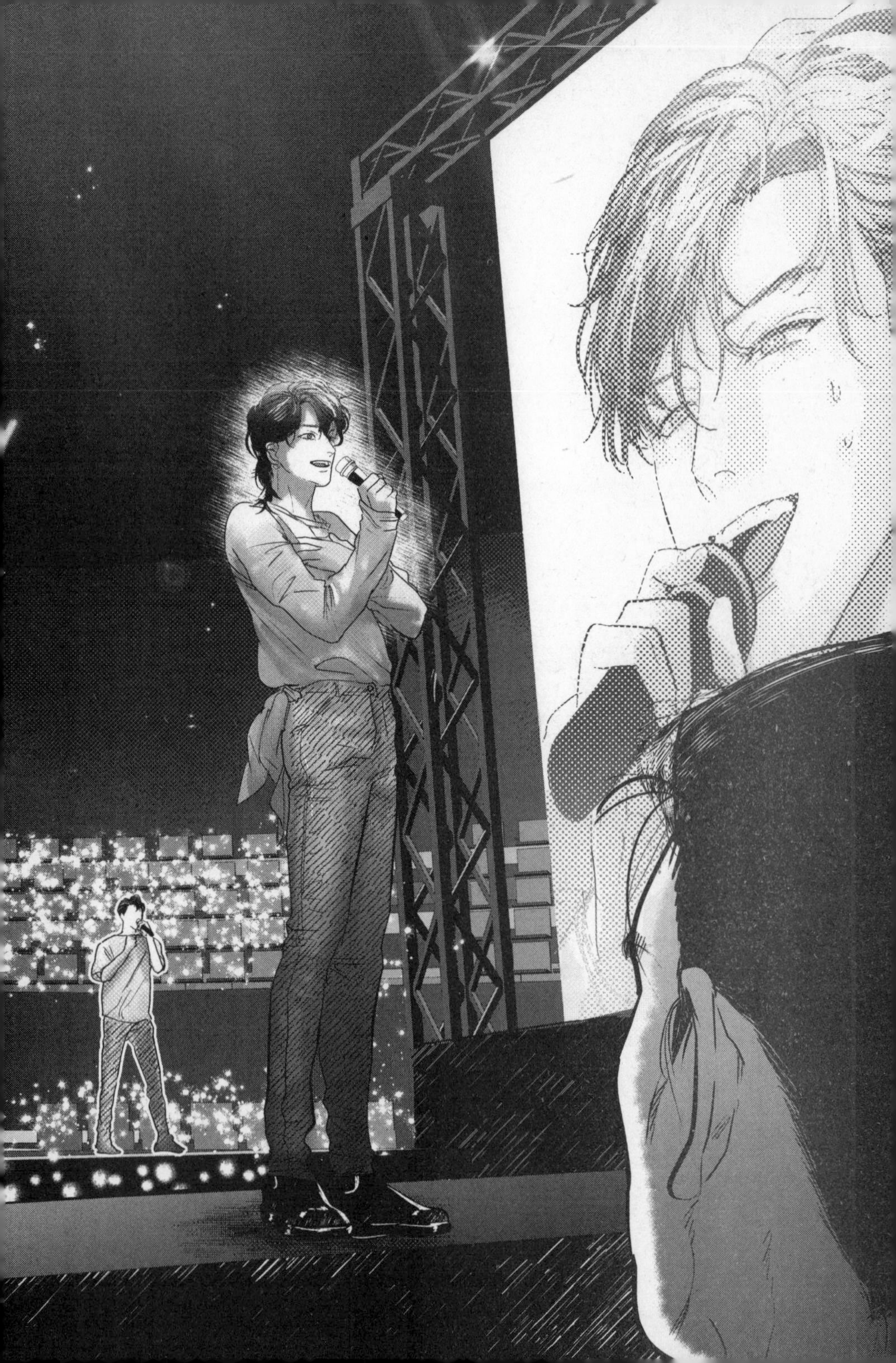

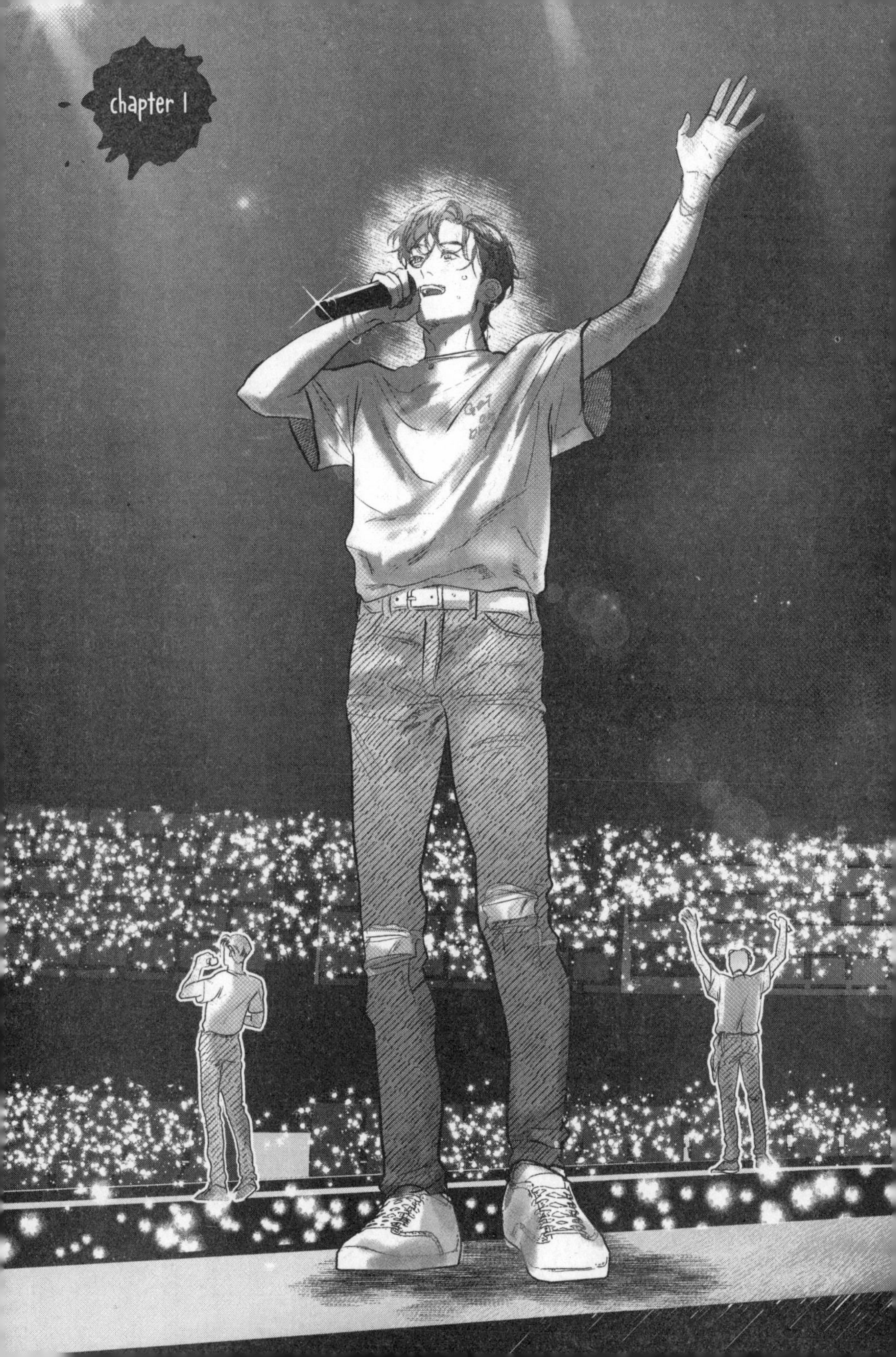
chapter 1

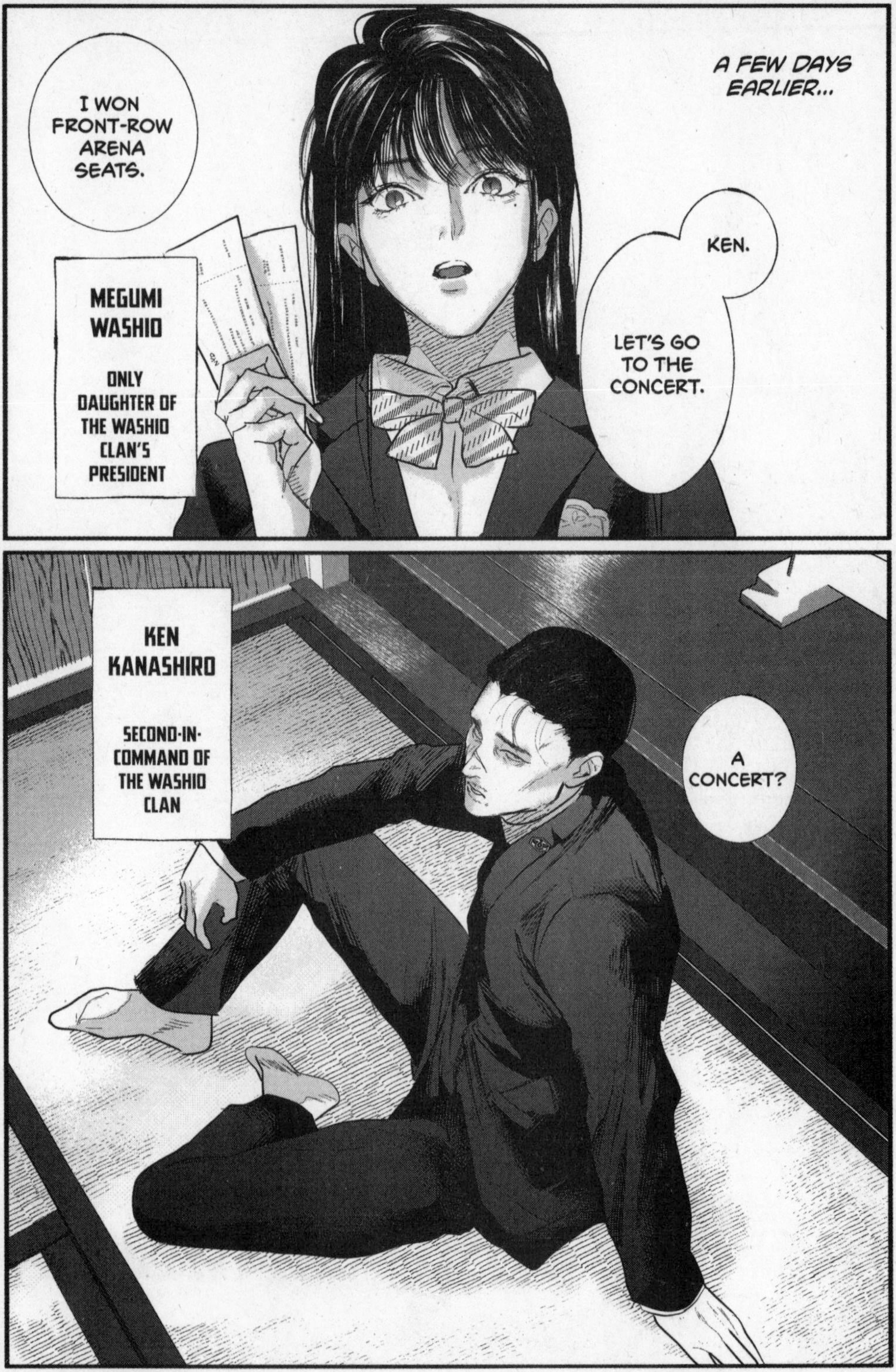
A FEW DAYS EARLIER...
KEN.
LET'S GO TO THE CONCERT.
MEGUMI WASHIO
ONLY DAUGHTER OF THE WASHIO CLAN'S PRESIDENT
I WON FRONT-ROW ARENA SEATS.
A CONCERT?
KEN KANASHIRO
SECOND-IN-COMMAND OF THE WASHIO CLAN

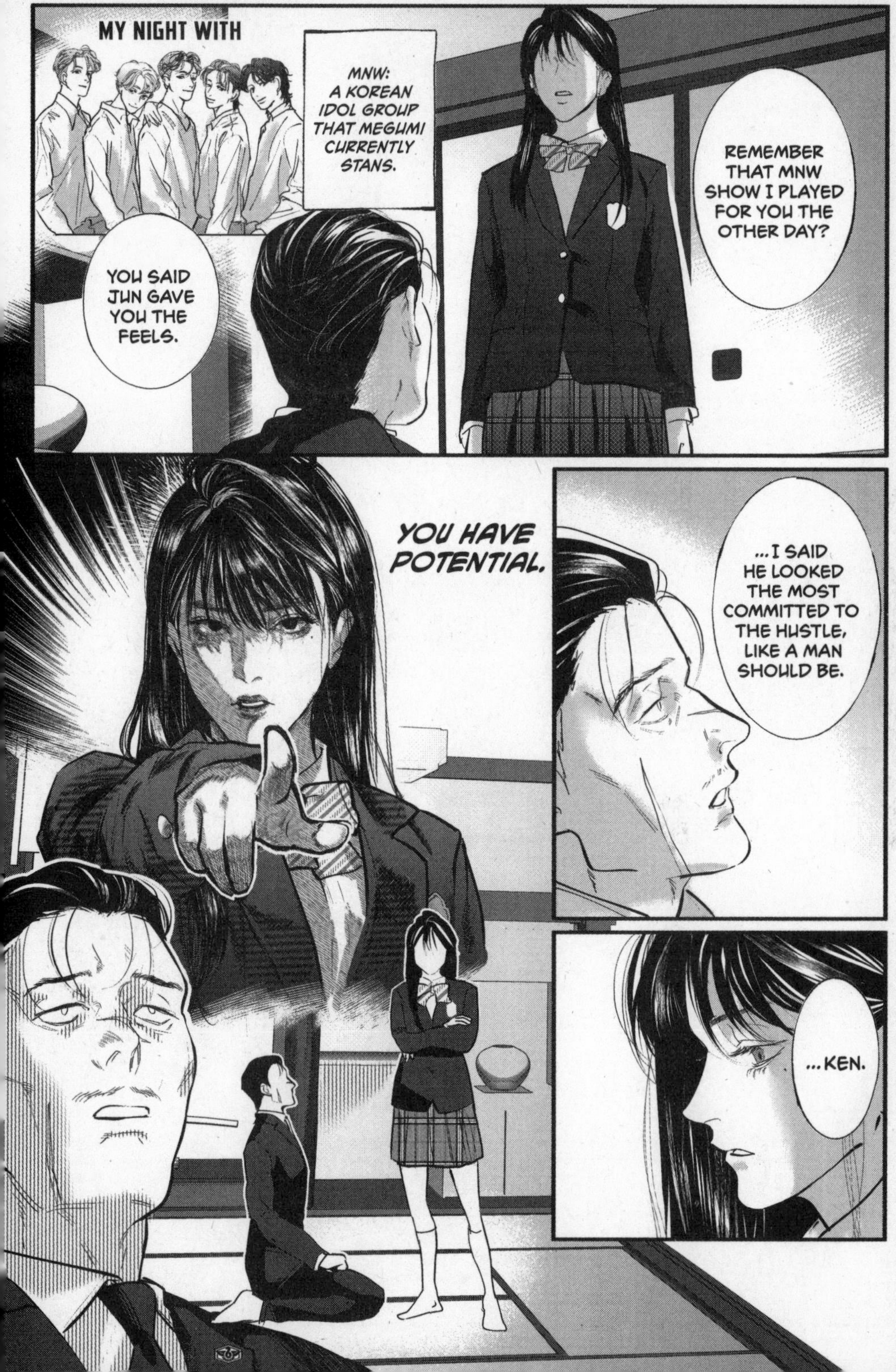
REMEMBER THAT MNW SHOW I PLAYED FOR YOU THE OTHER DAY?
MY NIGHT WITH
MNW: A KOREAN IDOL GROUP THAT MEGUMI CURRENTLY STANS.
YOU SAID JUN GAVE YOU THE FEELS.
...I SAID HE LOOKED THE MOST COMMITTED TO THE HUSTLE, LIKE A MAN SHOULD BE.
...KEN.
YOU HAVE POTENTIAL.

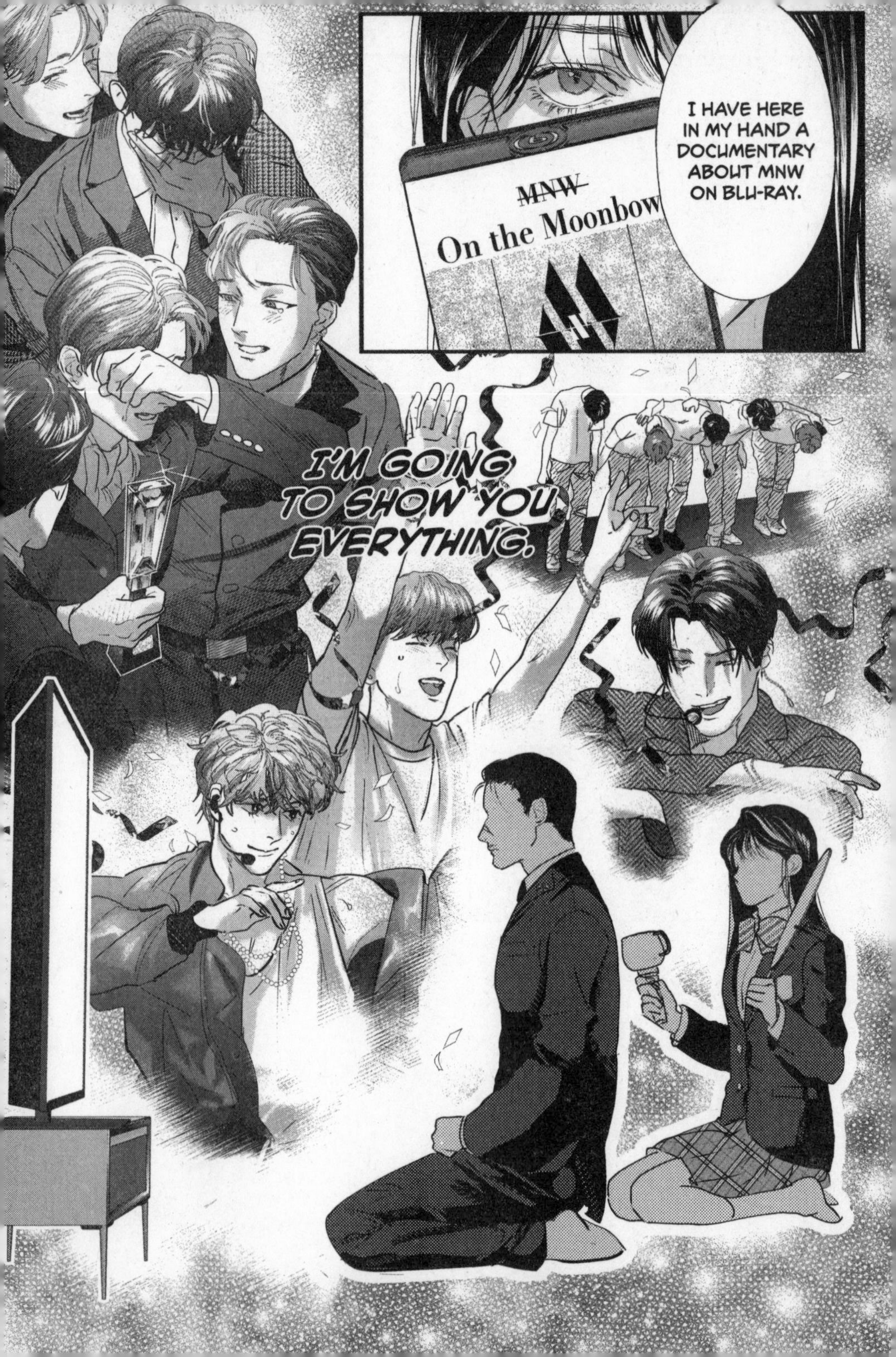
I HAVE HERE IN MY HAND A DOCUMENTARY ABOUT MNW ON BLU-RAY.
MNW
On the Moonbow
I'M GOING TO SHOW YOU EVERYTHING.

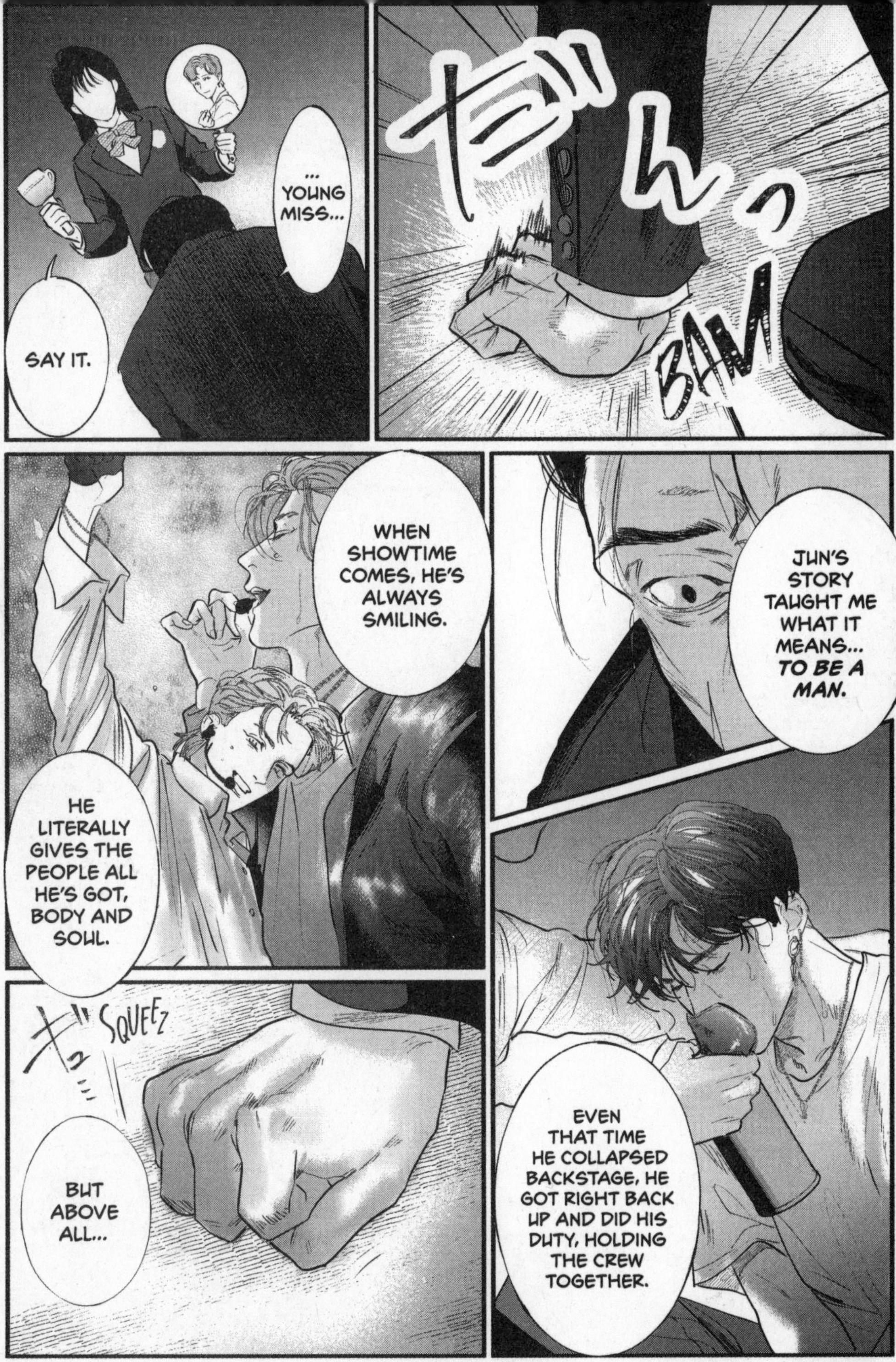
だんっ
BAM
... YOUNG MISS...
SAY IT.
JUN'S STORY TAUGHT ME WHAT IT MEANS... *TO BE A MAN.*
WHEN SHOWTIME COMES, HE'S ALWAYS SMILING.
HE LITERALLY GIVES THE PEOPLE ALL HE'S GOT, BODY AND SOUL.
EVEN THAT TIME HE COLLAPSED BACKSTAGE, HE GOT RIGHT BACK UP AND DID HIS DUTY, HOLDING THE CREW TOGETHER.
ギュッ
SQUEEZ
BUT ABOVE ALL...

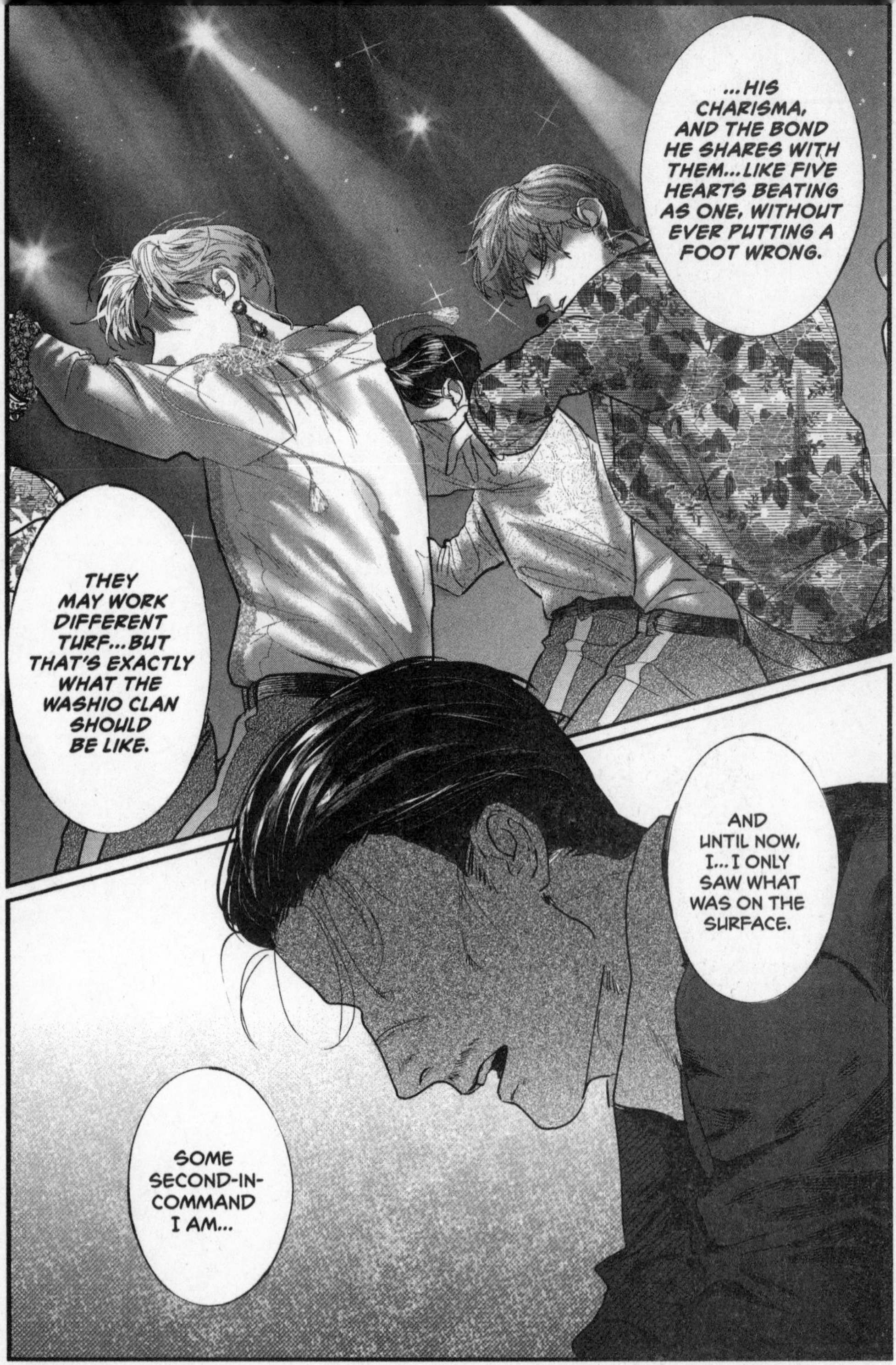
...HIS CHARISMA, AND THE BOND HE SHARES WITH THEM...LIKE FIVE HEARTS BEATING AS ONE, WITHOUT EVER PUTTING A FOOT WRONG.
THEY MAY WORK DIFFERENT TURF...BUT THAT'S EXACTLY WHAT THE WASHIO CLAN SHOULD BE LIKE.
AND UNTIL NOW, I...I ONLY SAW WHAT WAS ON THE SURFACE.
SOME SECOND-IN-COMMAND I AM...

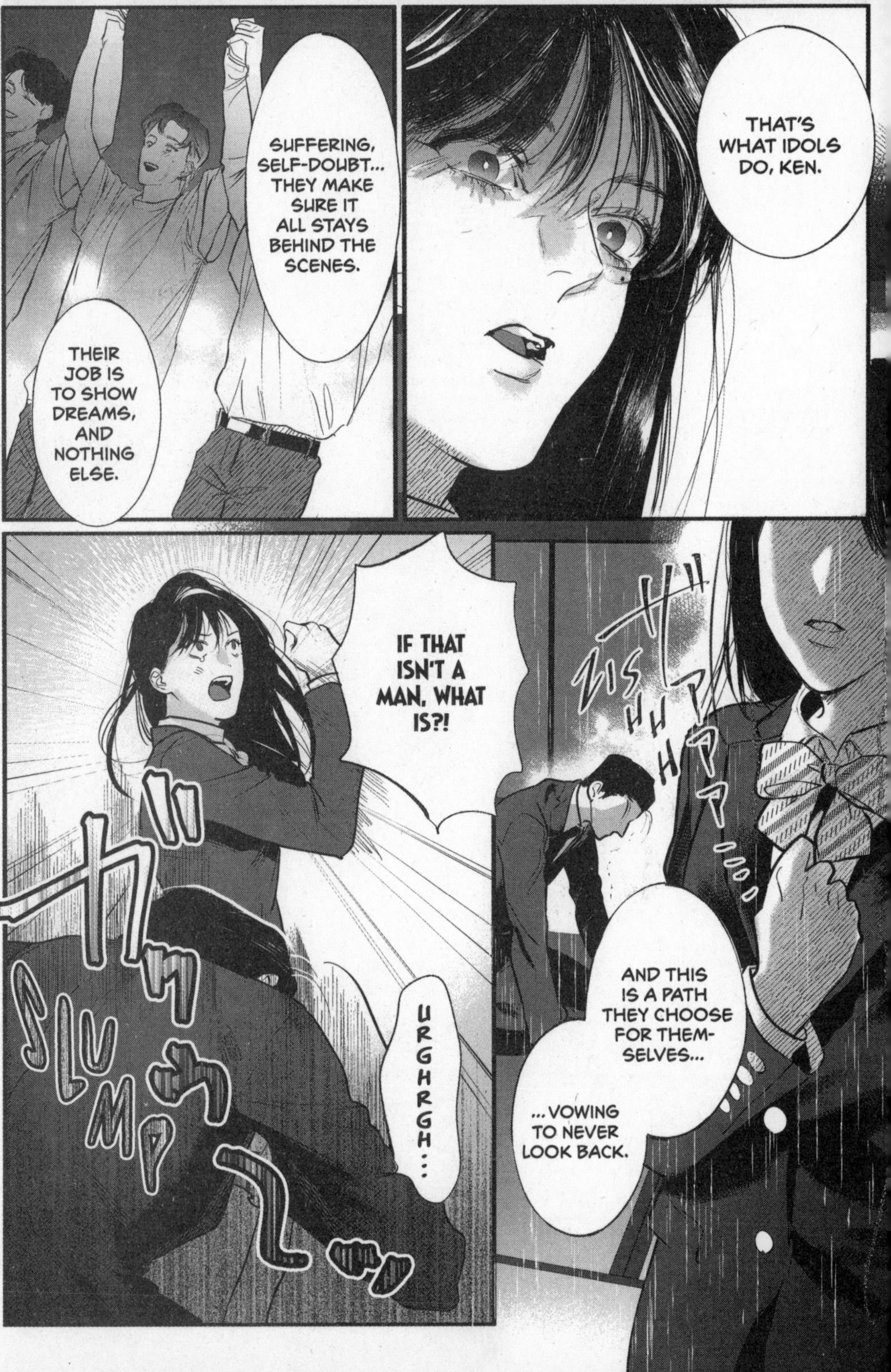
THAT'S WHAT IDOLS DO, KEN.
SUFFERING, SELF-DOUBT... THEY MAKE SURE IT ALL STAYS BEHIND THE SCENES.
THEIR JOB IS TO SHOW DREAMS, AND NOTHING ELSE.
ZISHHH
AND THIS IS A PATH THEY CHOOSE FOR THEM-SELVES...
...VOWING TO NEVER LOOK BACK.
IF THAT ISN'T A MAN, WHAT IS?!
URGHRGH...
SLUMP

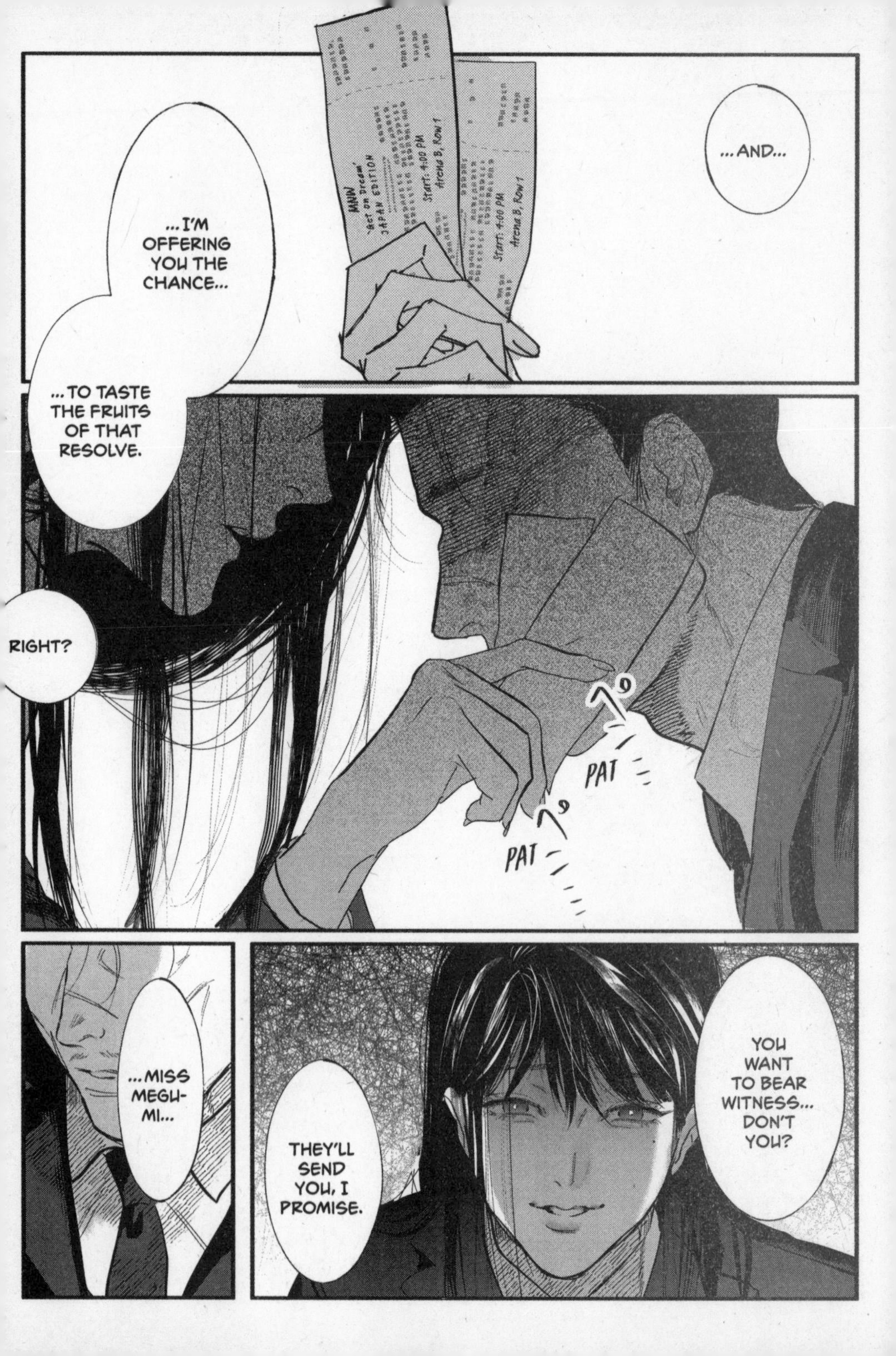
...AND...
...I'M OFFERING YOU THE CHANCE...
...TO TASTE THE FRUITS OF THAT RESOLVE.
Start: 4:00 PM
Arena B, Row 1
RIGHT?
PAT
PAT
YOU WANT TO BEAR WITNESS... DON'T YOU?
THEY'LL SEND YOU, I PROMISE.
...MISS MEGUMI...

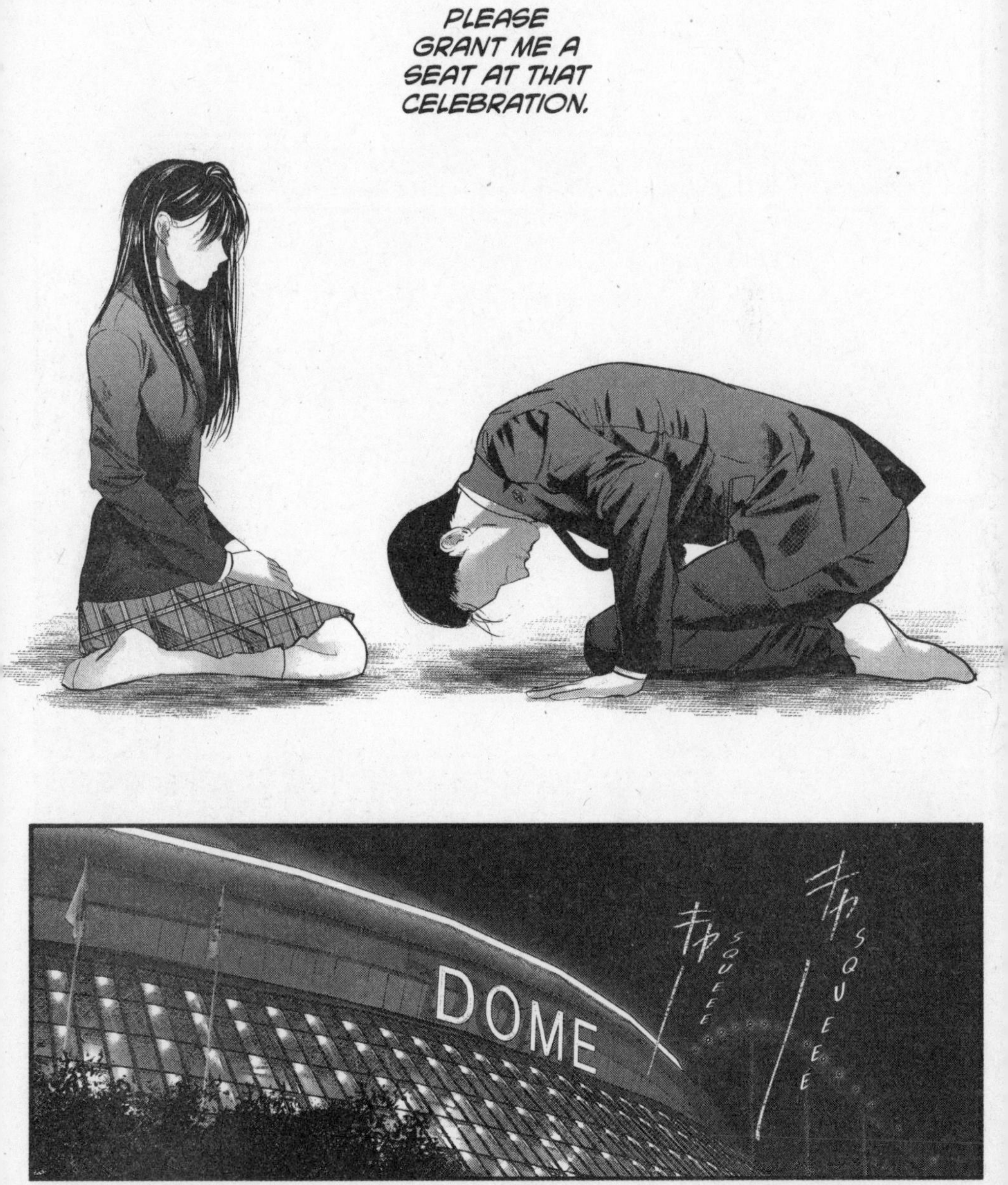
PLEASE GRANT ME A SEAT AT THAT CELEBRATION.
SQUEEE
SQUEEE
DOME

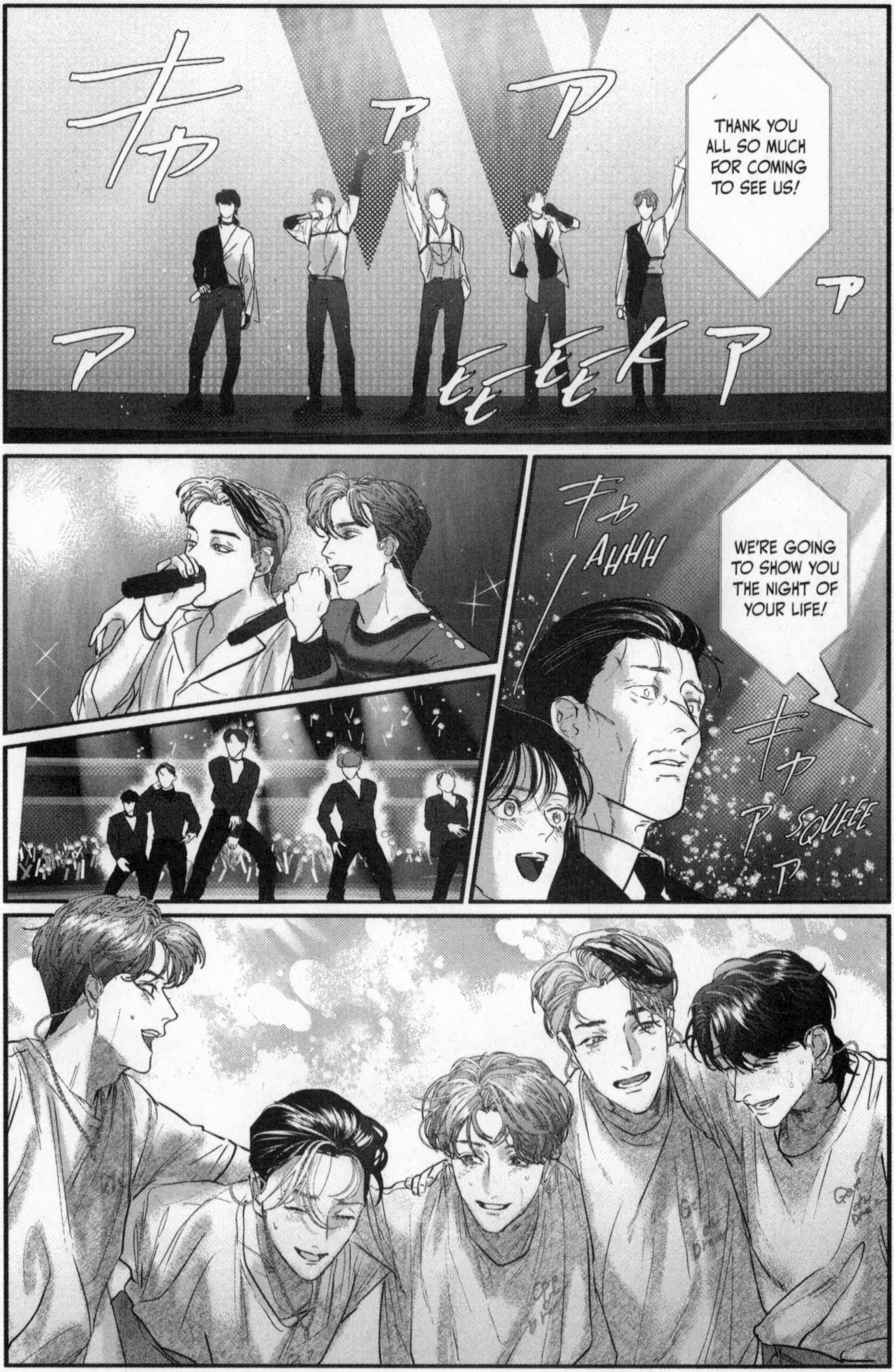
THANK YOU ALL SO MUCH FOR COMING TO SEE US!
AHHH
WE'RE GOING TO SHOW YOU THE NIGHT OF YOUR LIFE!
SQUEEEE

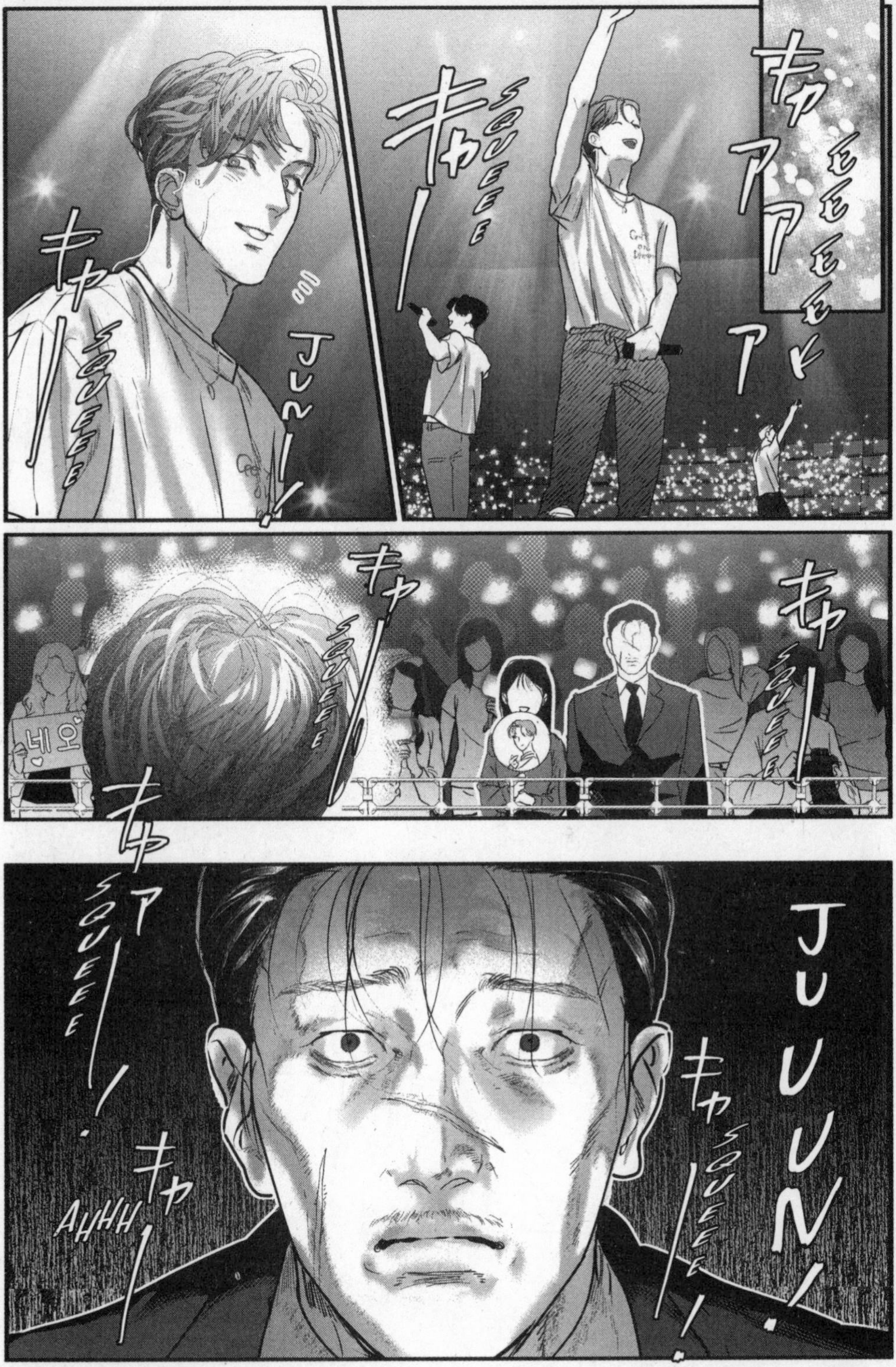

キャアアア
EEEEEK
キャー
SQUEEEE
キャー
SQUEEEE
JUN!
キャー
SQUEEEE
キャー
SQUEEE
네오
JUUUN!
キャ
SQUEEEE!
キャアー!
SQUEEEE
キャー
AHHH

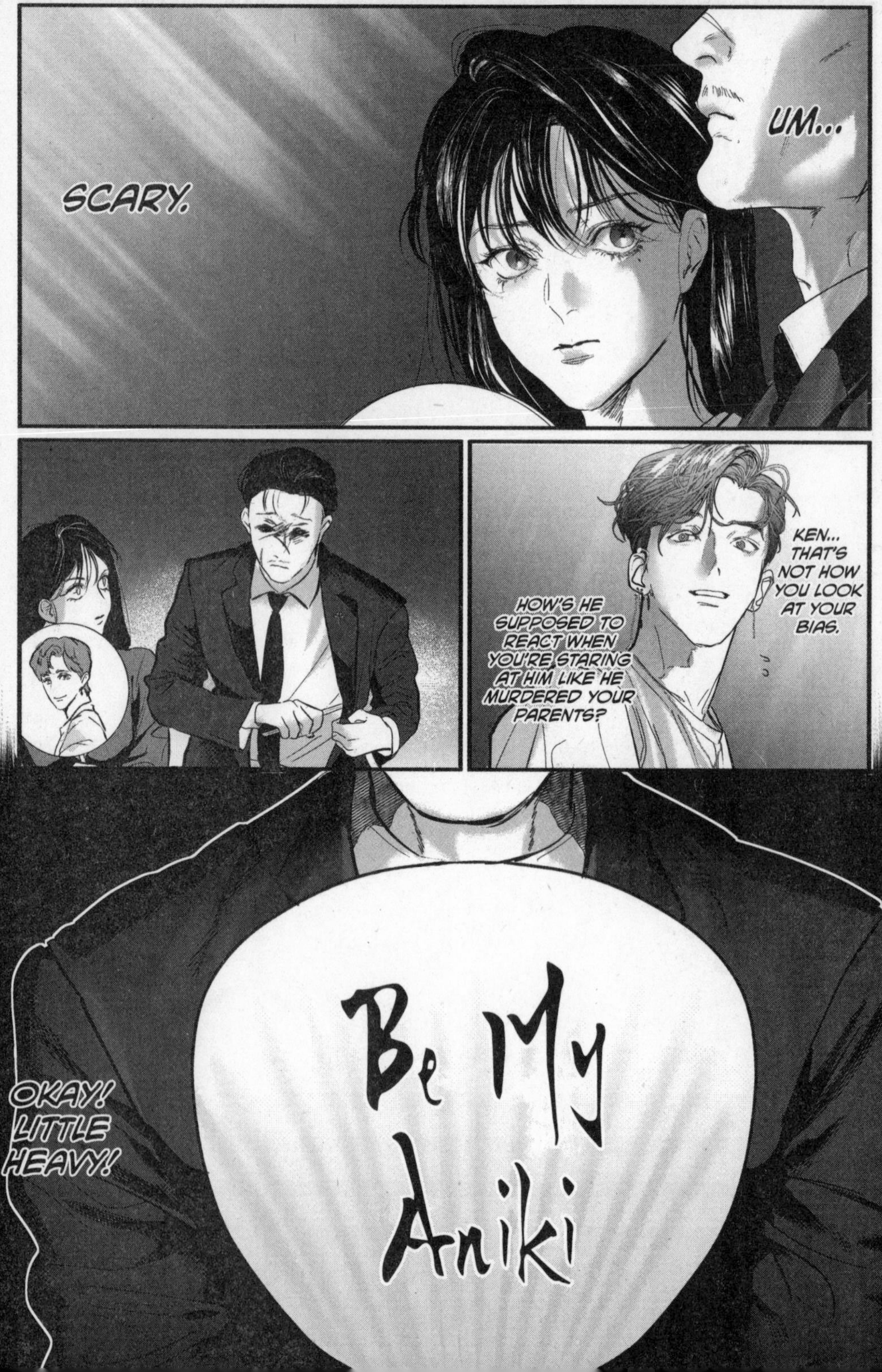
UM...
SCARY.
KEN... THAT'S NOT HOW YOU LOOK AT YOUR BIAS.
HOW'S HE SUPPOSED TO REACT WHEN YOU'RE STARING AT HIM LIKE HE MURDERED YOUR PARENTS?
Be My Aniki
OKAY! LITTLE HEAVY!

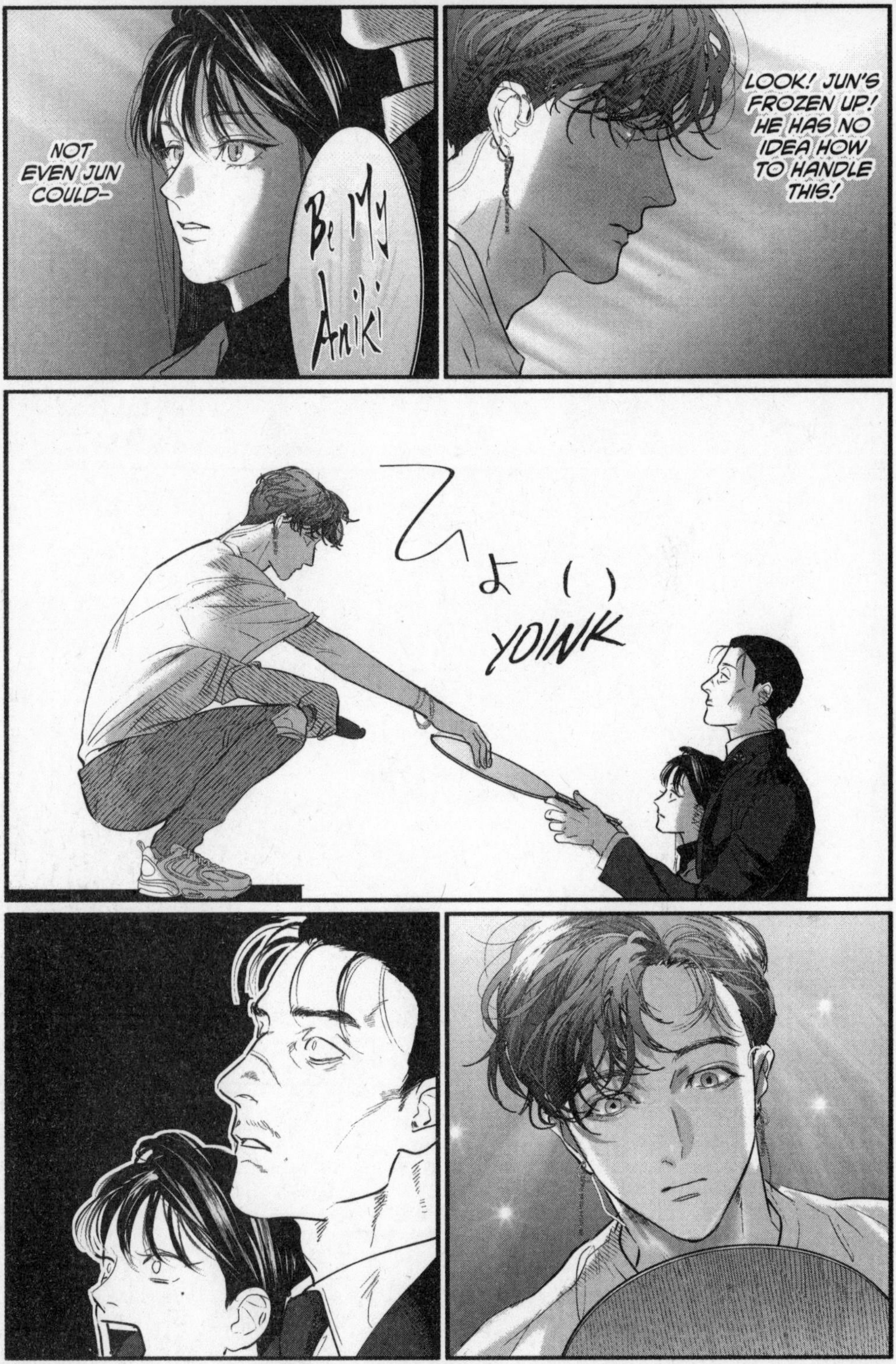
LOOK! JUN'S FROZEN UP! HE HAS NO IDEA HOW TO HANDLE THIS!
NOT EVEN JUN COULD–
Be My Aniki
ひょい
YOINK

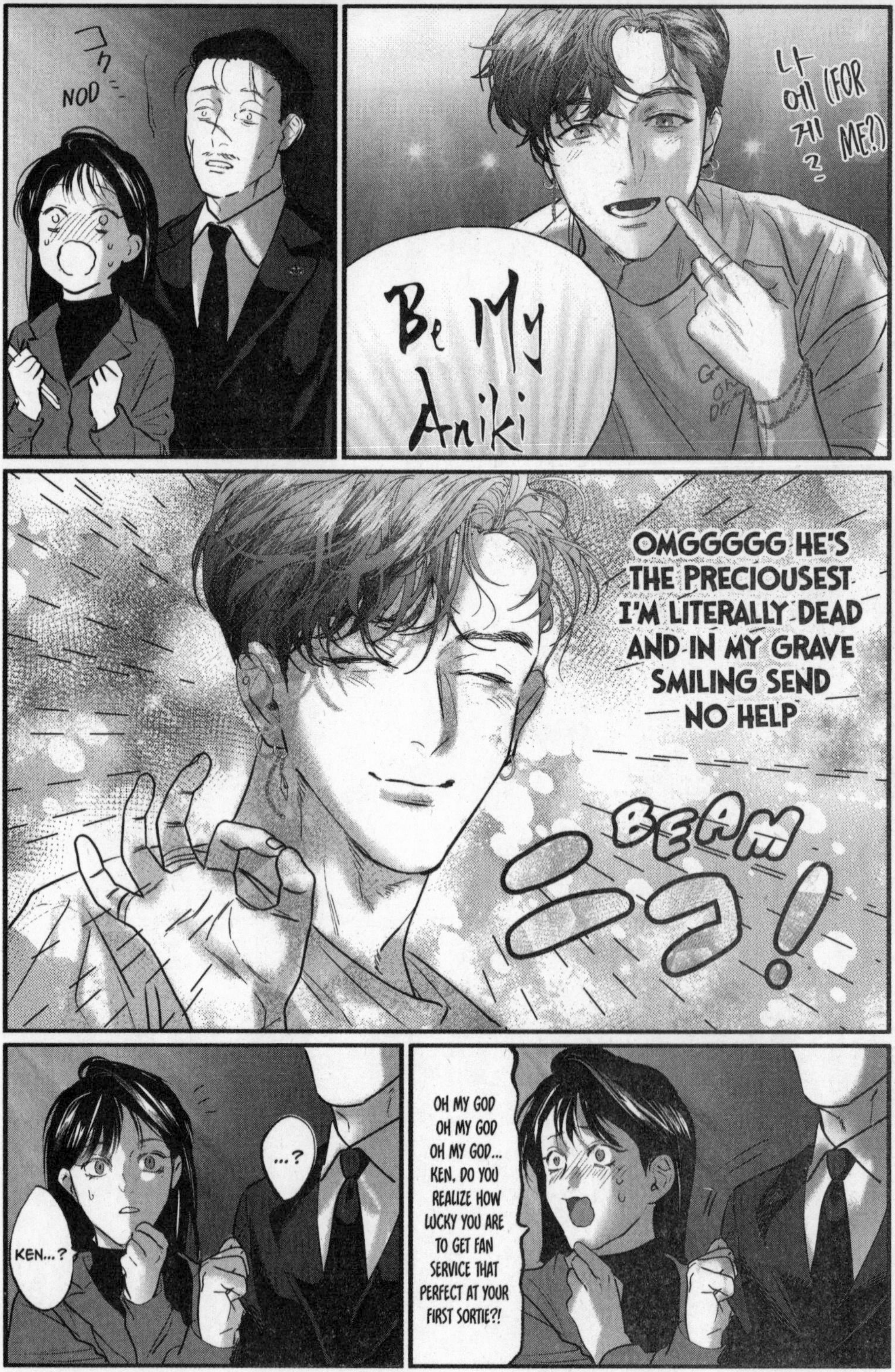
나에게?
(FOR ME?)
Be My Aniki
コク
NOD
OMGGGGG HE'S THE PRECIOUSEST I'M LITERALLY DEAD AND IN MY GRAVE SMILING SEND NO HELP
BEAM
ニコ!
OH MY GOD OH MY GOD OH MY GOD... KEN, DO YOU REALIZE HOW LUCKY YOU ARE TO GET FAN SERVICE THAT PERFECT AT YOUR FIRST SORTIE?!
...?
KEN...?

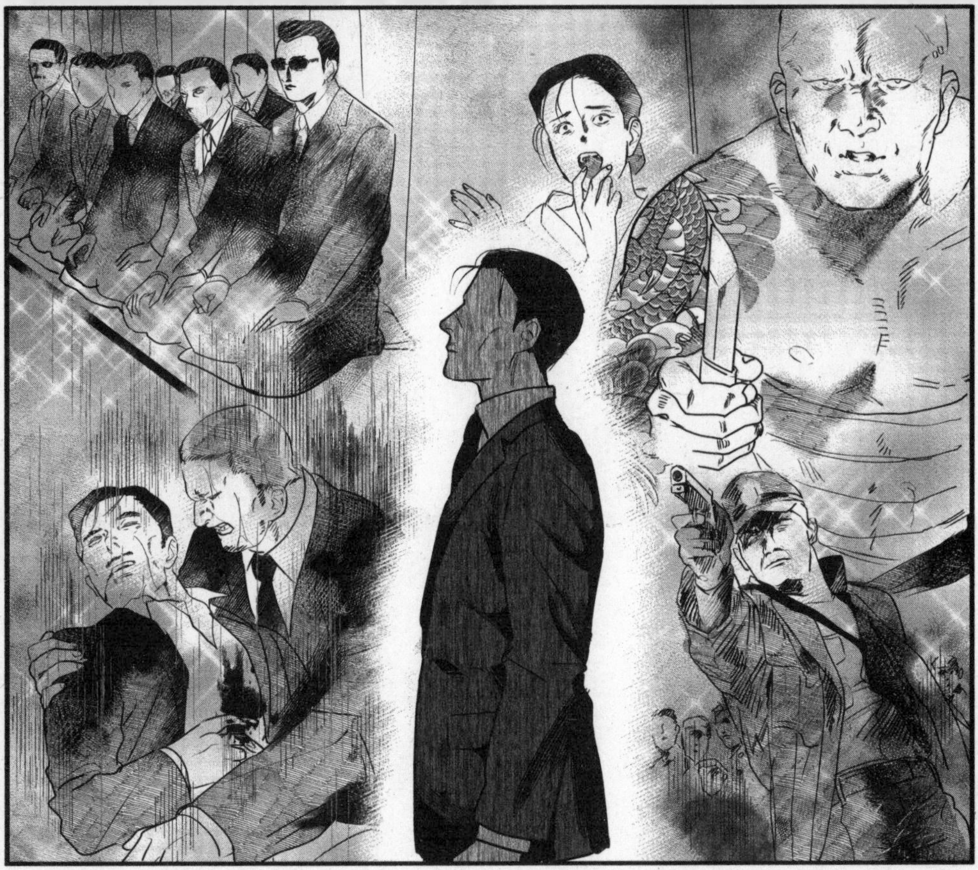
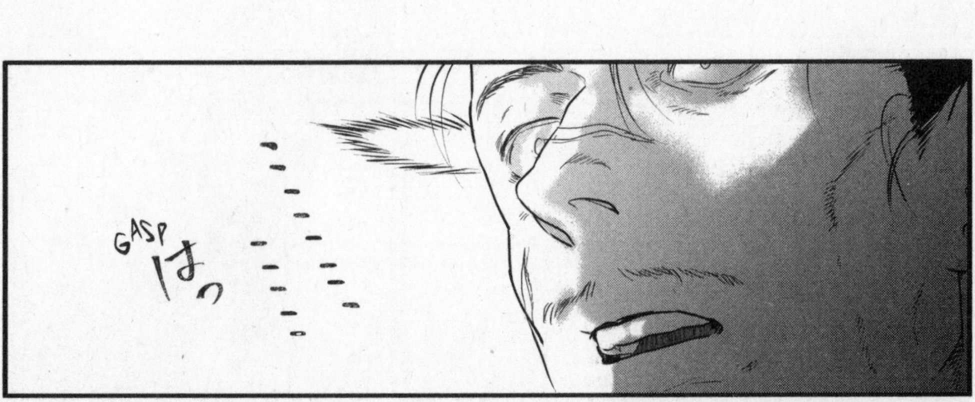
GASP
はっ

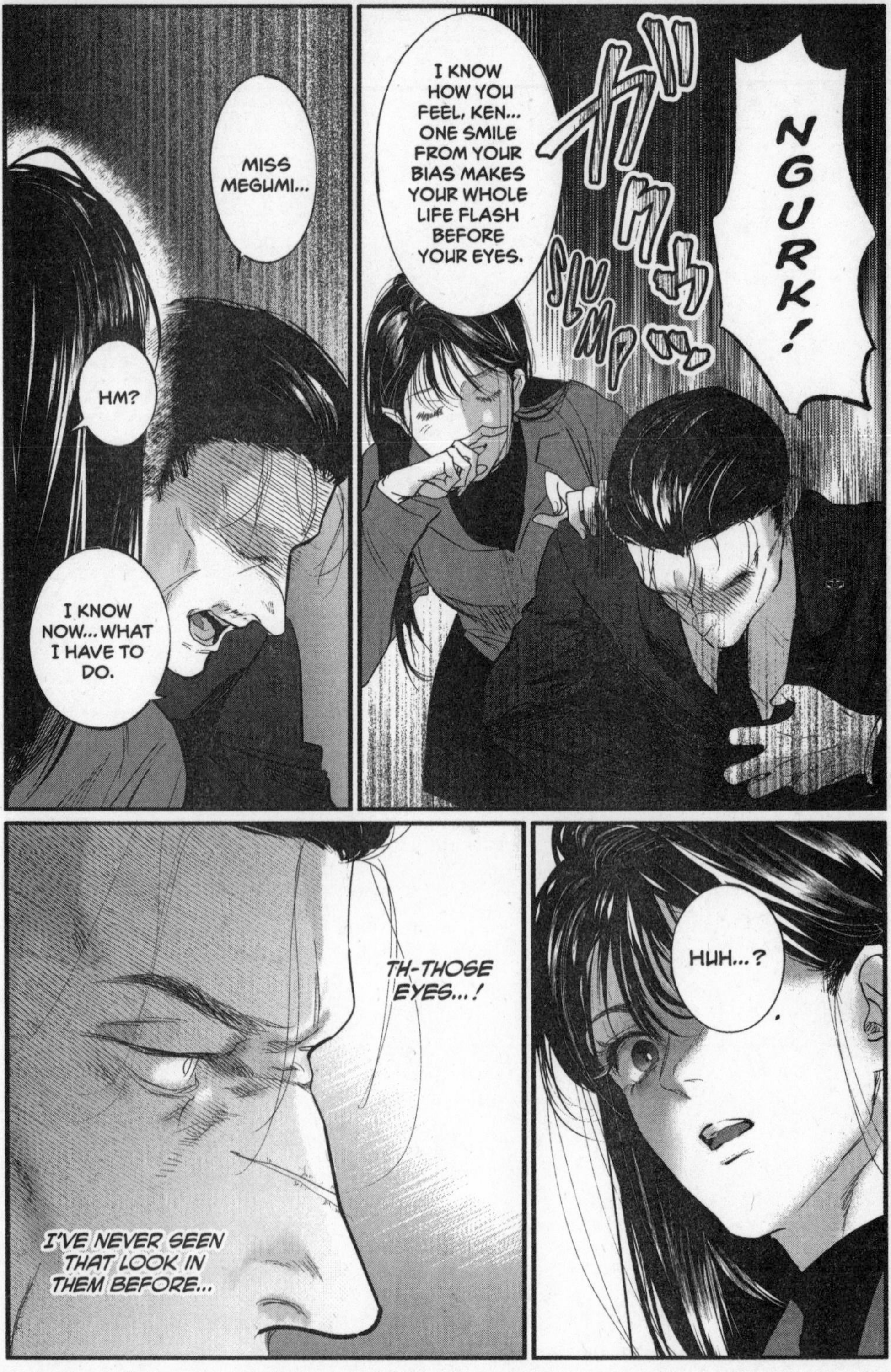
NGURK!
I KNOW HOW YOU FEEL, KEN... ONE SMILE FROM YOUR BIAS MAKES YOUR WHOLE LIFE FLASH BEFORE YOUR EYES.
SLUMP
MISS MEGUMI...
HM?
I KNOW NOW... WHAT I HAVE TO DO.
HUH...?
TH-THOSE EYES...!
I'VE NEVER SEEN THAT LOOK IN THEM BEFORE...

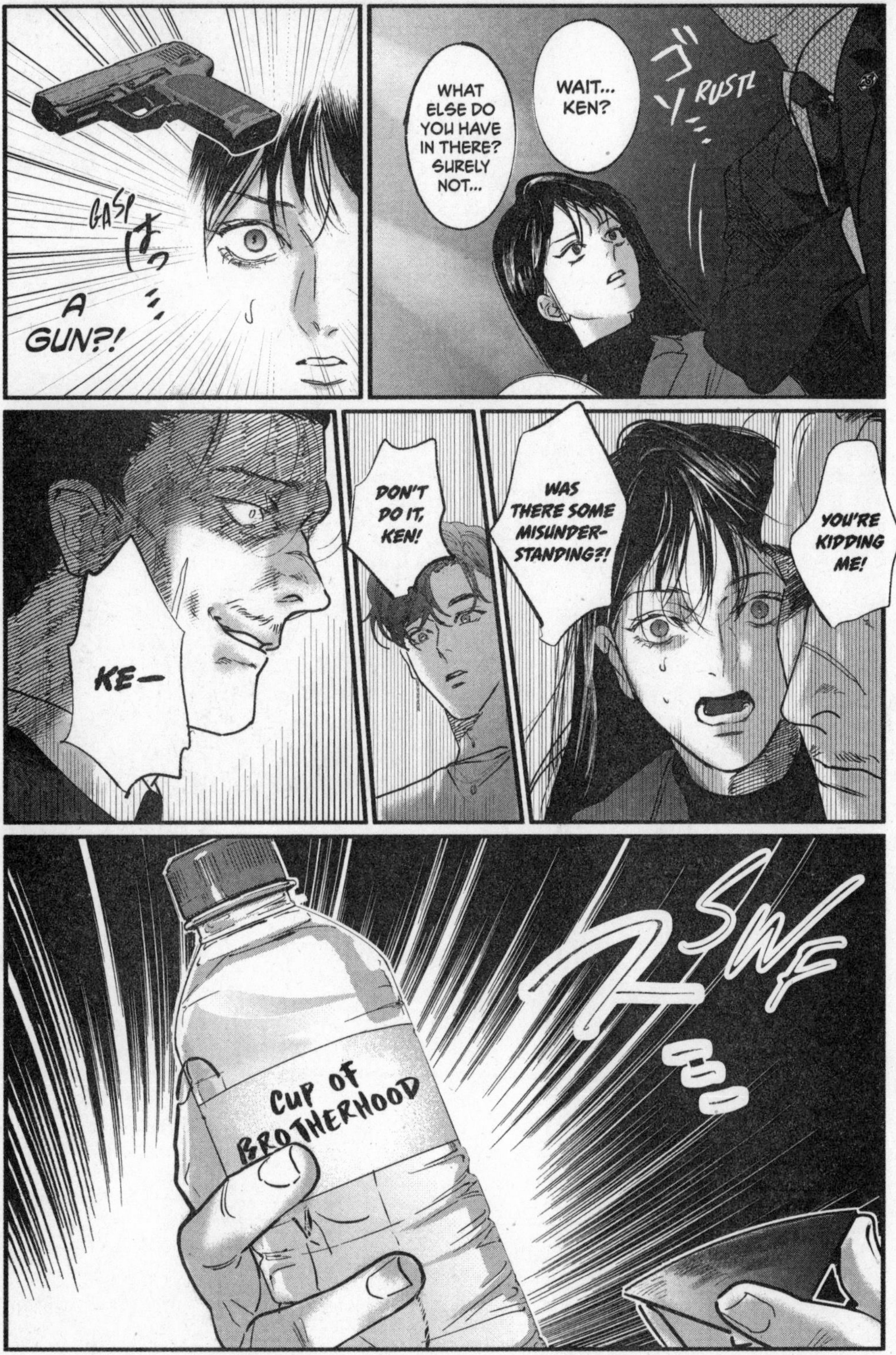
RUSTL
WAIT... KEN?
WHAT ELSE DO YOU HAVE IN THERE? SURELY NOT...
GASP
A GUN?!
YOU'RE KIDDING ME!
WAS THERE SOME MISUNDER-STANDING?!
DON'T DO IT, KEN!
KE—
SWF
CUP OF BROTHERHOOD

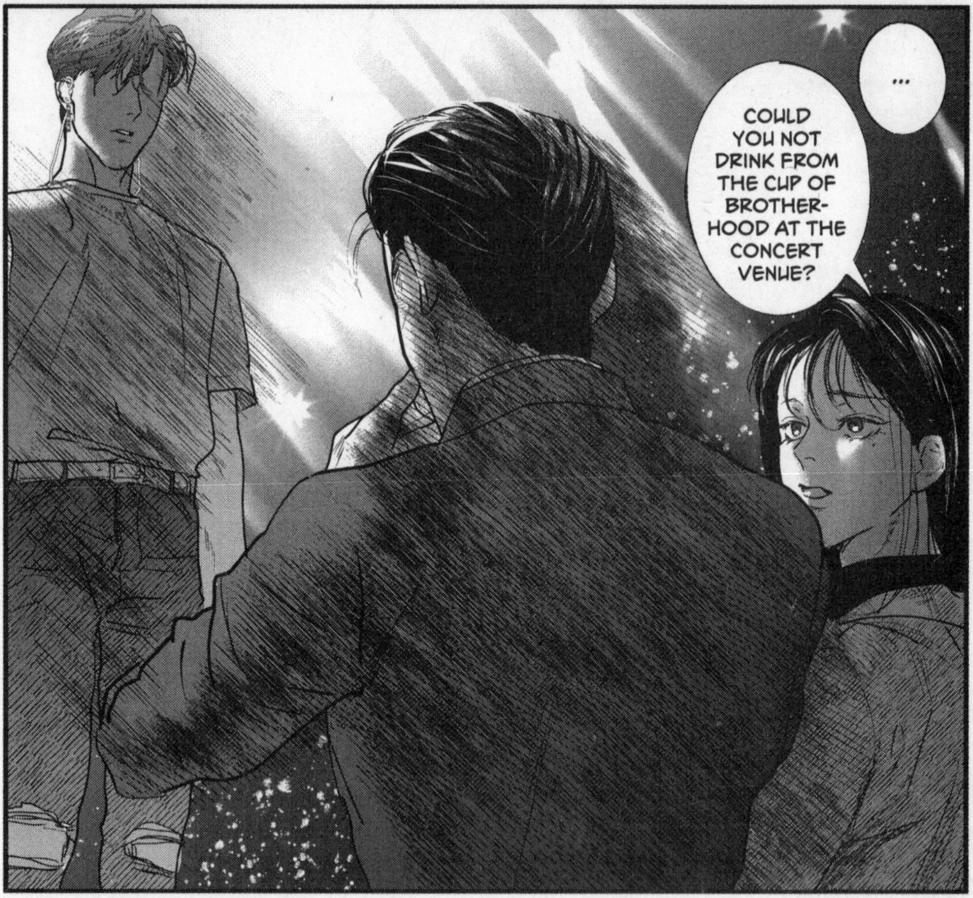
...
COULD YOU NOT DRINK FROM THE CUP OF BROTHER-HOOD AT THE CONCERT VENUE?

*Cheers: Name for MNW fans

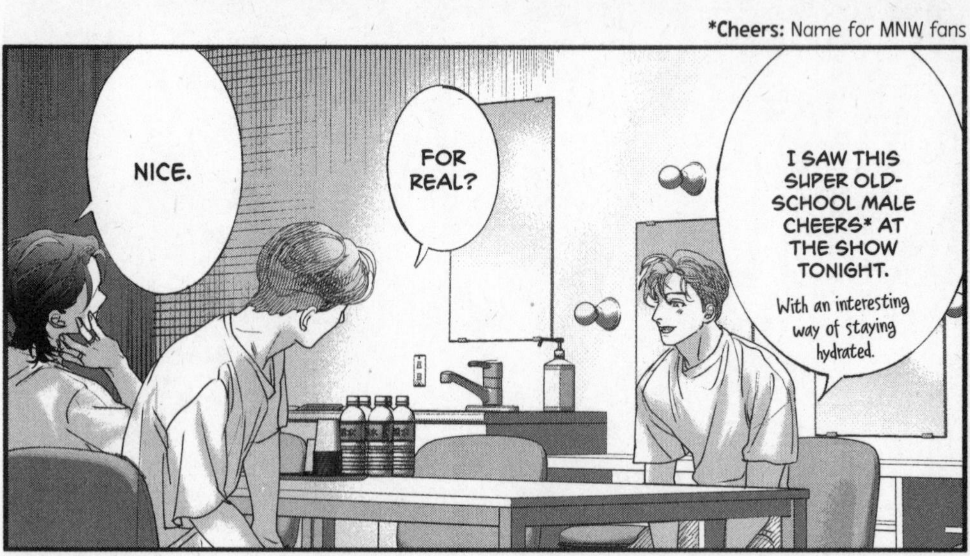
I SAW THIS SUPER OLD-SCHOOL MALE CHEERS* AT THE SHOW TONIGHT.
With an interesting way of staying hydrated.
FOR REAL?
NICE.

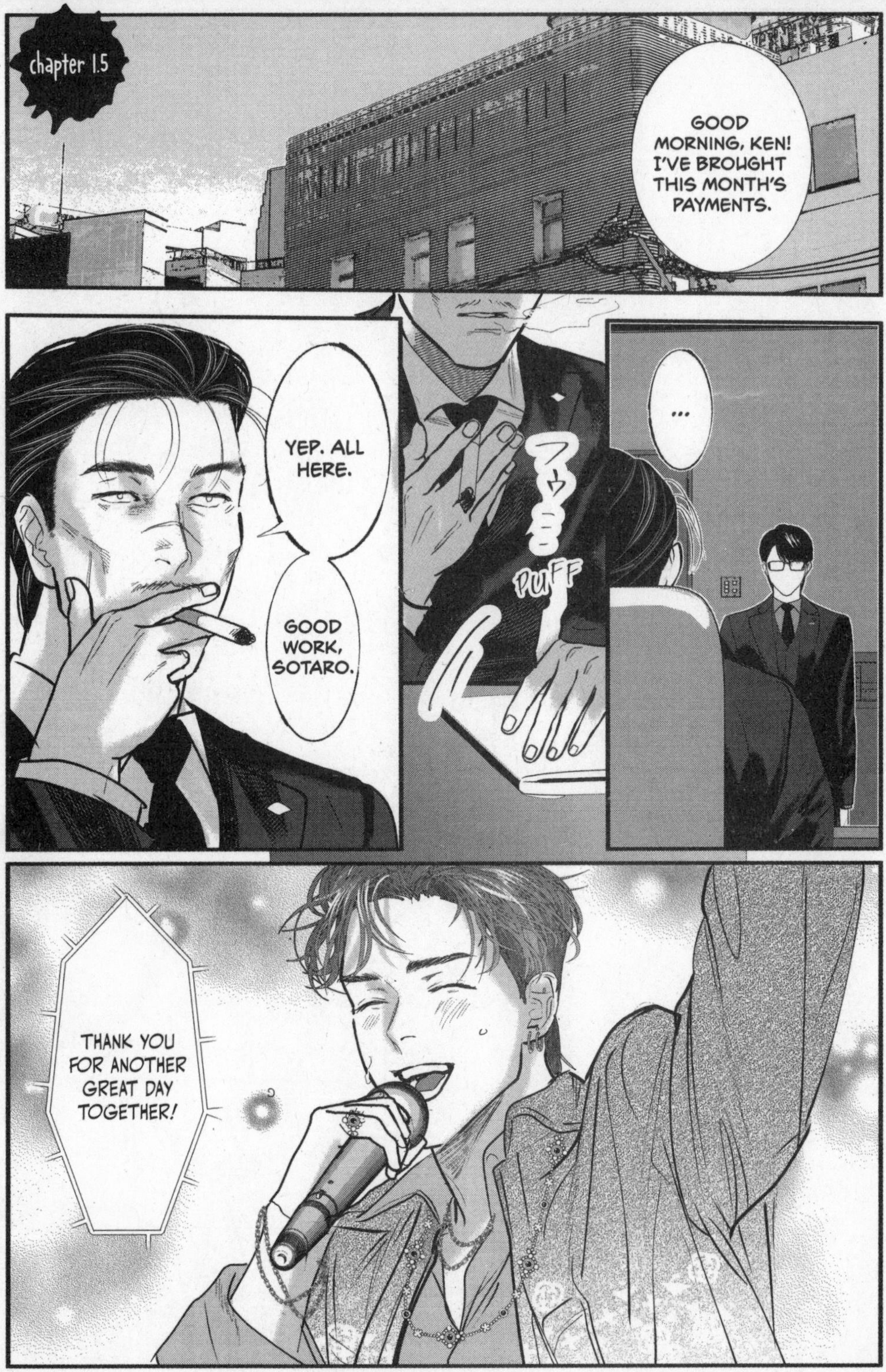
chapter 1.5
GOOD MORNING, KEN! I'VE BROUGHT THIS MONTH'S PAYMENTS.
...
フゥー
PUFF
YEP. ALL HERE.
GOOD WORK, SOTARO.
THANK YOU FOR ANOTHER GREAT DAY TOGETHER!

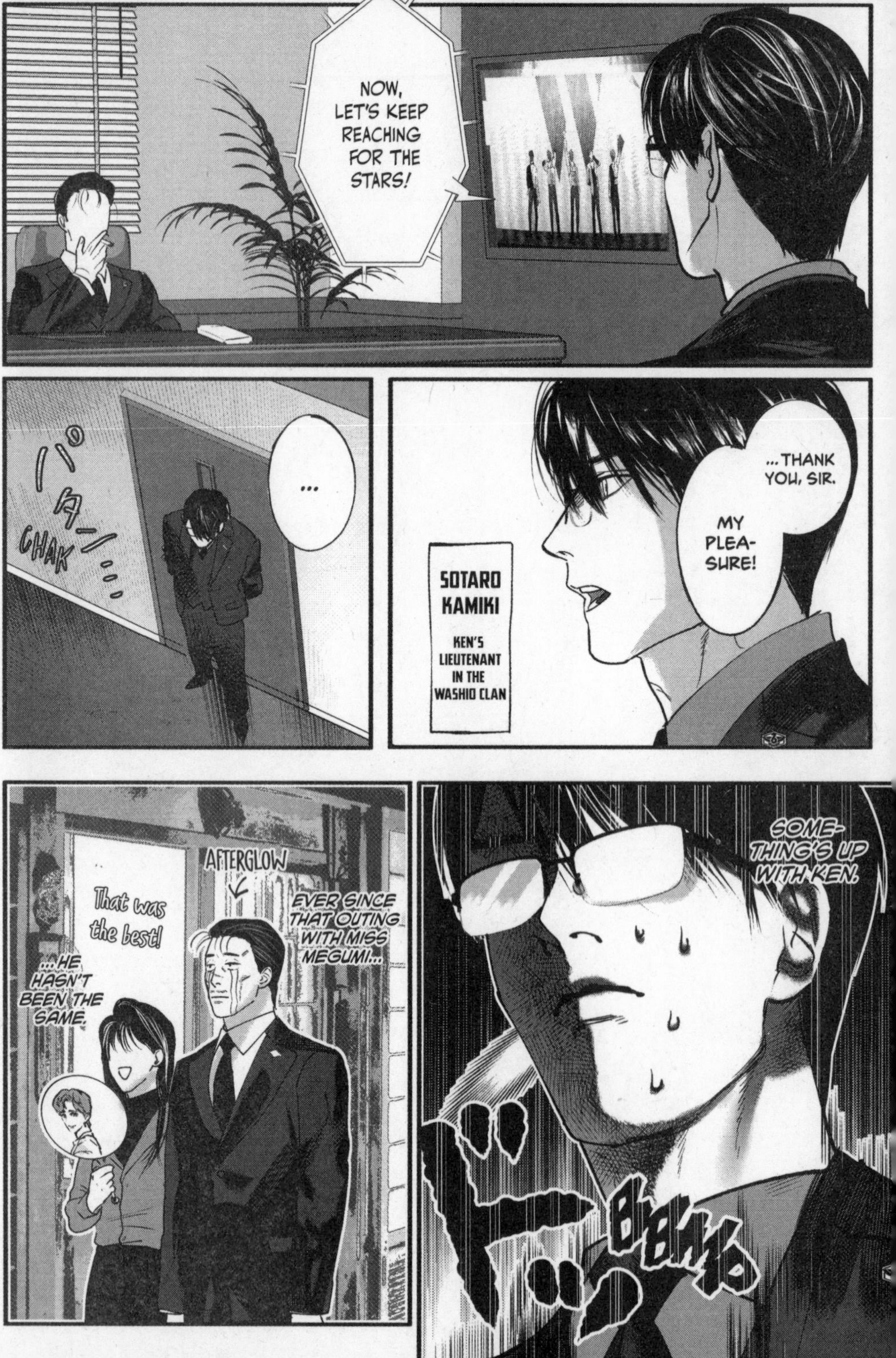
NOW, LET'S KEEP REACHING FOR THE STARS!
...THANK YOU, SIR.
MY PLEASURE!
SOTARO KAMIKI
KEN'S LIEUTENANT IN THE WASHIO CLAN
...
パタン
CHAK
SOMETHING'S UP WITH KEN.
EVER SINCE THAT OUTING WITH MISS MEGUMI...
AFTERGLOW
That was the best!
...HE HASN'T BEEN THE SAME.

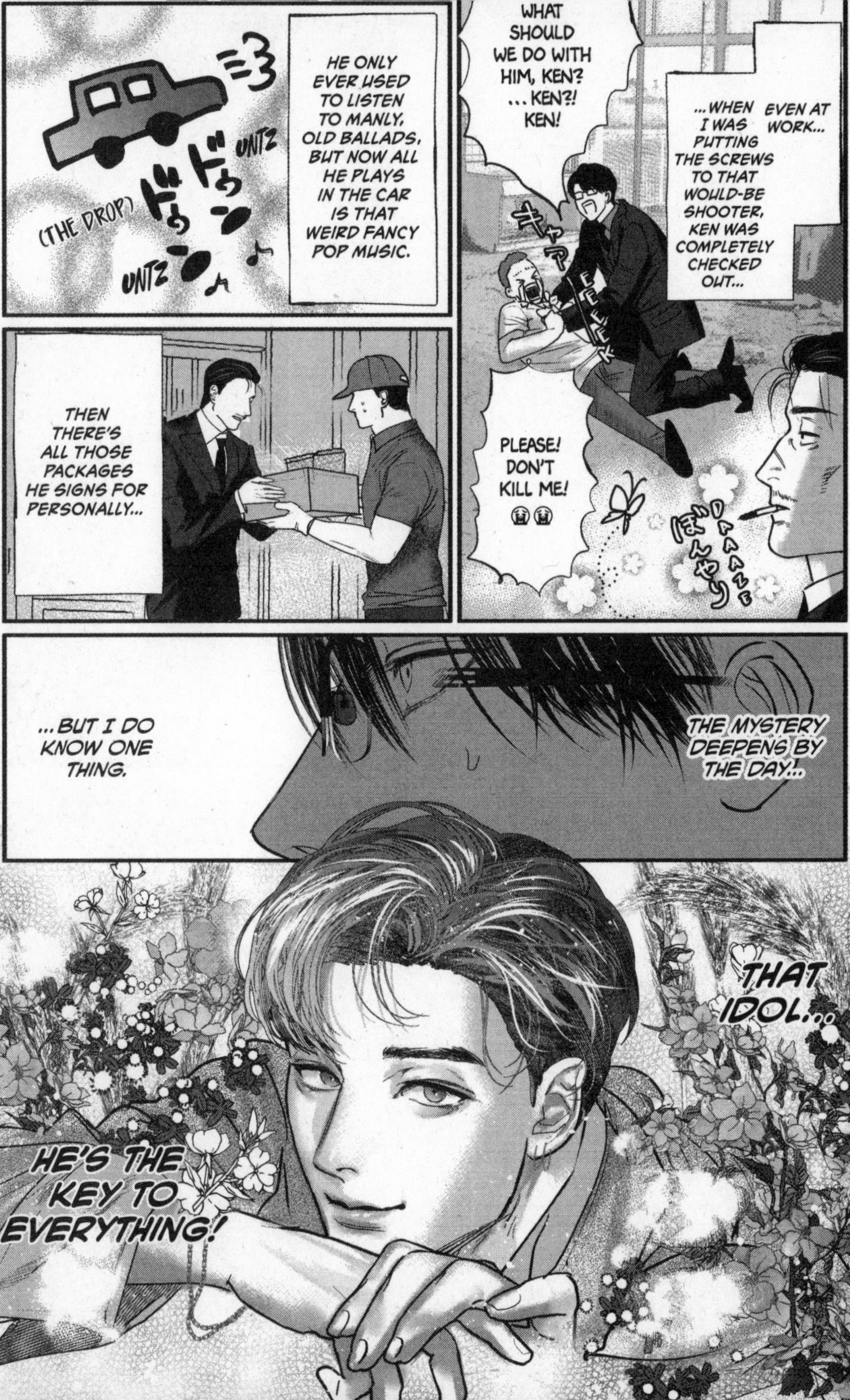
EVEN AT WORK...
...WHEN I WAS PUTTING THE SCREWS TO THAT WOULD-BE SHOOTER, KEN WAS COMPLETELY CHECKED OUT...
WHAT SHOULD WE DO WITH HIM, KEN? ...KEN?! KEN!
キャア
EEEEEK
PLEASE! DON'T KILL ME!
ぼんやり
DAAAAZE
HE ONLY EVER USED TO LISTEN TO MANLY, OLD BALLADS, BUT NOW ALL HE PLAYS IN THE CAR IS THAT WEIRD FANCY POP MUSIC.
UNTZ
(THE DROP)
UNTZ
THEN THERE'S ALL THOSE PACKAGES HE SIGNS FOR PERSONALLY...
THE MYSTERY DEEPENS BY THE DAY...
...BUT I DO KNOW ONE THING.
THAT IDOL...
HE'S THE KEY TO EVERYTHING!

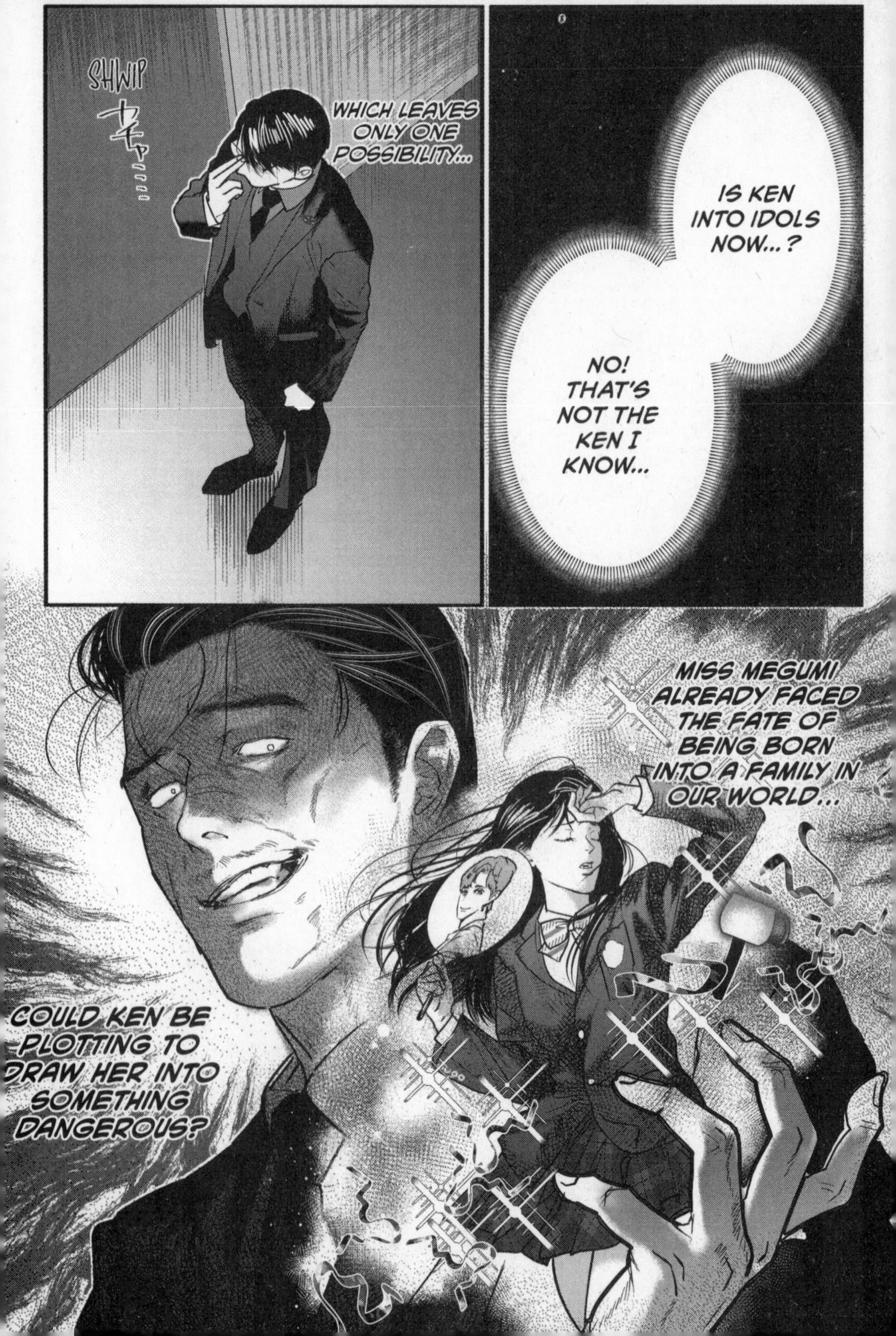
IS KEN INTO IDOLS NOW...?
NO! THAT'S NOT THE KEN I KNOW...
SHWIP
WHICH LEAVES ONLY ONE POSSIBILITY...
MISS MEGUMI ALREADY FACED THE FATE OF BEING BORN INTO A FAMILY IN OUR WORLD...
COULD KEN BE PLOTTING TO DRAW HER INTO SOMETHING DANGEROUS?

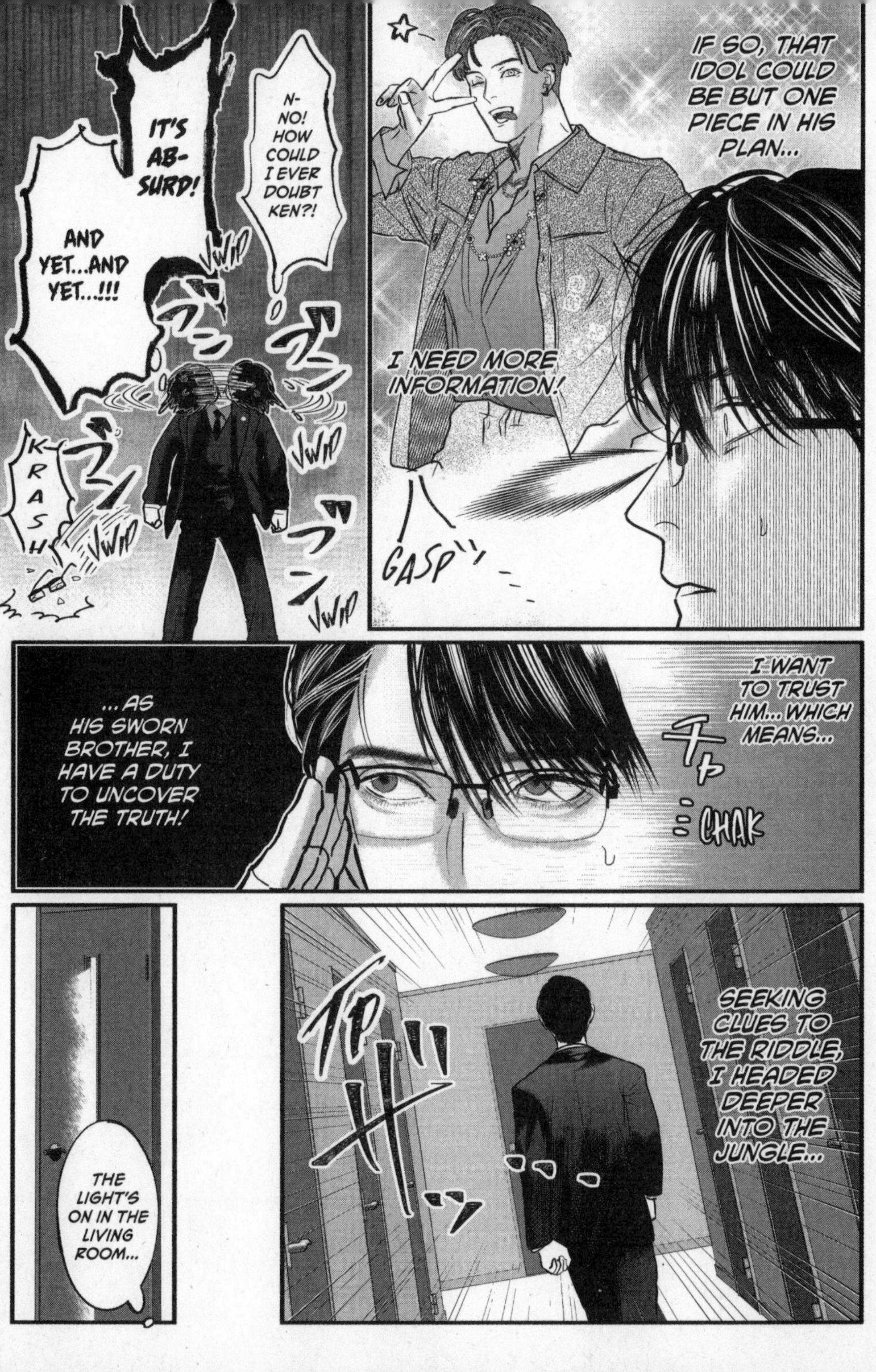
IF SO, THAT IDOL COULD BE BUT ONE PIECE IN HIS PLAN...
I NEED MORE INFORMATION!
GASP
N-NO! HOW COULD I EVER DOUBT KEN?!
IT'S ABSURD!
AND YET...AND YET...!!!
JWIP
JWIP
KRASH
JWIP
JWIP
I WANT TO TRUST HIM...WHICH MEANS...
CHAK
...AS HIS SWORN BROTHER, I HAVE A DUTY TO UNCOVER THE TRUTH!
SEEKING CLUES TO THE RIDDLE, I HEADED DEEPER INTO THE JUNGLE...
THE LIGHT'S ON IN THE LIVING ROOM...

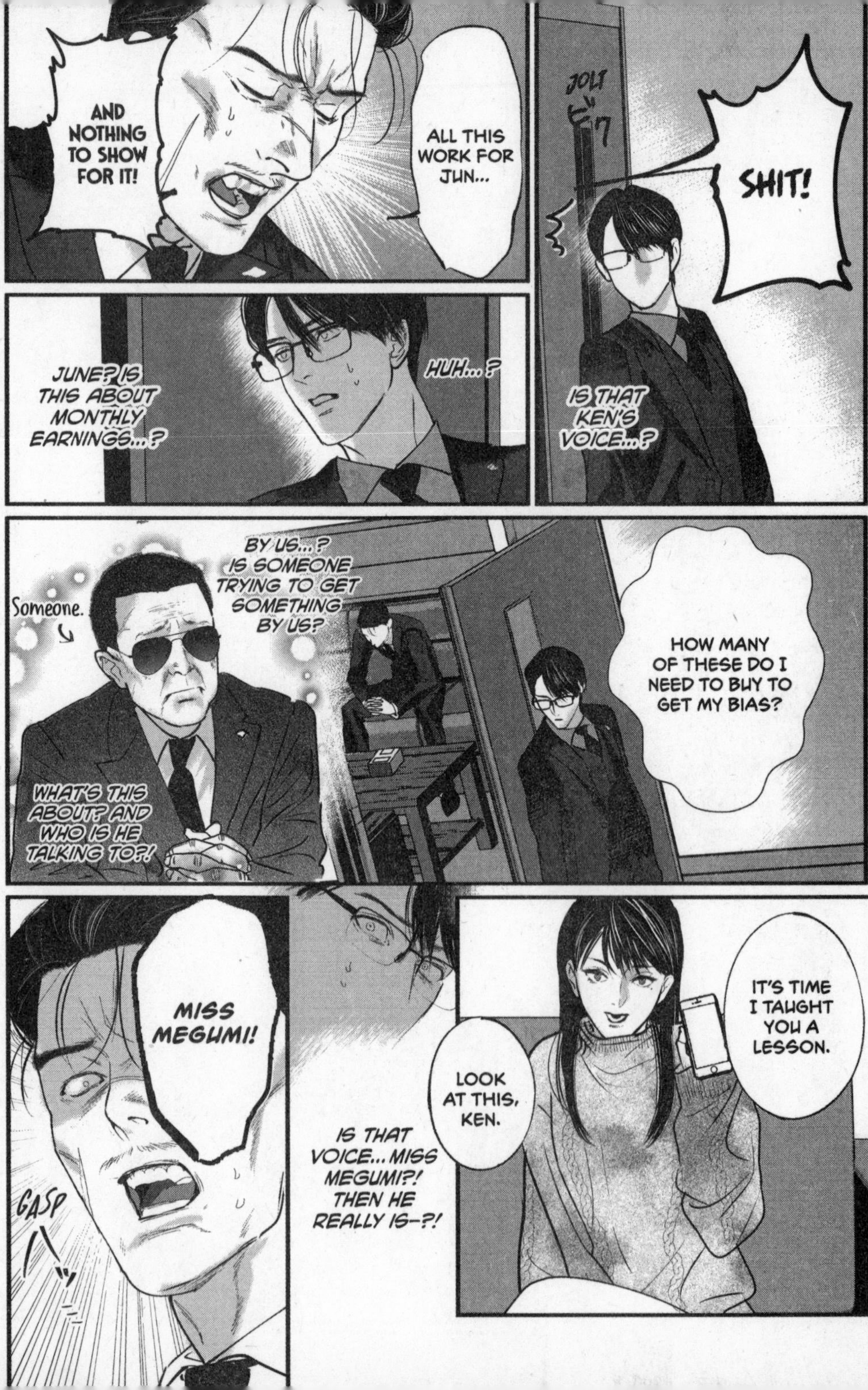
JOLT
SHIT!
IS THAT KEN'S VOICE...?
ALL THIS WORK FOR JUN...
AND NOTHING TO SHOW FOR IT!
HUH...?
JUNE? IS THIS ABOUT MONTHLY EARNINGS...?
HOW MANY OF THESE DO I NEED TO BUY TO GET MY BIAS?
BY US...? IS SOMEONE TRYING TO GET SOMETHING BY US?
Someone.
WHAT'S THIS ABOUT? AND WHO IS HE TALKING TO?!
IT'S TIME I TAUGHT YOU A LESSON.
LOOK AT THIS, KEN.
IS THAT VOICE...MISS MEGUMI?! THEN HE REALLY IS–?!
MISS MEGUMI!
GASP

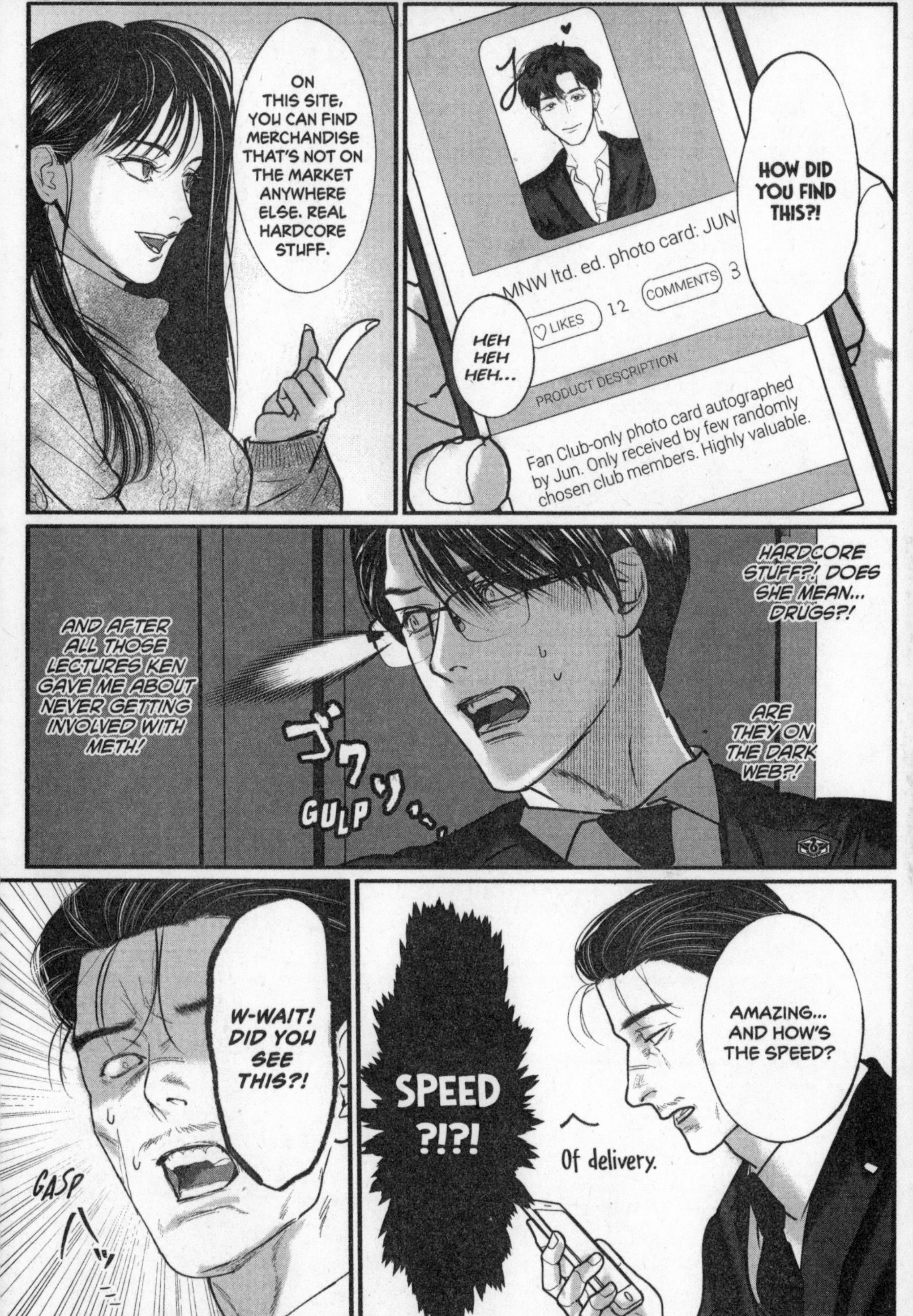
HOW DID YOU FIND THIS?!
MNW ltd. ed. photo card: JUN
LIKES 12
COMMENTS 3
PRODUCT DESCRIPTION
Fan Club-only photo card autographed by Jun. Only received by few randomly chosen club members. Highly valuable.
HEH HEH HEH...
ON THIS SITE, YOU CAN FIND MERCHANDISE THAT'S NOT ON THE MARKET ANYWHERE ELSE. REAL HARDCORE STUFF.
HARDCORE STUFF?! DOES SHE MEAN... DRUGS?!
ARE THEY ON THE DARK WEB?!
AND AFTER ALL THOSE LECTURES KEN GAVE ME ABOUT NEVER GETTING INVOLVED WITH METH!
GULP
AMAZING... AND HOW'S THE SPEED?
SPEED ?!?!
Of delivery.
W-WAIT! DID YOU SEE THIS?!
GASP

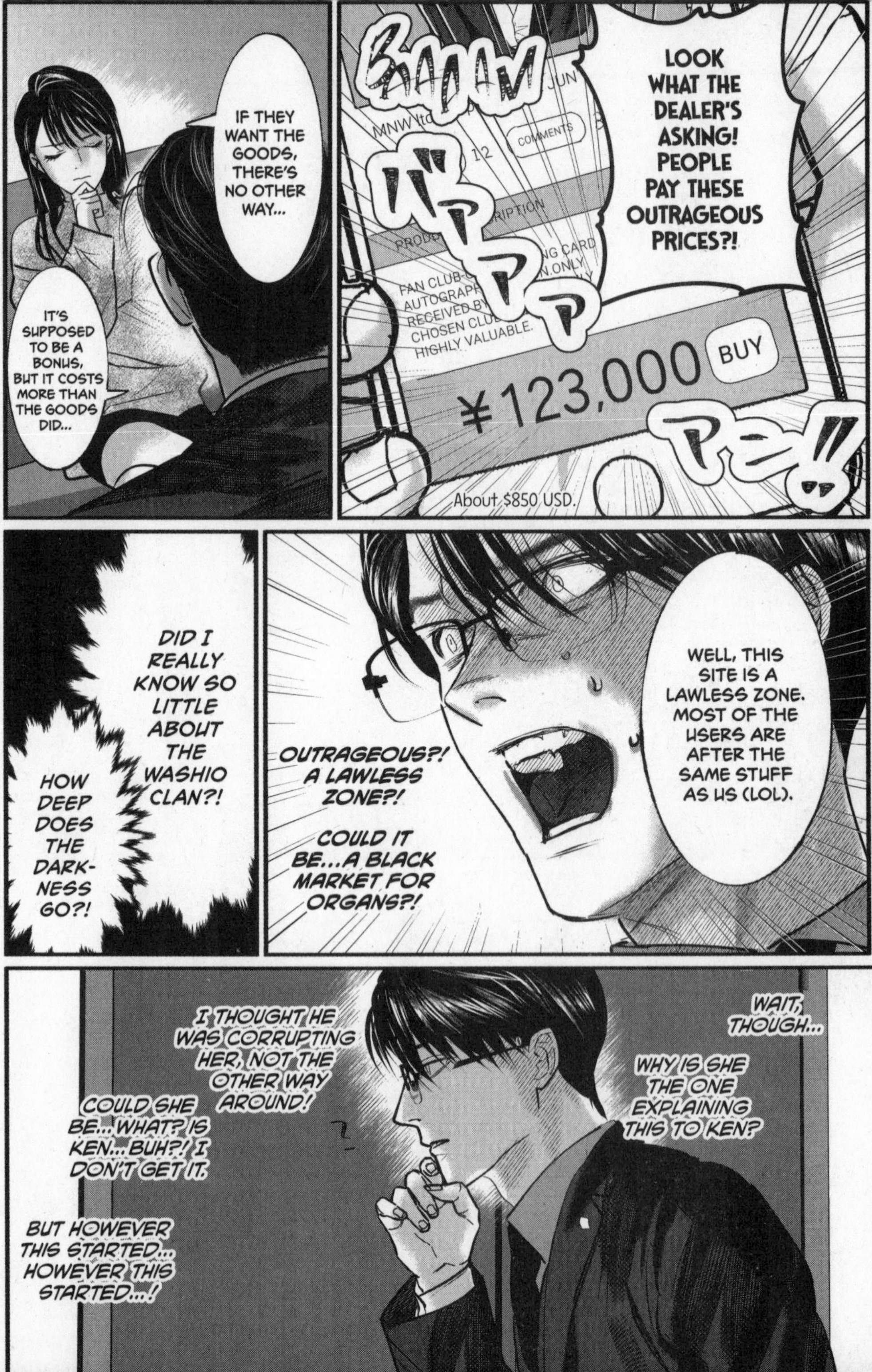
LOOK WHAT THE DEALER'S ASKING! PEOPLE PAY THESE OUTRAGEOUS PRICES?!
COMMENTS
¥123,000
BUY
About $850 USD.
IF THEY WANT THE GOODS, THERE'S NO OTHER WAY...
IT'S SUPPOSED TO BE A BONUS, BUT IT COSTS MORE THAN THE GOODS DID...
WELL, THIS SITE IS A LAWLESS ZONE. MOST OF THE USERS ARE AFTER THE SAME STUFF AS US (LOL).
OUTRAGEOUS?! A LAWLESS ZONE?!
COULD IT BE...A BLACK MARKET FOR ORGANS?!
DID I REALLY KNOW SO LITTLE ABOUT THE WASHIO CLAN?!
HOW DEEP DOES THE DARK-NESS GO?!
WAIT, THOUGH...
WHY IS SHE THE ONE EXPLAINING THIS TO KEN?
I THOUGHT HE WAS CORRUPTING HER, NOT THE OTHER WAY AROUND!
COULD SHE BE... WHAT? IS KEN... BUH?! I DON'T GET IT.
BUT HOWEVER THIS STARTED... HOWEVER THIS STARTED...!

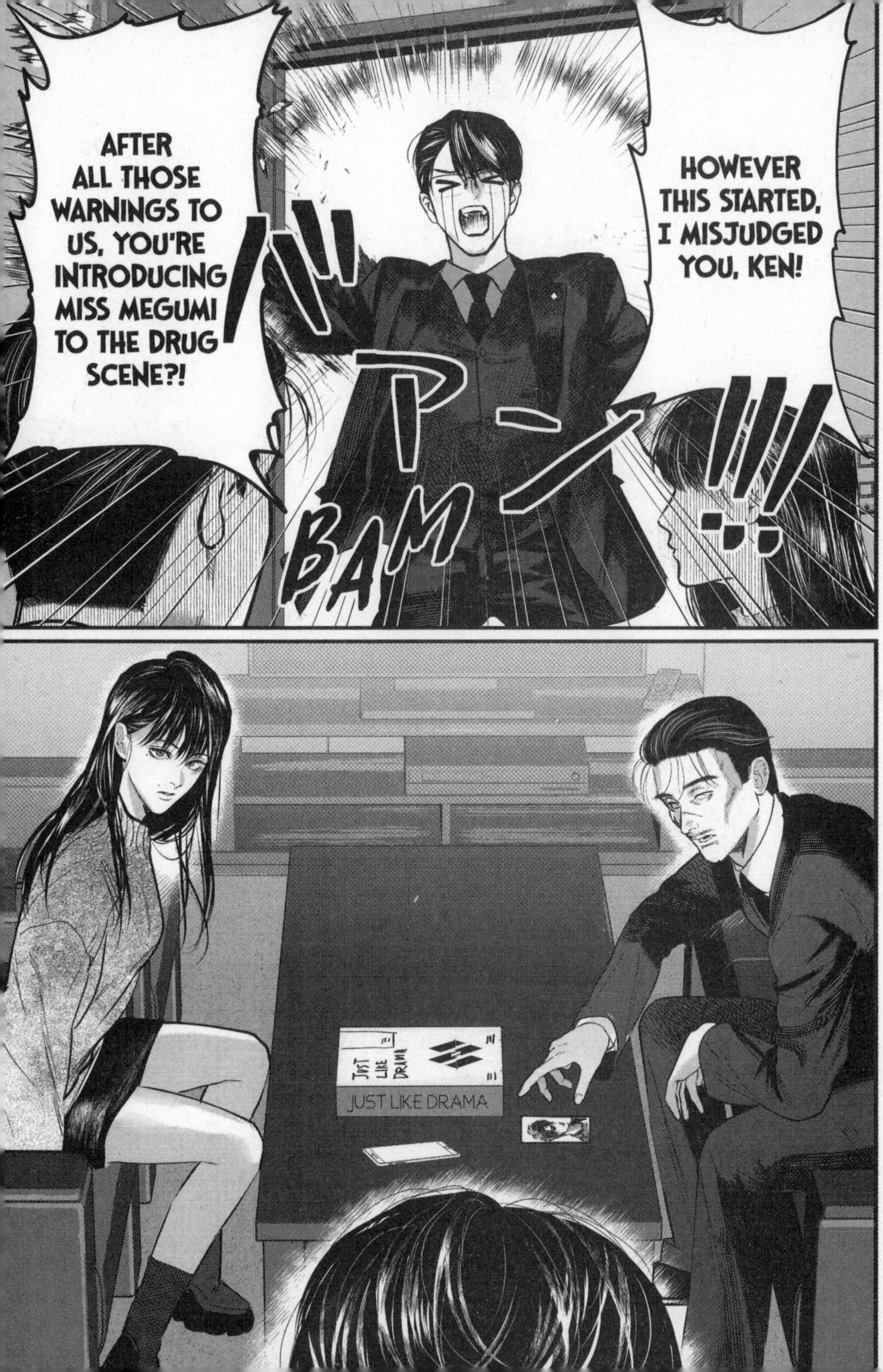
HOWEVER THIS STARTED, I MISJUDGED YOU, KEN!
AFTER ALL THOSE WARNINGS TO US, YOU'RE INTRODUCING MISS MEGUMI TO THE DRUG SCENE?!
バアーン!!!
BAM
JUST LIKE DRAMA
JUST LIKE DRAMA

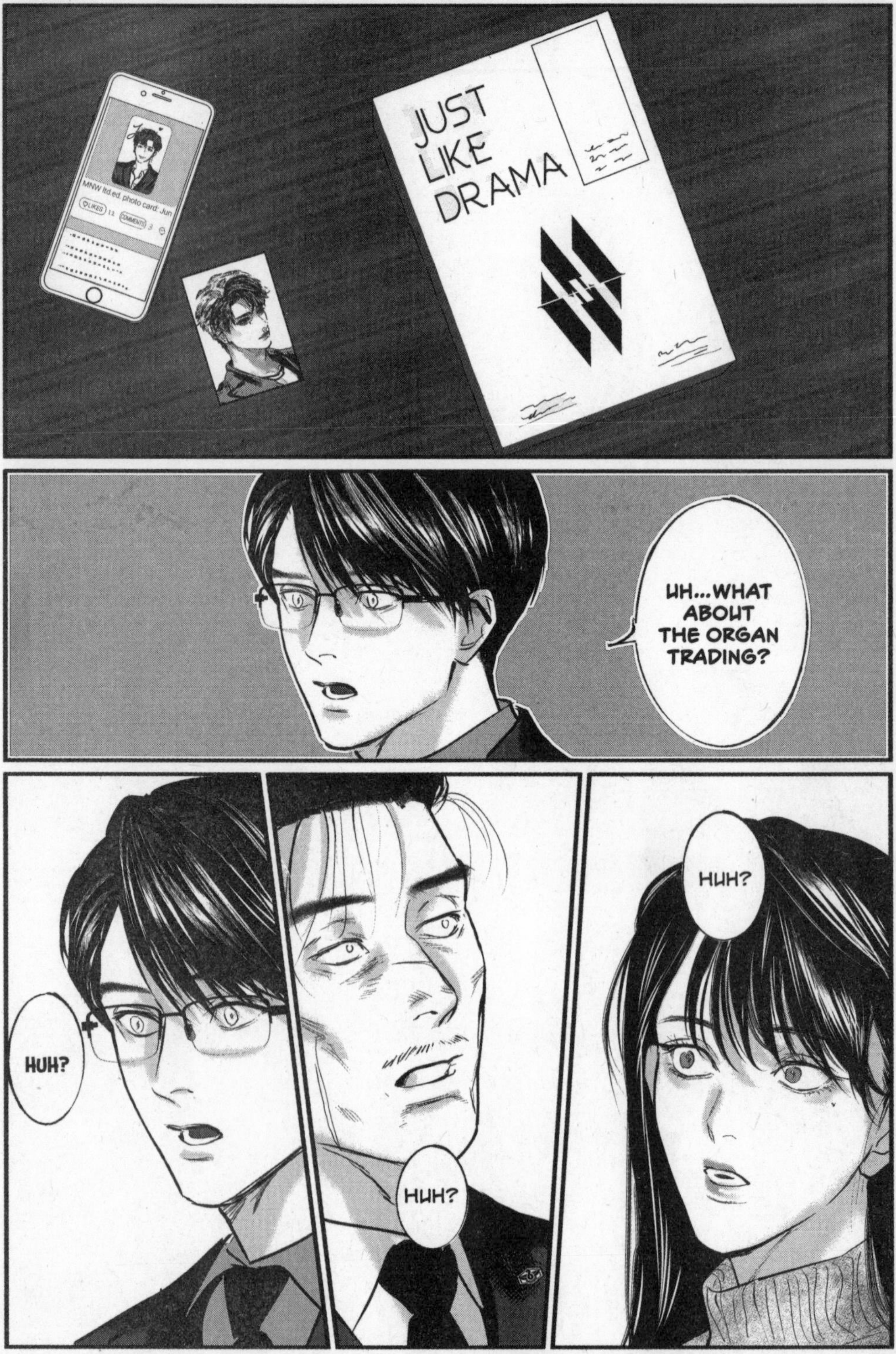
JUST LIKE DRAMA
MNW ltd.ed. photo card: Jun
LIKES 12
COMMENTS 3
UH...WHAT ABOUT THE ORGAN TRADING?
HUH?
HUH?
HUH?

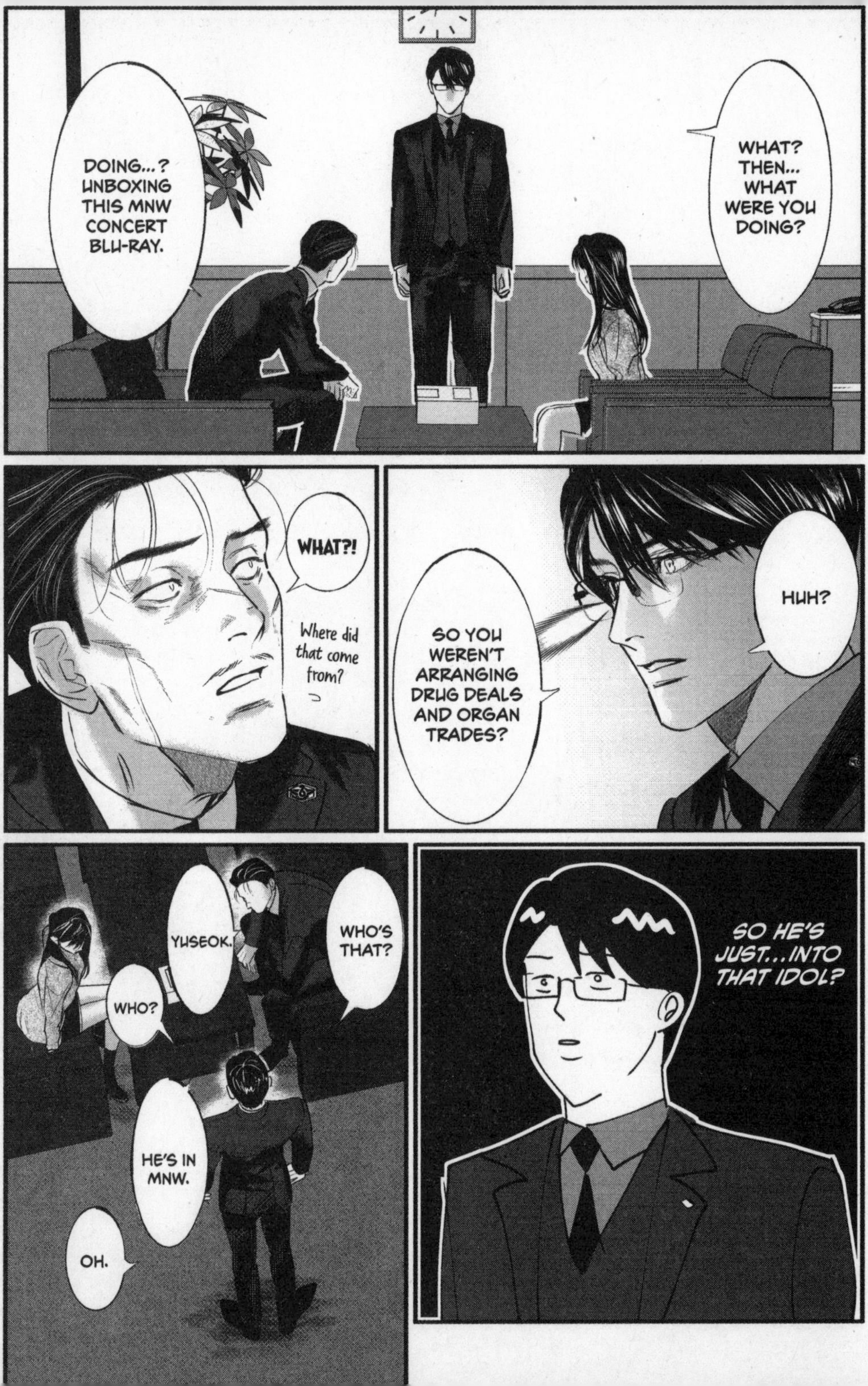
WHAT? THEN... WHAT WERE YOU DOING?
DOING...? UNBOXING THIS MNW CONCERT BLU-RAY.
HUH?
SO YOU WEREN'T ARRANGING DRUG DEALS AND ORGAN TRADES?
WHAT?!
Where did that come from?
SO HE'S JUST...INTO THAT IDOL?
WHO'S THAT?
YUSEOK.
WHO?
HE'S IN MNW.
OH.

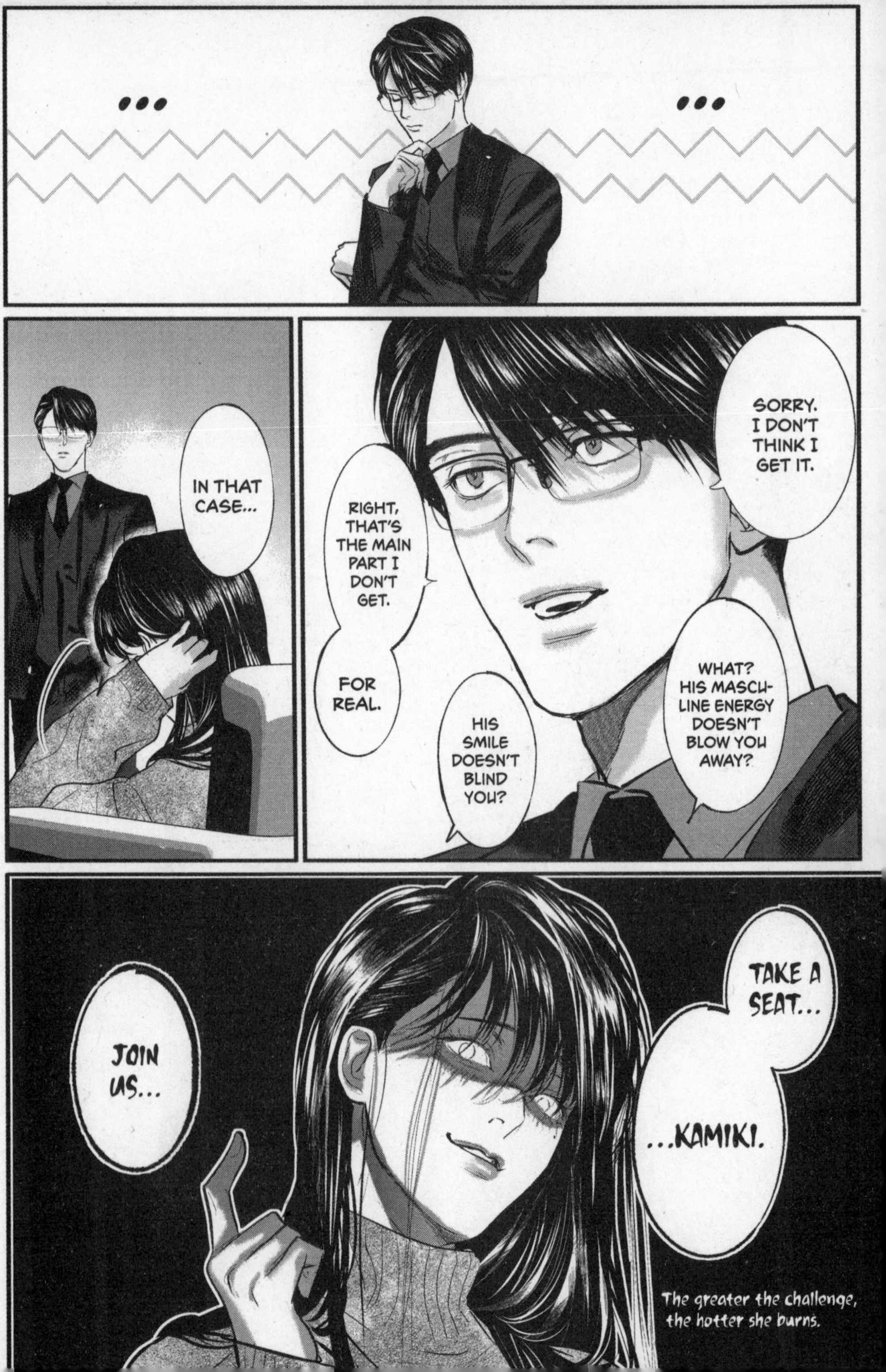
...
...
SORRY. I DON'T THINK I GET IT.
RIGHT, THAT'S THE MAIN PART I DON'T GET.
WHAT? HIS MASCU-LINE ENERGY DOESN'T BLOW YOU AWAY?
FOR REAL.
HIS SMILE DOESN'T BLIND YOU?
IN THAT CASE...
TAKE A SEAT...
...KAMIKI.
JOIN US...
The greater the challenge, the hotter she burns.

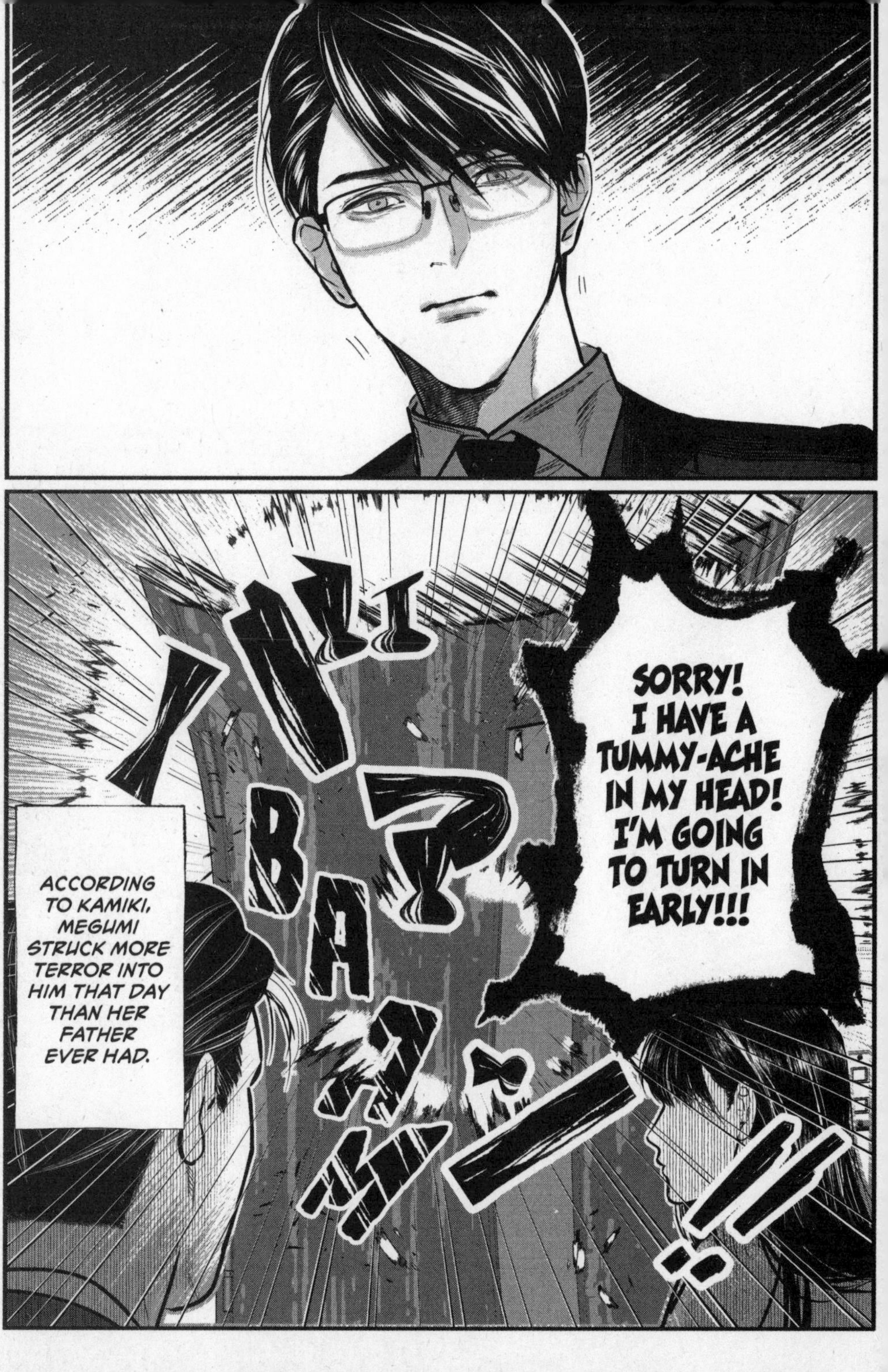
SORRY! I HAVE A TUMMY-ACHE IN MY HEAD! I'M GOING TO TURN IN EARLY!!!
ACCORDING TO KAMIKI, MEGUMI STRUCK MORE TERROR INTO HIM THAT DAY THAN HER FATHER EVER HAD.

THE YAKUZA'S Bias

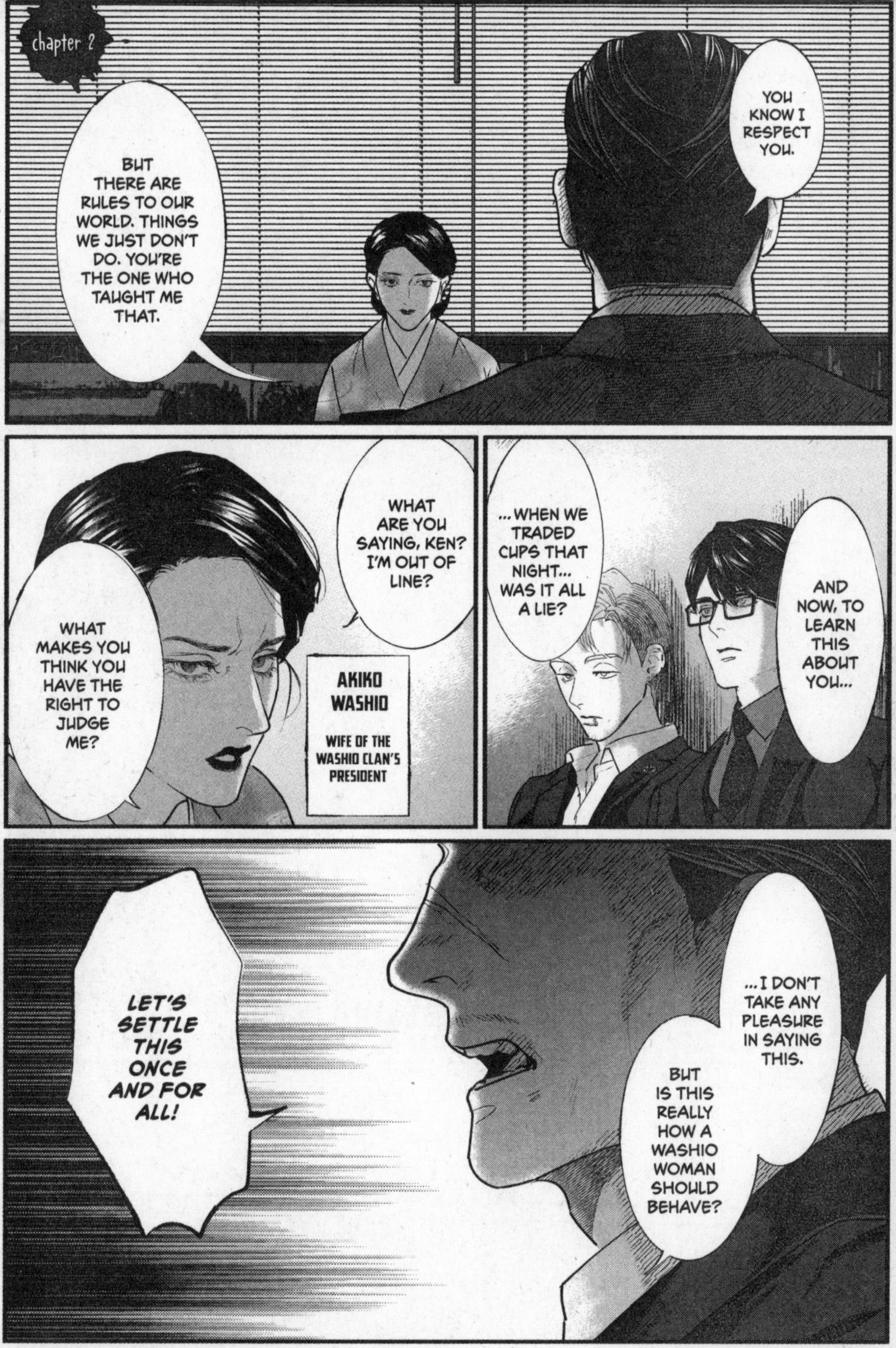
chapter 2
YOU KNOW I RESPECT YOU.
BUT THERE ARE RULES TO OUR WORLD. THINGS WE JUST DON'T DO. YOU'RE THE ONE WHO TAUGHT ME THAT.
AND NOW, TO LEARN THIS ABOUT YOU...
...WHEN WE TRADED CUPS THAT NIGHT... WAS IT ALL A LIE?
WHAT ARE YOU SAYING, KEN? I'M OUT OF LINE?
AKIKO WASHIO
WIFE OF THE WASHIO CLAN'S PRESIDENT
WHAT MAKES YOU THINK YOU HAVE THE RIGHT TO JUDGE ME?
...I DON'T TAKE ANY PLEASURE IN SAYING THIS.
BUT IS THIS REALLY HOW A WASHIO WOMAN SHOULD BEHAVE?
LET'S SETTLE THIS ONCE AND FOR ALL!

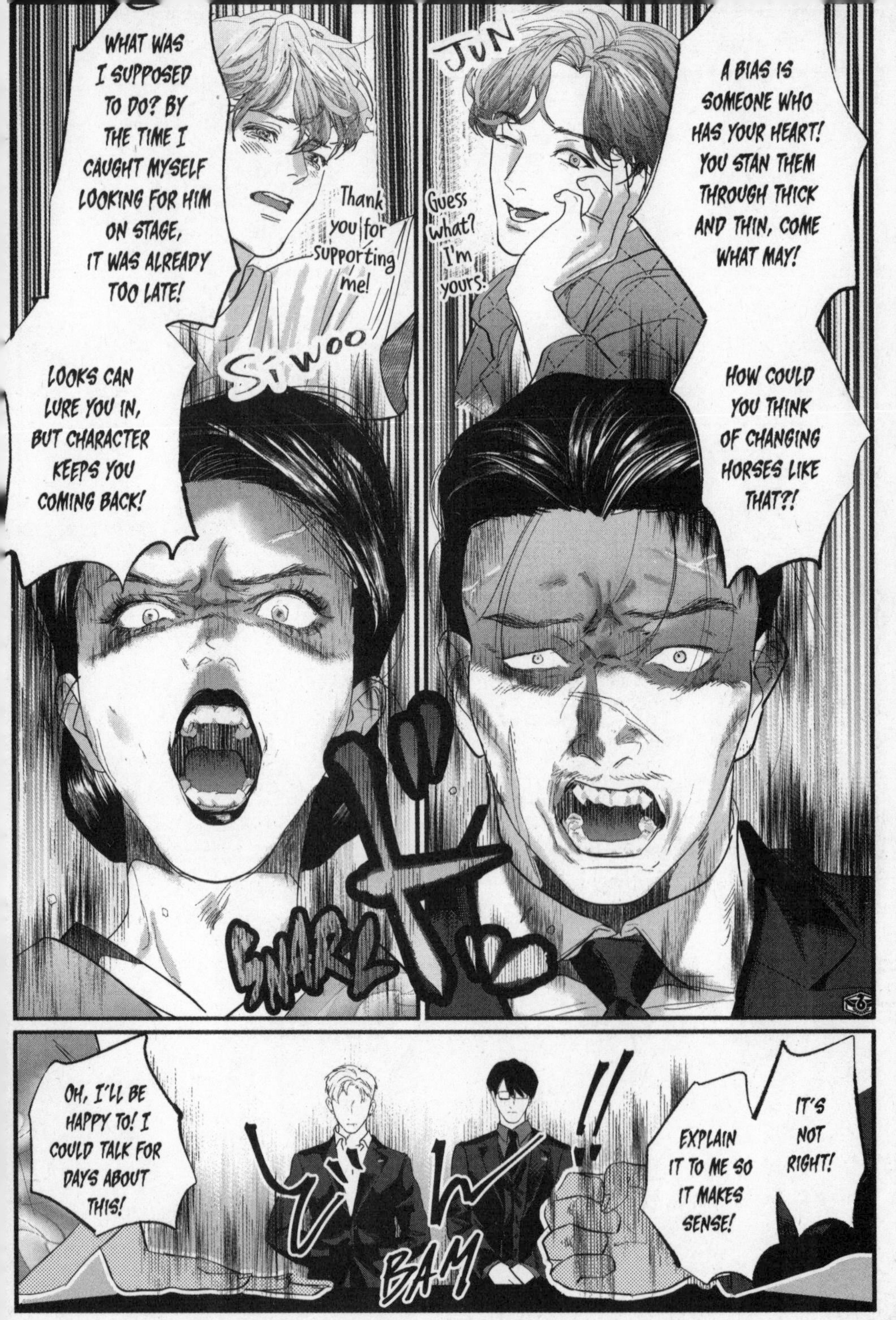
JUN
A BIAS IS SOMEONE WHO HAS YOUR HEART! YOU STAN THEM THROUGH THICK AND THIN, COME WHAT MAY!
Guess what? I'm yours!
HOW COULD YOU THINK OF CHANGING HORSES LIKE THAT?!
WHAT WAS I SUPPOSED TO DO? BY THE TIME I CAUGHT MYSELF LOOKING FOR HIM ON STAGE, IT WAS ALREADY TOO LATE!
Thank you for supporting me!
SIWOO
LOOKS CAN LURE YOU IN, BUT CHARACTER KEEPS YOU COMING BACK!
SNARL
IT'S NOT RIGHT!
EXPLAIN IT TO ME SO IT MAKES SENSE!
BAM
OH, I'LL BE HAPPY TO! I COULD TALK FOR DAYS ABOUT THIS!

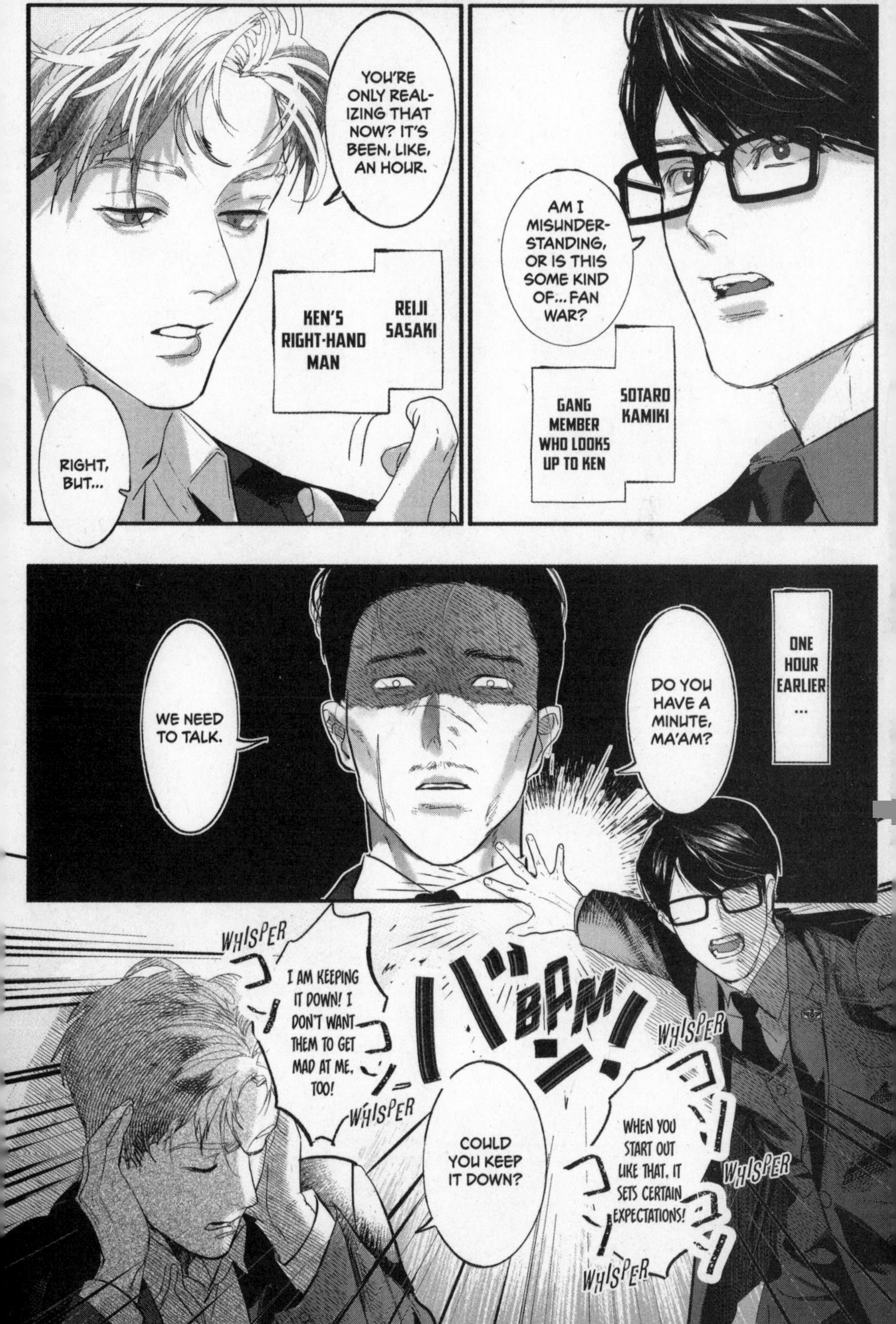
AM I MISUNDERSTANDING, OR IS THIS SOME KIND OF... FAN WAR?
SOTARO KAMIKI
GANG MEMBER WHO LOOKS UP TO KEN
YOU'RE ONLY REALIZING THAT NOW? IT'S BEEN, LIKE, AN HOUR.
REIJI SASAKI
KEN'S RIGHT-HAND MAN
RIGHT, BUT...
ONE HOUR EARLIER...
DO YOU HAVE A MINUTE, MA'AM?
WE NEED TO TALK.
BAM
WHISPER
WHISPER
WHEN YOU START OUT LIKE THAT, IT SETS CERTAIN EXPECTATIONS!
WHISPER
COULD YOU KEEP IT DOWN?
WHISPER
I AM KEEPING IT DOWN! I DON'T WANT THEM TO GET MAD AT ME, TOO!
WHISPER

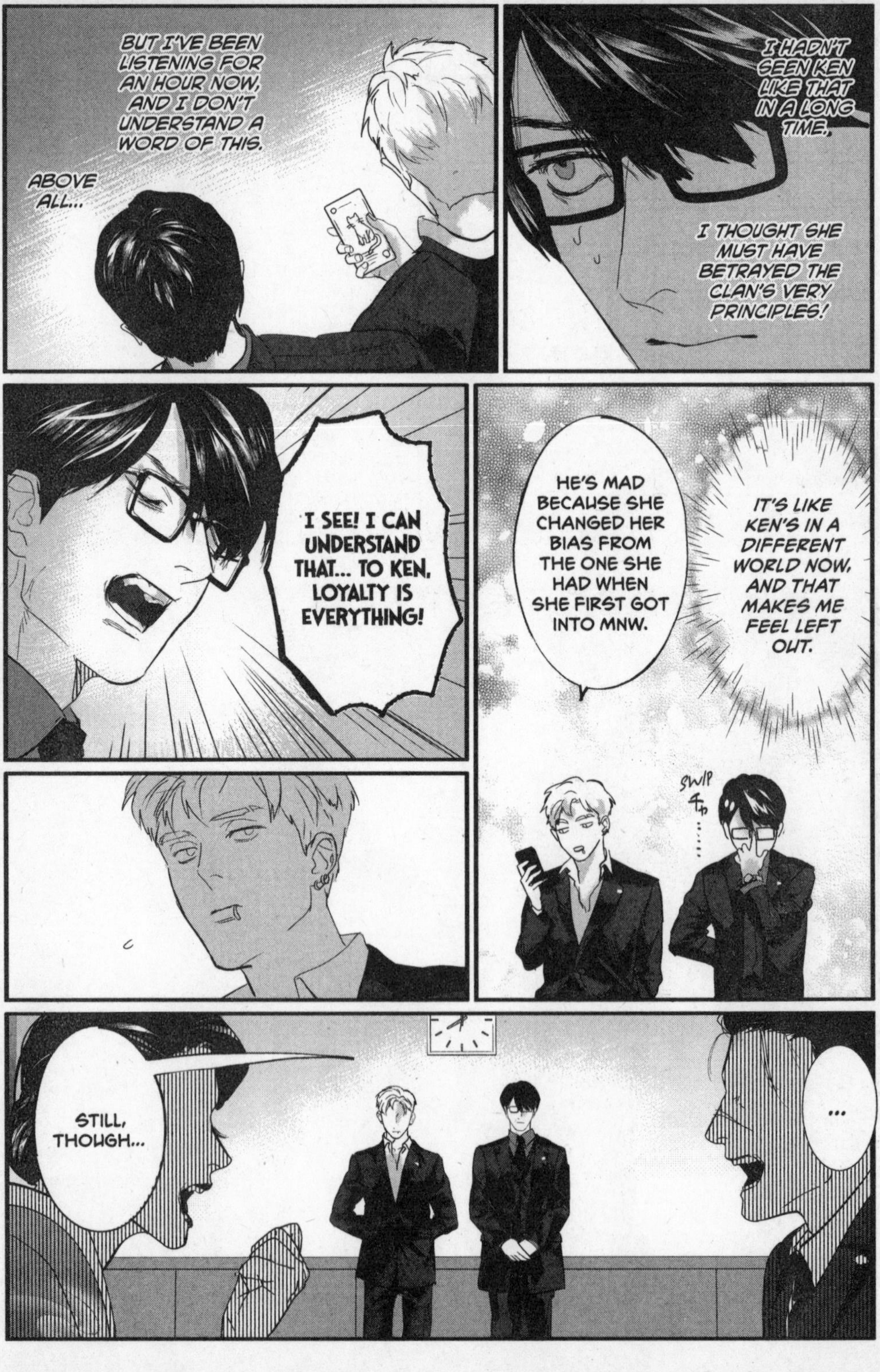
I HADN'T SEEN KEN LIKE THAT IN A LONG TIME.
I THOUGHT SHE MUST HAVE BETRAYED THE CLAN'S VERY PRINCIPLES!
BUT I'VE BEEN LISTENING FOR AN HOUR NOW, AND I DON'T UNDERSTAND A WORD OF THIS.
ABOVE ALL...
IT'S LIKE KEN'S IN A DIFFERENT WORLD NOW, AND THAT MAKES ME FEEL LEFT OUT.
HE'S MAD BECAUSE SHE CHANGED HER BIAS FROM THE ONE SHE HAD WHEN SHE FIRST GOT INTO MNW.
SWIP
......
I SEE! I CAN UNDERSTAND THAT... TO KEN, LOYALTY IS EVERYTHING!
...
STILL, THOUGH...

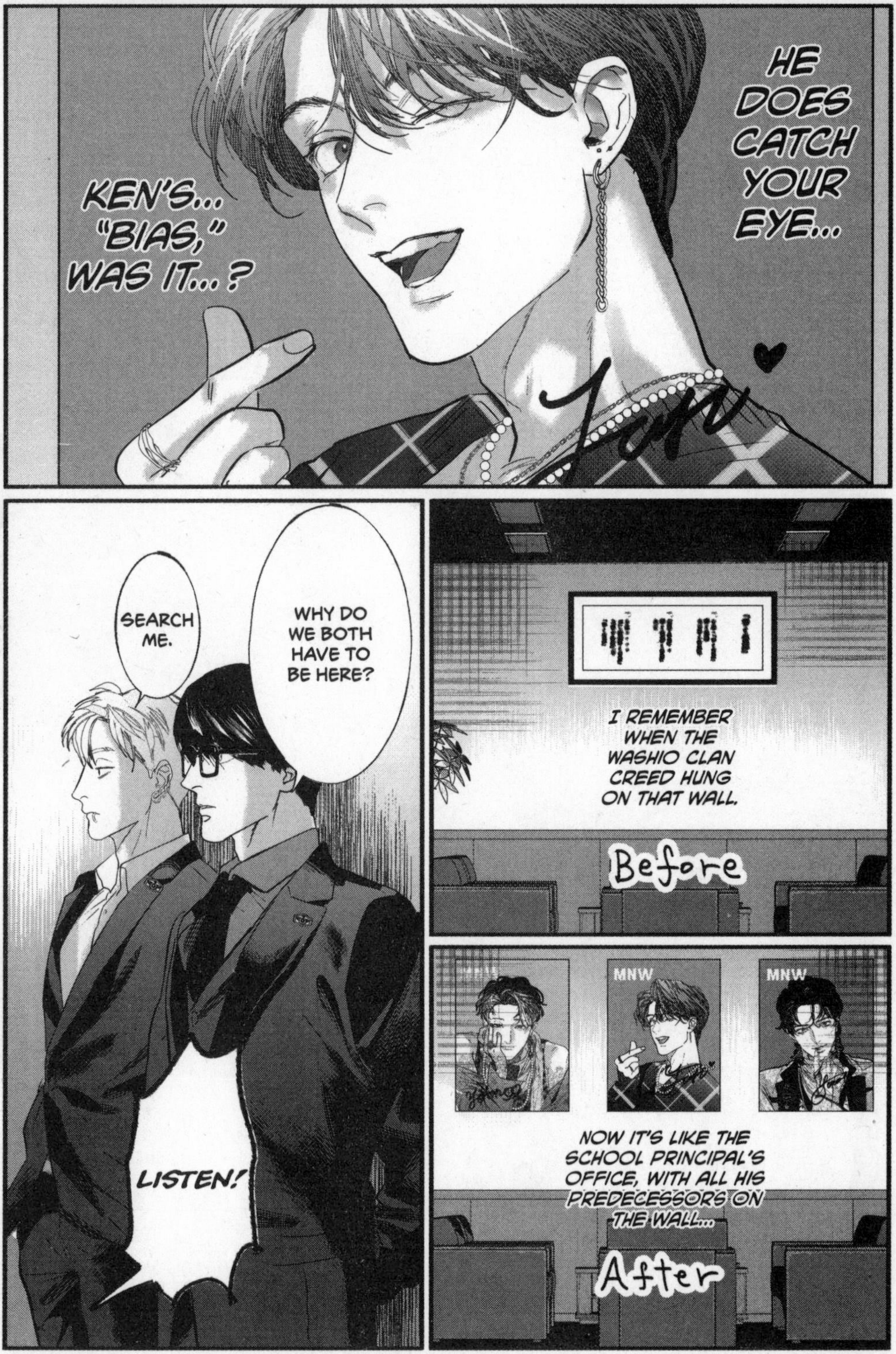
HE DOES CATCH YOUR EYE...
KEN'S... "BIAS," WAS IT...?
I REMEMBER WHEN THE WASHIO CLAN CREED HUNG ON THAT WALL.
Before
MNW
MNW
NOW IT'S LIKE THE SCHOOL PRINCIPAL'S OFFICE, WITH ALL HIS PREDECESSORS ON THE WALL...
After
WHY DO WE BOTH HAVE TO BE HERE?
SEARCH ME.
LISTEN!

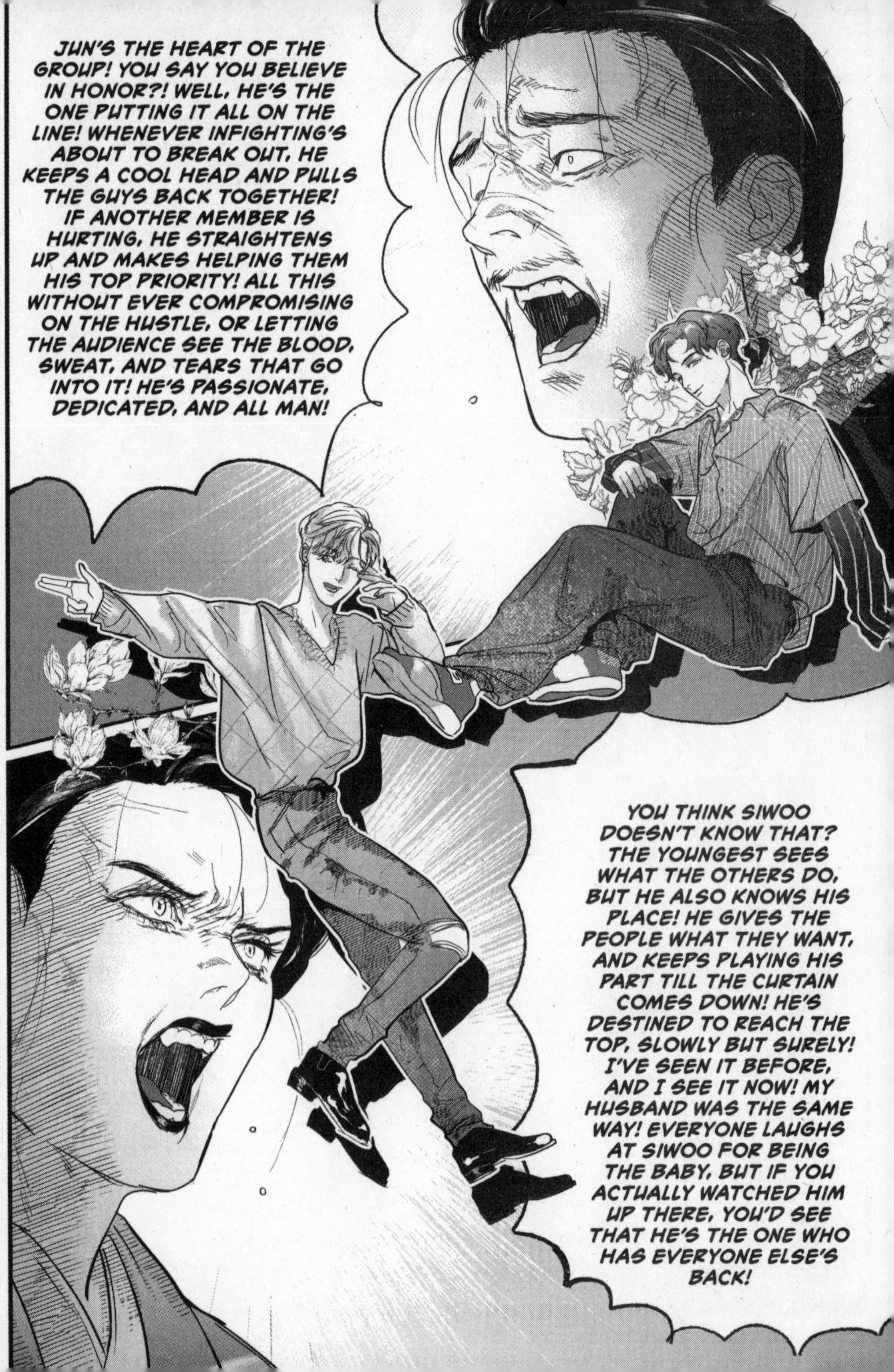
JUN'S THE HEART OF THE GROUP! YOU SAY YOU BELIEVE IN HONOR?! WELL, HE'S THE ONE PUTTING IT ALL ON THE LINE! WHENEVER INFIGHTING'S ABOUT TO BREAK OUT, HE KEEPS A COOL HEAD AND PULLS THE GUYS BACK TOGETHER! IF ANOTHER MEMBER IS HURTING, HE STRAIGHTENS UP AND MAKES HELPING THEM HIS TOP PRIORITY! ALL THIS WITHOUT EVER COMPROMISING ON THE HUSTLE, OR LETTING THE AUDIENCE SEE THE BLOOD, SWEAT, AND TEARS THAT GO INTO IT! HE'S PASSIONATE, DEDICATED, AND ALL MAN!
YOU THINK SIWOO DOESN'T KNOW THAT? THE YOUNGEST SEES WHAT THE OTHERS DO, BUT HE ALSO KNOWS HIS PLACE! HE GIVES THE PEOPLE WHAT THEY WANT, AND KEEPS PLAYING HIS PART TILL THE CURTAIN COMES DOWN! HE'S DESTINED TO REACH THE TOP, SLOWLY BUT SURELY! I'VE SEEN IT BEFORE, AND I SEE IT NOW! MY HUSBAND WAS THE SAME WAY! EVERYONE LAUGHS AT SIWOO FOR BEING THE BABY, BUT IF YOU ACTUALLY WATCHED HIM UP THERE, YOU'D SEE THAT HE'S THE ONE WHO HAS EVERYONE ELSE'S BACK!

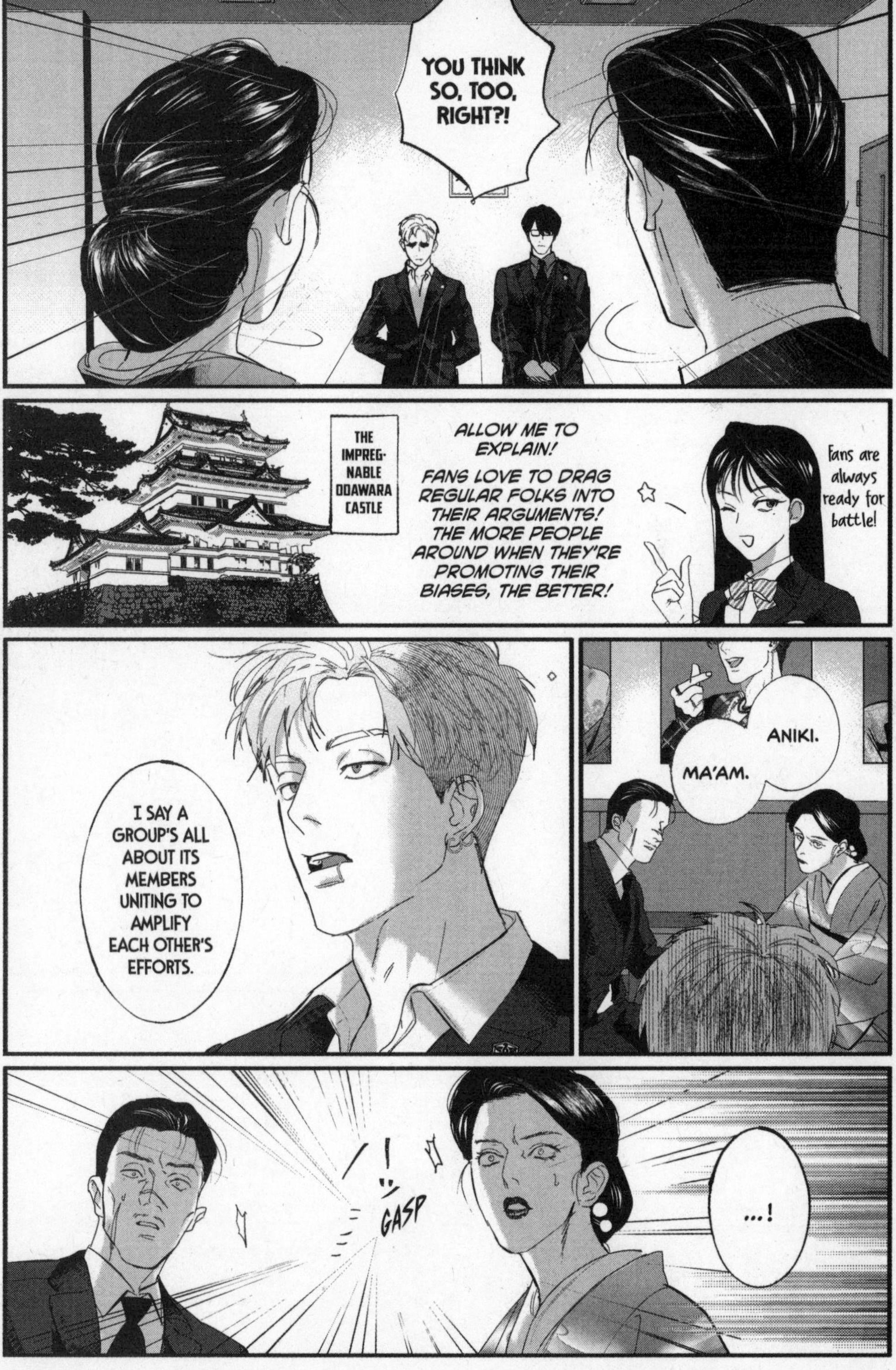
YOU THINK SO, TOO, RIGHT?!
Fans are always ready for battle!
ALLOW ME TO EXPLAIN!
FANS LOVE TO DRAG REGULAR FOLKS INTO THEIR ARGUMENTS! THE MORE PEOPLE AROUND WHEN THEY'RE PROMOTING THEIR BIASES, THE BETTER!
THE IMPREG-NABLE ODAWARA CASTLE
ANIKI.
MA'AM.
I SAY A GROUP'S ALL ABOUT ITS MEMBERS UNITING TO AMPLIFY EACH OTHER'S EFFORTS.
...!
GASP
!

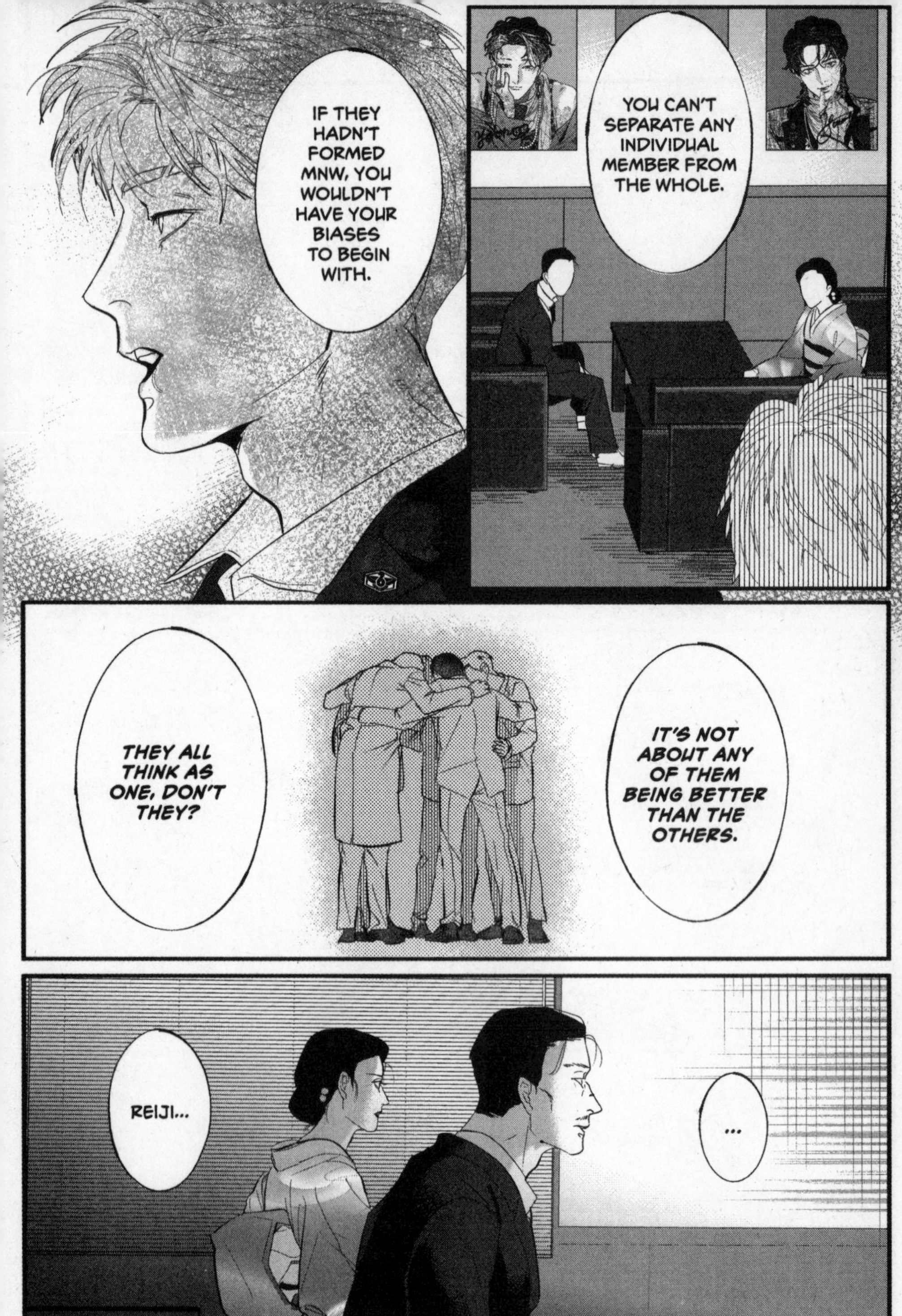
YOU CAN'T SEPARATE ANY INDIVIDUAL MEMBER FROM THE WHOLE.
IF THEY HADN'T FORMED MNW, YOU WOULDN'T HAVE YOUR BIASES TO BEGIN WITH.
IT'S NOT ABOUT ANY OF THEM BEING BETTER THAN THE OTHERS.
THEY ALL THINK AS ONE, DON'T THEY?
...
REIJI...

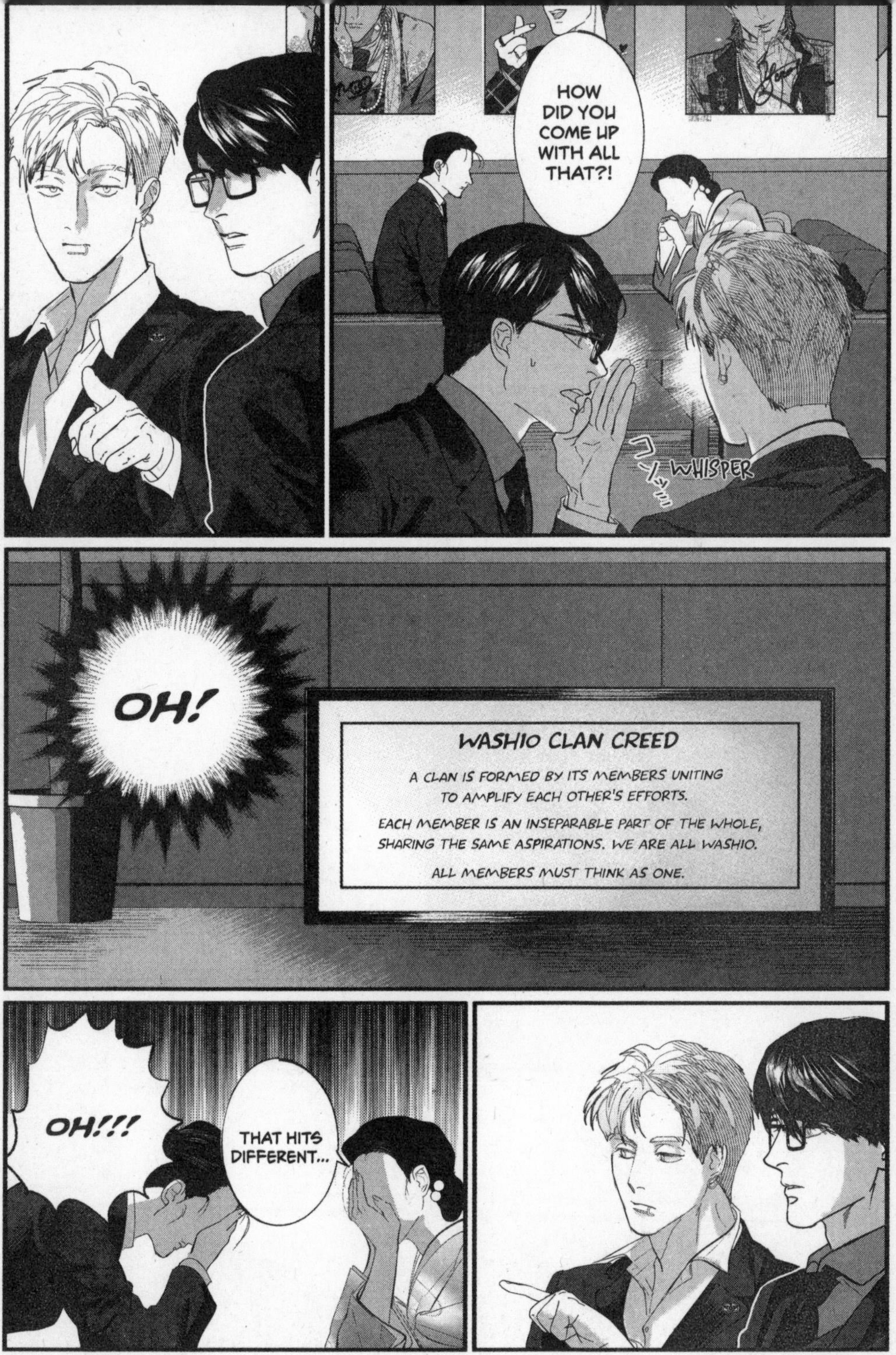
HOW DID YOU COME UP WITH ALL THAT?!
WHISPER
WASHIO CLAN CREED
A CLAN IS FORMED BY ITS MEMBERS UNITING TO AMPLIFY EACH OTHER'S EFFORTS.
EACH MEMBER IS AN INSEPARABLE PART OF THE WHOLE, SHARING THE SAME ASPIRATIONS. WE ARE ALL WASHIO.
ALL MEMBERS MUST THINK AS ONE.
OH!
THAT HITS DIFFERENT...
OH!!!

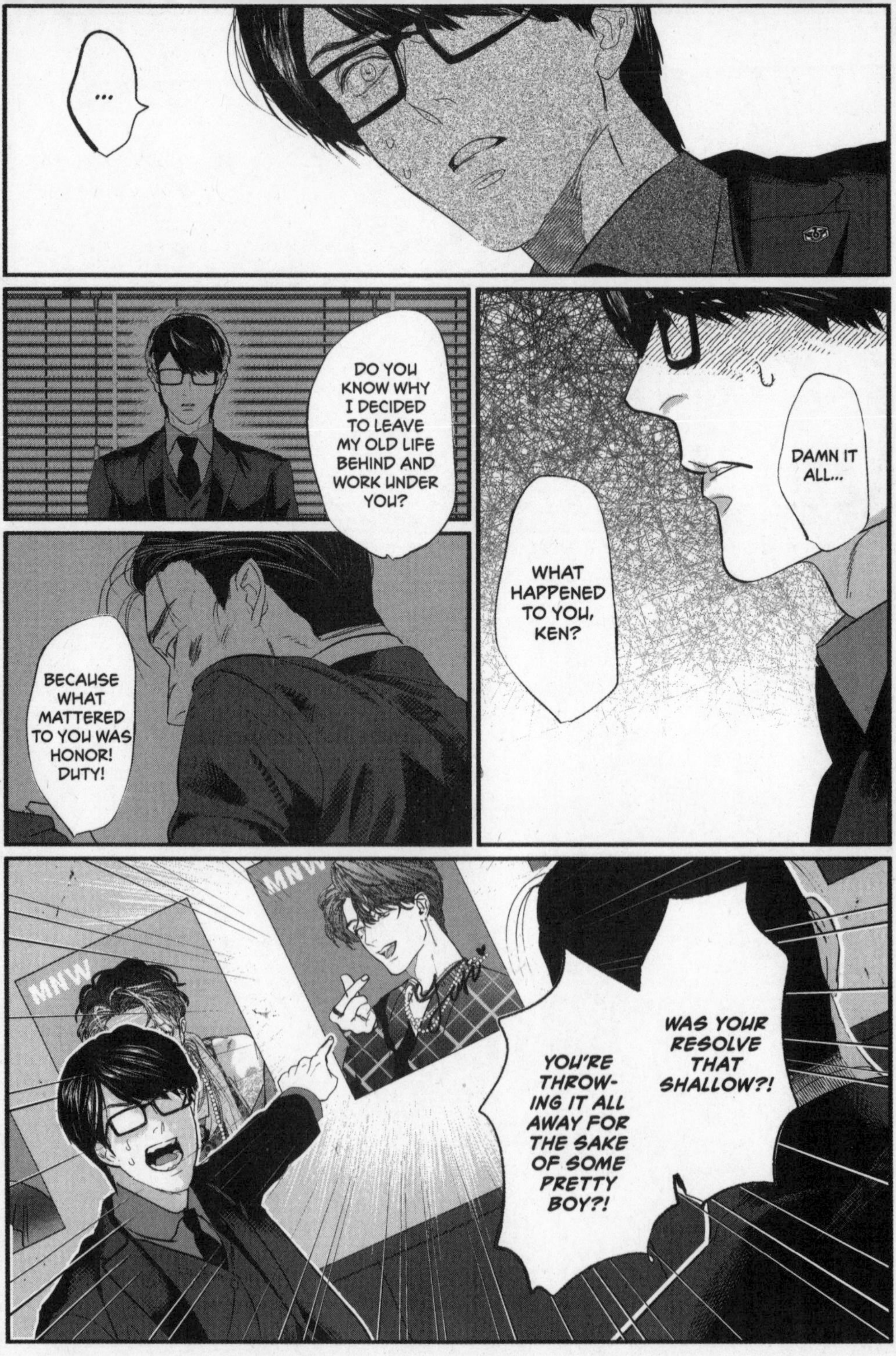
...
DAMN IT ALL...
WHAT HAPPENED TO YOU, KEN?
DO YOU KNOW WHY I DECIDED TO LEAVE MY OLD LIFE BEHIND AND WORK UNDER YOU?
BECAUSE WHAT MATTERED TO YOU WAS HONOR! DUTY!
MNW
WAS YOUR RESOLVE THAT SHALLOW?!
YOU'RE THROWING IT ALL AWAY FOR THE SAKE OF SOME PRETTY BOY?!
MNW

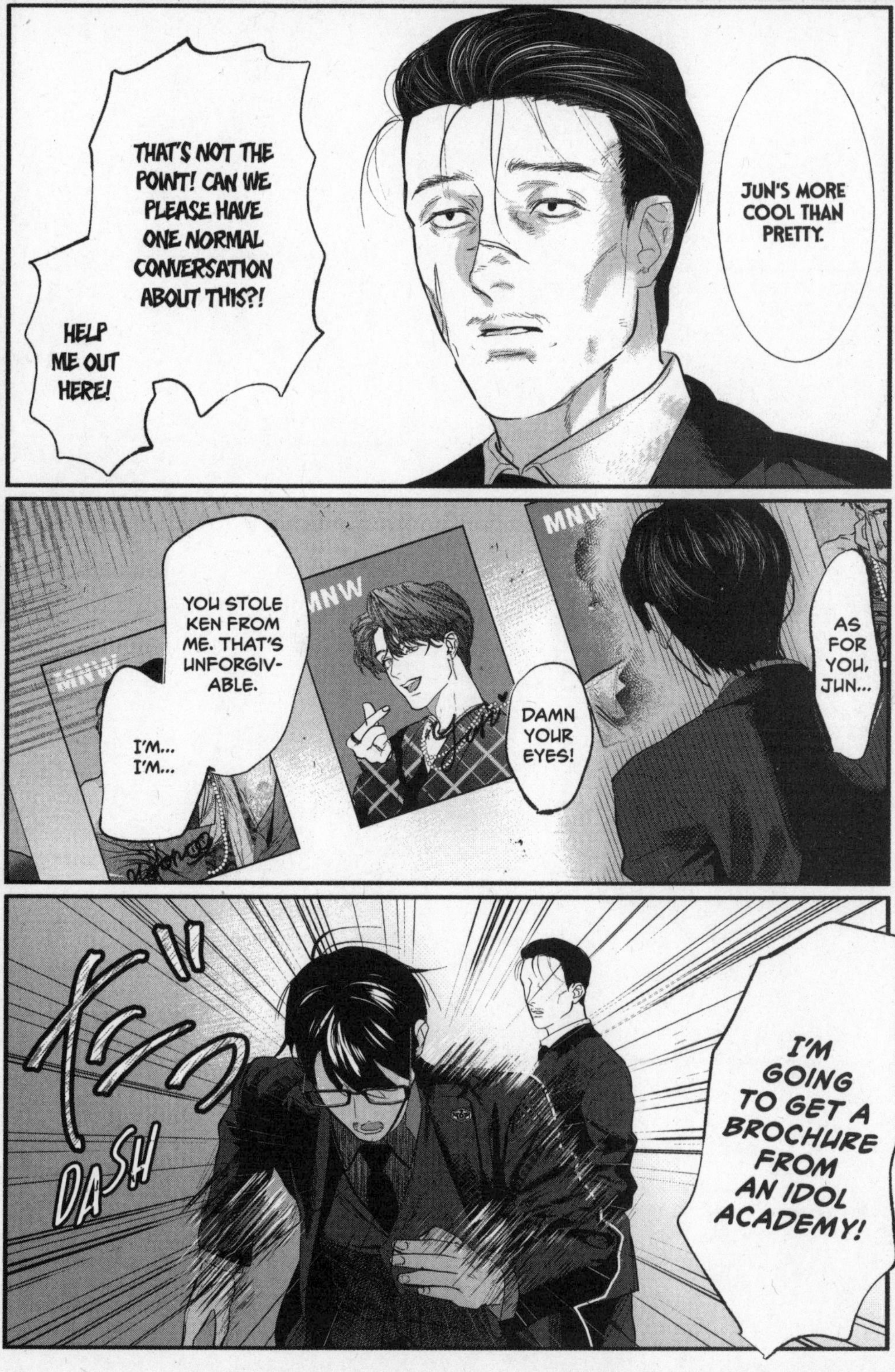
JUN'S MORE COOL THAN PRETTY.
THAT'S NOT THE POINT! CAN WE PLEASE HAVE ONE NORMAL CONVERSATION ABOUT THIS?!
HELP ME OUT HERE!
AS FOR YOU, JUN...
DAMN YOUR EYES!
YOU STOLE KEN FROM ME. THAT'S UNFORGIVABLE.
I'M... I'M...
I'M GOING TO GET A BROCHURE FROM AN IDOL ACADEMY!
DASH

THE YAKUZA'S Bias

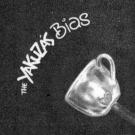

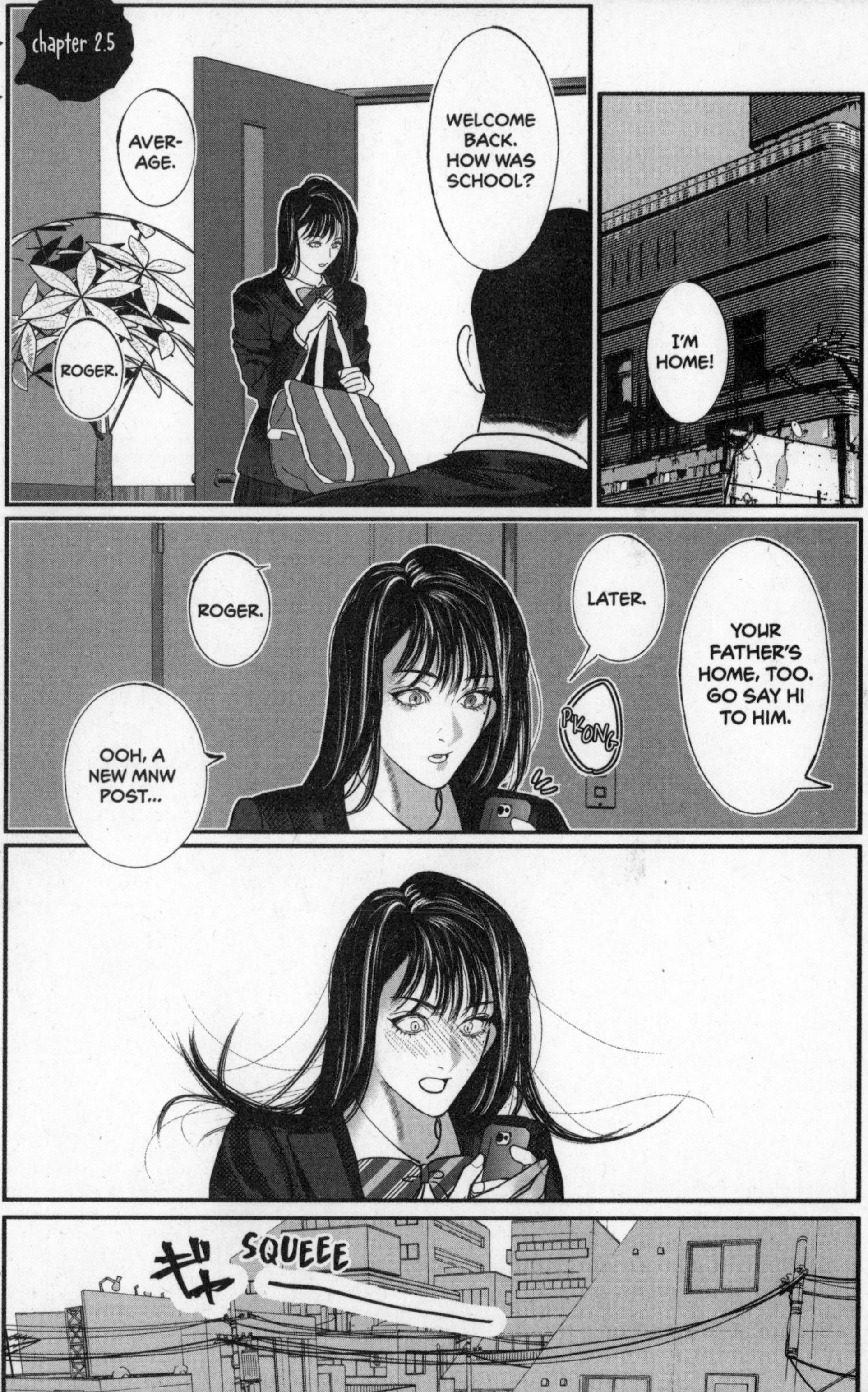
chapter 2.5
I'M HOME!
WELCOME BACK. HOW WAS SCHOOL?
AVER-AGE.
ROGER.
YOUR FATHER'S HOME, TOO. GO SAY HI TO HIM.
LATER.
PIKONG
ROGER.
OOH, A NEW MNW POST...
SQUEEE
ギャ

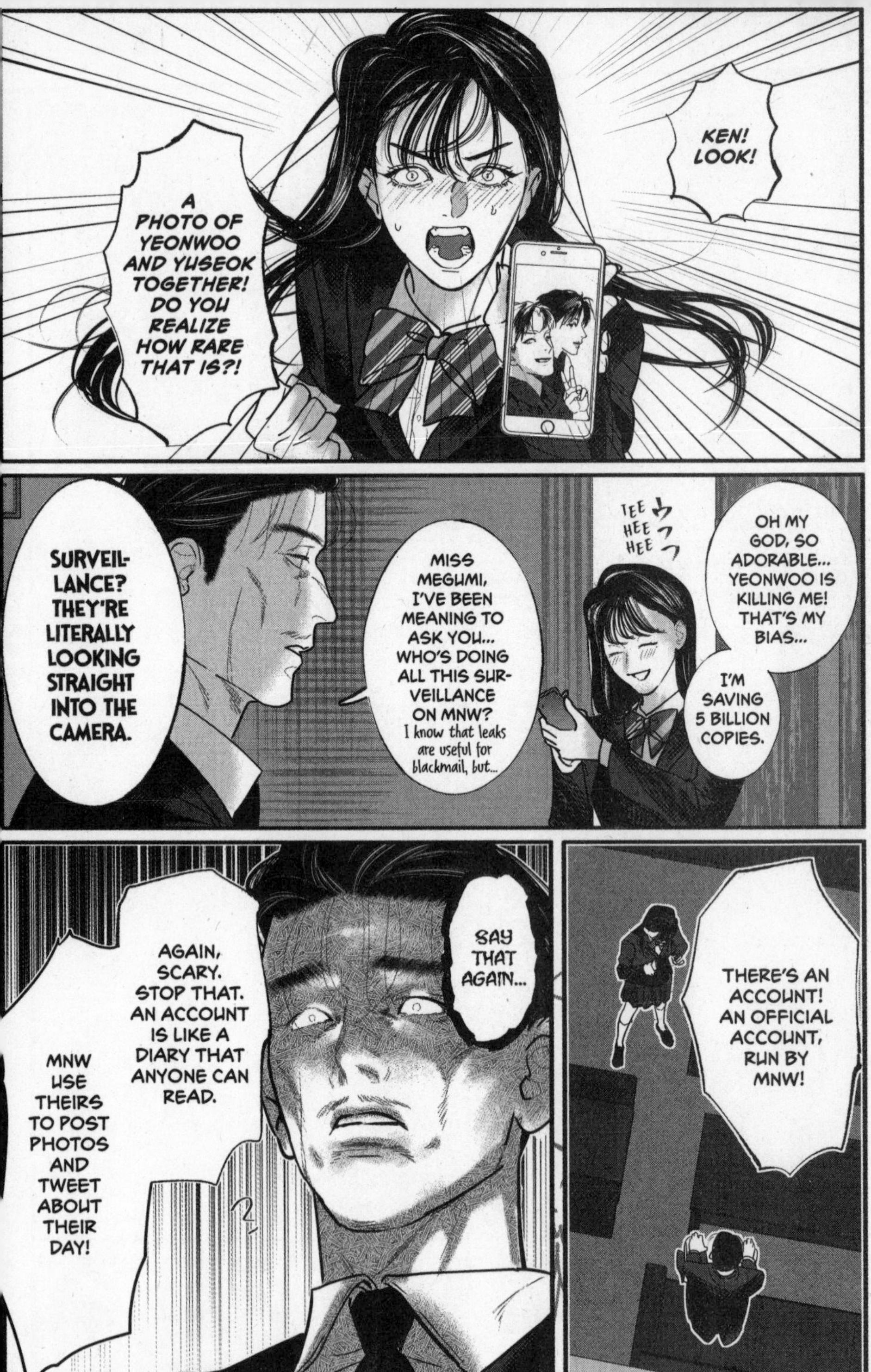
KEN! LOOK!
A PHOTO OF YEONWOO AND YUSEOK TOGETHER! DO YOU REALIZE HOW RARE THAT IS?!
OH MY GOD, SO ADORABLE... YEONWOO IS KILLING ME! THAT'S MY BIAS...
TEE HEE HEE
I'M SAVING 5 BILLION COPIES.
MISS MEGUMI, I'VE BEEN MEANING TO ASK YOU... WHO'S DOING ALL THIS SURVEILLANCE ON MNW?
I know that leaks are useful for blackmail, but...
SURVEIL-LANCE? THEY'RE LITERALLY LOOKING STRAIGHT INTO THE CAMERA.
THERE'S AN ACCOUNT! AN OFFICIAL ACCOUNT, RUN BY MNW!
SAY THAT AGAIN...
AGAIN, SCARY. STOP THAT. AN ACCOUNT IS LIKE A DIARY THAT ANYONE CAN READ.
MNW USE THEIRS TO POST PHOTOS AND TWEET ABOUT THEIR DAY!

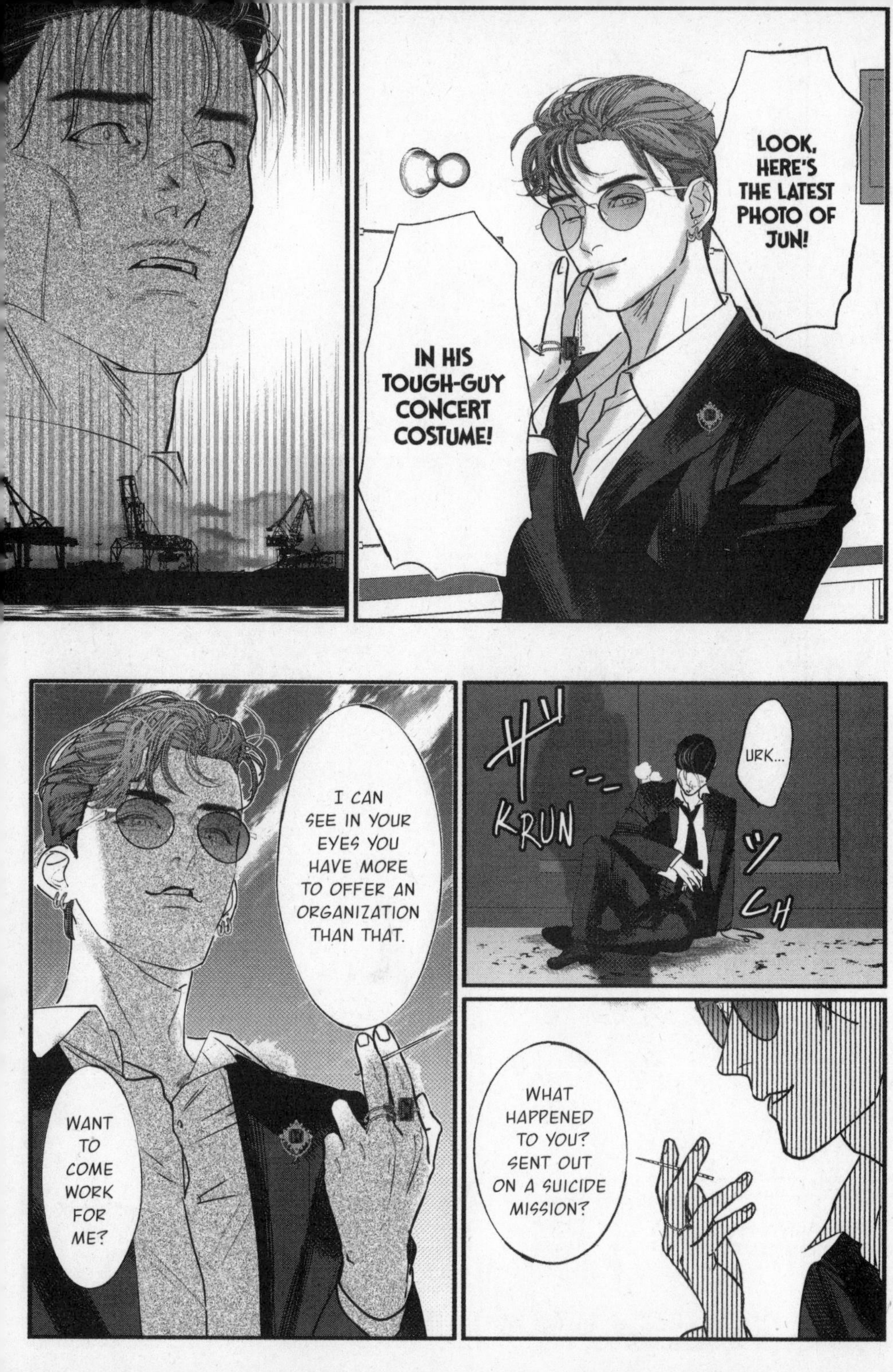
LOOK, HERE'S THE LATEST PHOTO OF JUN!
IN HIS TOUGH-GUY CONCERT COSTUME!
URK...
KRUN
CH
WHAT HAPPENED TO YOU? SENT OUT ON A SUICIDE MISSION?
I CAN SEE IN YOUR EYES YOU HAVE MORE TO OFFER AN ORGANIZATION THAN THAT.
WANT TO COME WORK FOR ME?

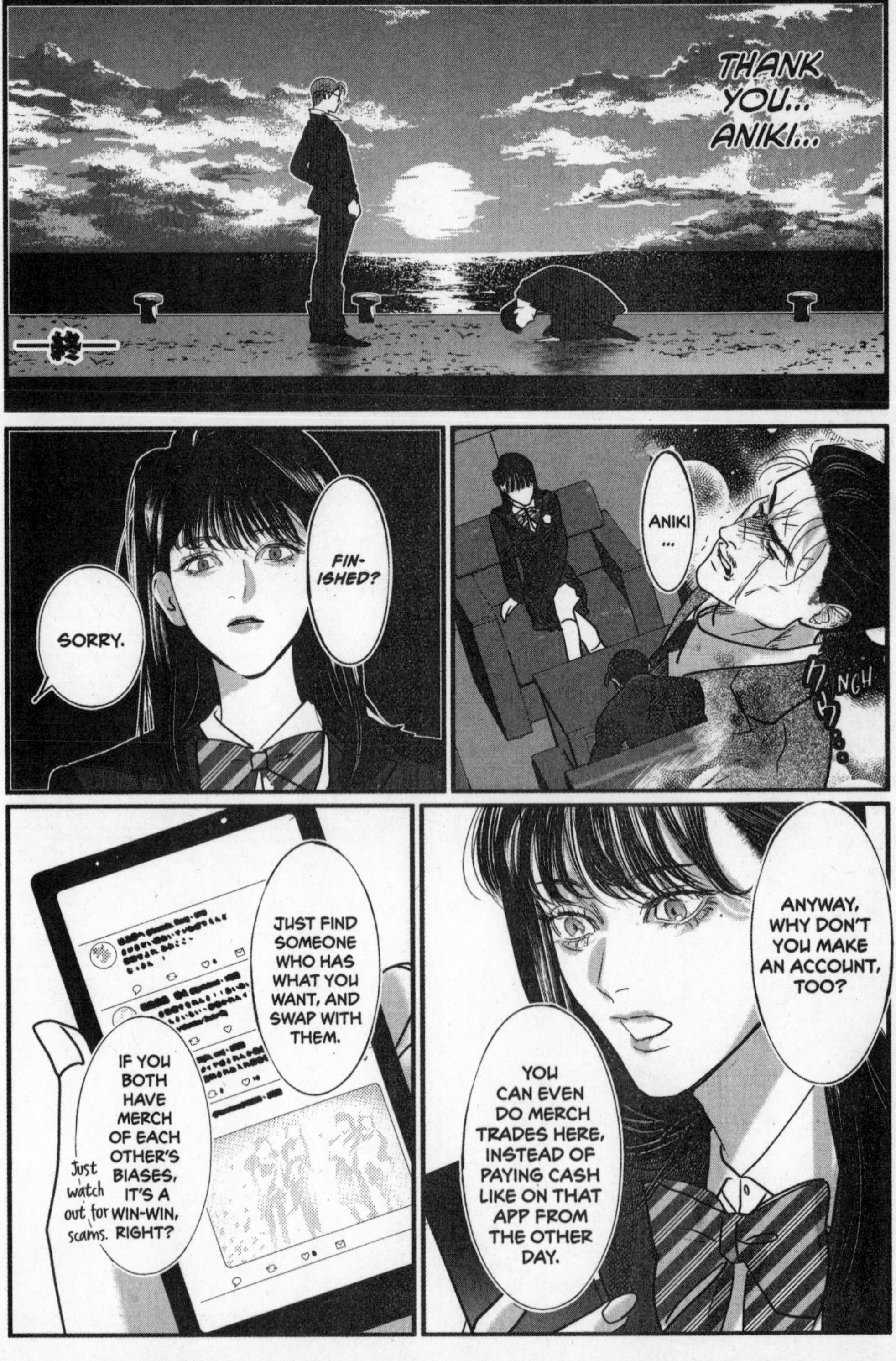
THANK YOU... ANIKI...
—終—
ANIKI ...
NGH
FIN-ISHED?
SORRY.
ANYWAY, WHY DON'T YOU MAKE AN ACCOUNT, TOO?
YOU CAN EVEN DO MERCH TRADES HERE, INSTEAD OF PAYING CASH LIKE ON THAT APP FROM THE OTHER DAY.
JUST FIND SOMEONE WHO HAS WHAT YOU WANT, AND SWAP WITH THEM.
IF YOU BOTH HAVE MERCH OF EACH OTHER'S BIASES, IT'S A WIN-WIN, RIGHT?
Just watch out for scams.

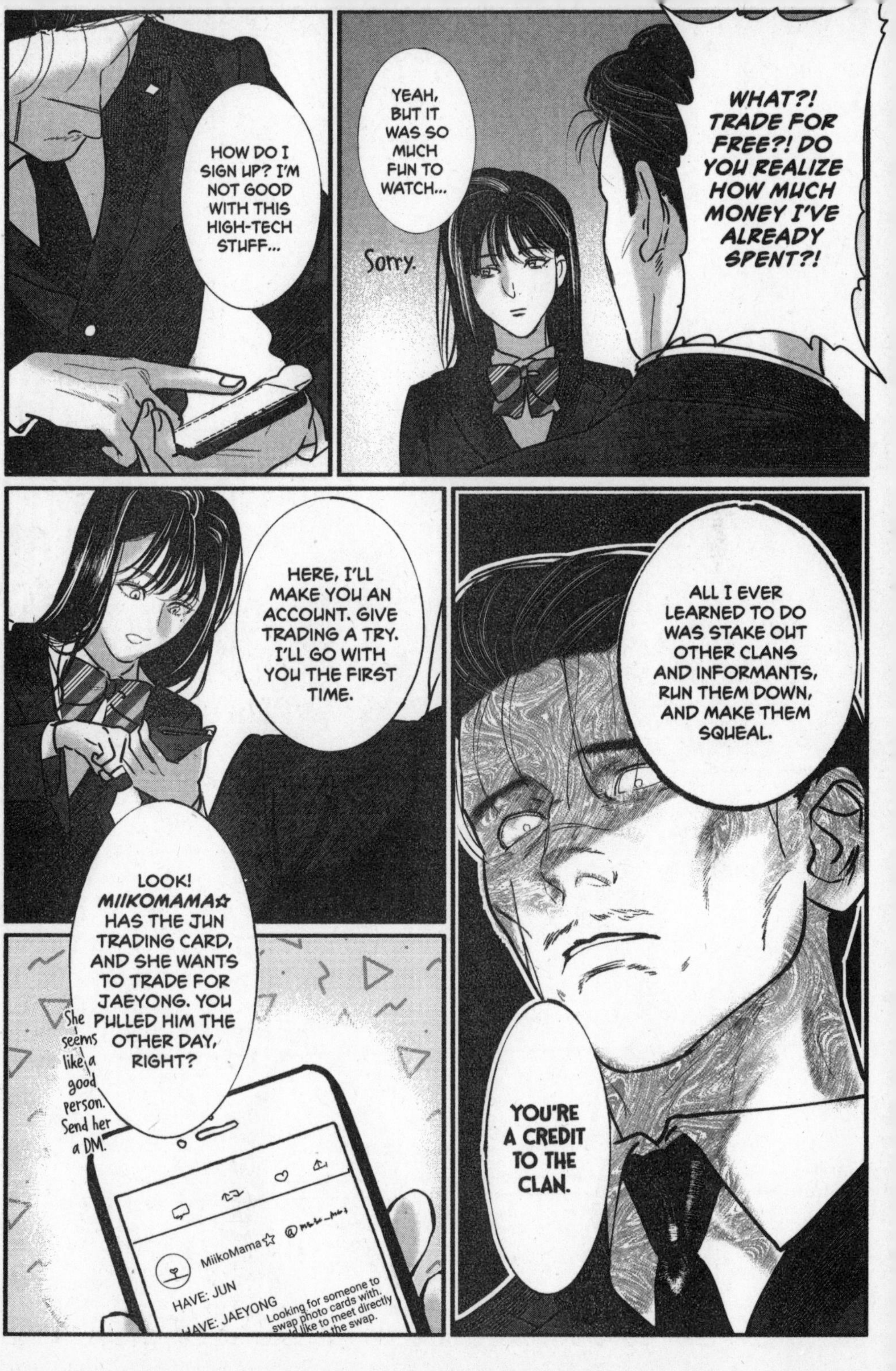
WHAT?! TRADE FOR FREE?! DO YOU REALIZE HOW MUCH MONEY I'VE ALREADY SPENT?!
YEAH, BUT IT WAS SO MUCH FUN TO WATCH...
Sorry.
HOW DO I SIGN UP? I'M NOT GOOD WITH THIS HIGH-TECH STUFF...
ALL I EVER LEARNED TO DO WAS STAKE OUT OTHER CLANS AND INFORMANTS, RUN THEM DOWN, AND MAKE THEM SQUEAL.
YOU'RE A CREDIT TO THE CLAN.
HERE, I'LL MAKE YOU AN ACCOUNT. GIVE TRADING A TRY. I'LL GO WITH YOU THE FIRST TIME.
LOOK! MIIKOMAMA☆ HAS THE JUN TRADING CARD, AND SHE WANTS TO TRADE FOR JAEYONG. YOU PULLED HIM THE OTHER DAY, RIGHT?
She seems like a good person. Send her a DM.
MiikoMama☆
HAVE: JUN
HAVE: JAEYONG
Looking for someone to swap photo cards with.

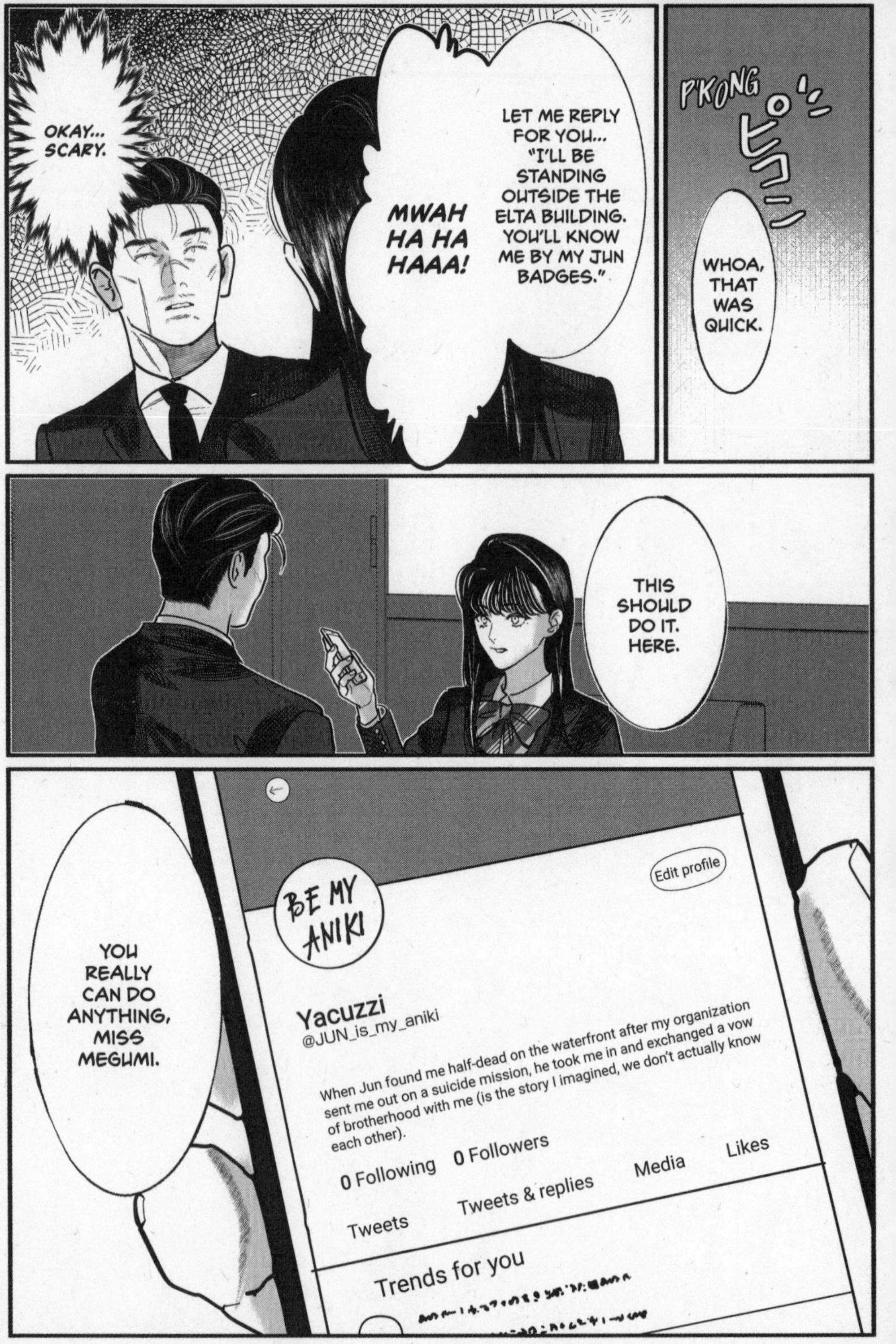
P'KONG
ピコーン
WHOA, THAT WAS QUICK.
LET ME REPLY FOR YOU... "I'LL BE STANDING OUTSIDE THE ELTA BUILDING. YOU'LL KNOW ME BY MY JUN BADGES."
MWAH HA HA HAAA!
OKAY... SCARY.
THIS SHOULD DO IT. HERE.
Edit profile
BE MY ANIKI
Yacuzzi
@JUN_is_my_aniki
When Jun found me half-dead on the waterfront after my organization sent me out on a suicide mission, he took me in and exchanged a vow of brotherhood with me (is the story I imagined, we don't actually know each other).
0 Following 0 Followers
Tweets Tweets & replies Media Likes
Trends for you
YOU REALLY CAN DO ANYTHING, MISS MEGUMI.

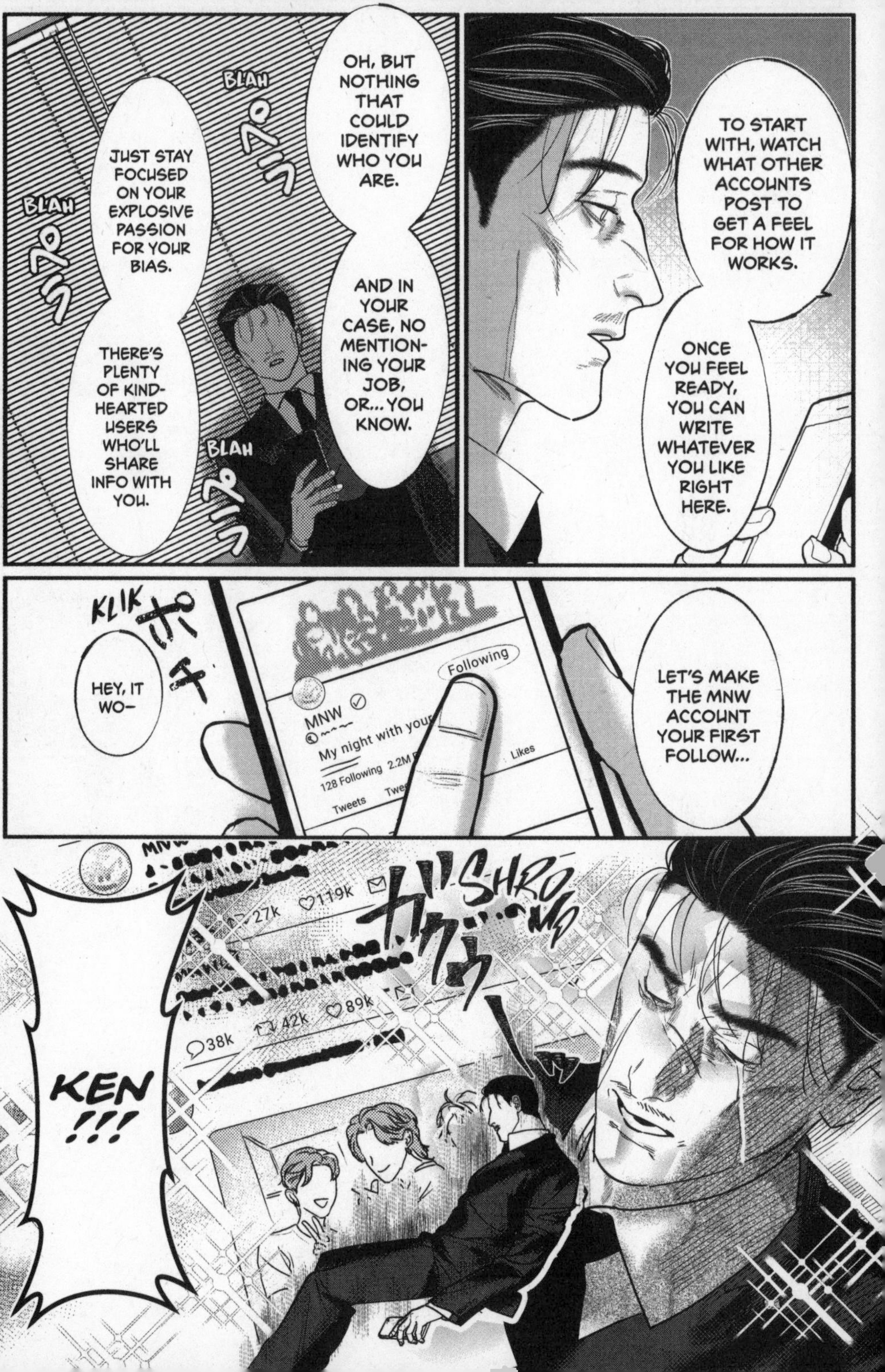
TO START WITH, WATCH WHAT OTHER ACCOUNTS POST TO GET A FEEL FOR HOW IT WORKS.
ONCE YOU FEEL READY, YOU CAN WRITE WHATEVER YOU LIKE RIGHT HERE.
OH, BUT NOTHING THAT COULD IDENTIFY WHO YOU ARE.
AND IN YOUR CASE, NO MENTIONING YOUR JOB, OR... YOU KNOW.
BLAH
JUST STAY FOCUSED ON YOUR EXPLOSIVE PASSION FOR YOUR BIAS.
BLAH
THERE'S PLENTY OF KIND-HEARTED USERS WHO'LL SHARE INFO WITH YOU.
BLAH
LET'S MAKE THE MNW ACCOUNT YOUR FIRST FOLLOW...
Following
MNW
My night with your
128 Following 2.2M
Likes
Tweets
KLIK
ポチ
HEY, IT WO-
SHROMP
KEN!!!

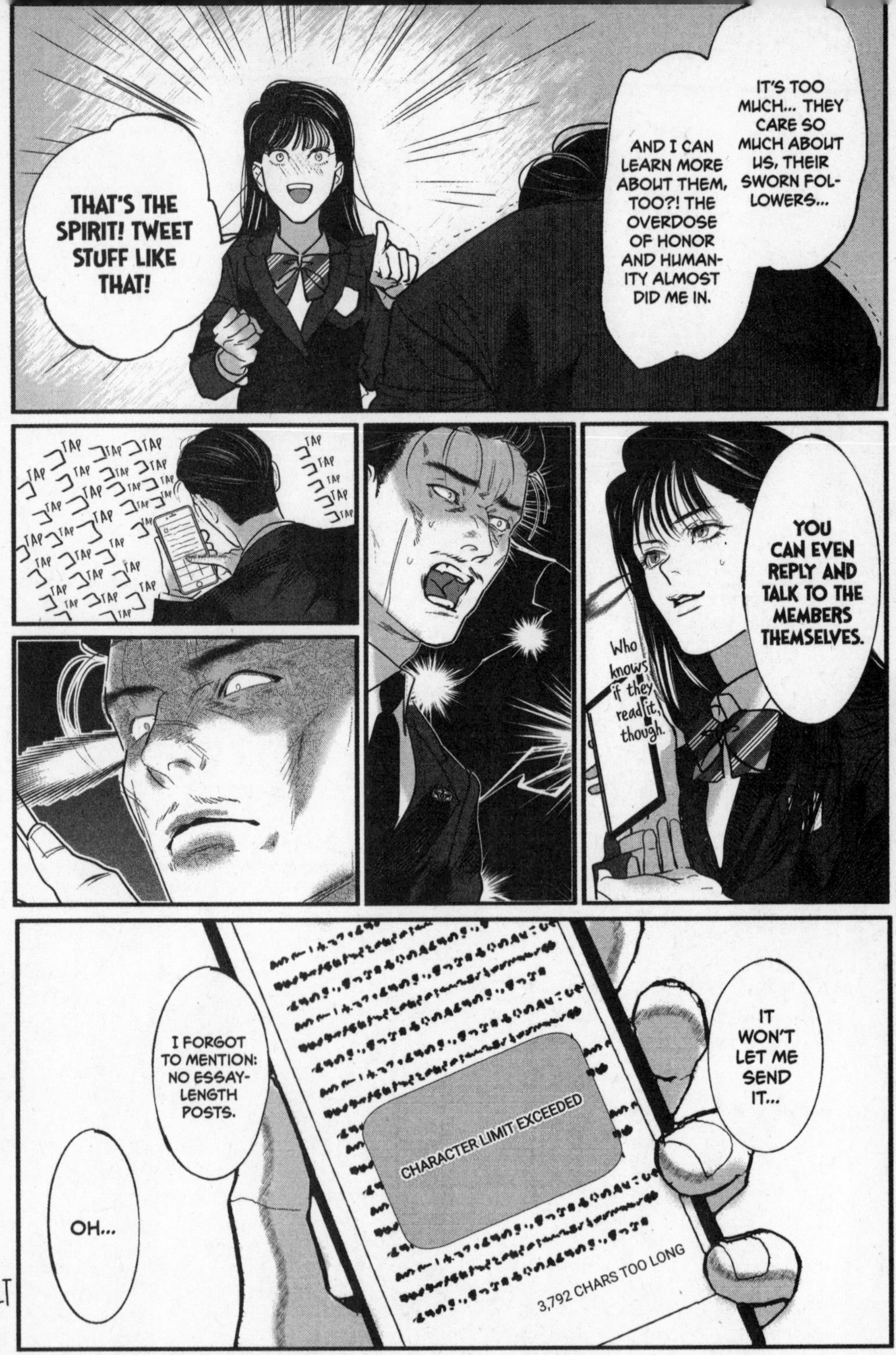
IT'S TOO MUCH... THEY CARE SO MUCH ABOUT US, THEIR SWORN FOL-LOWERS...
AND I CAN LEARN MORE ABOUT THEM, TOO?! THE OVERDOSE OF HONOR AND HUMAN-ITY ALMOST DID ME IN.
THAT'S THE SPIRIT! TWEET STUFF LIKE THAT!
YOU CAN EVEN REPLY AND TALK TO THE MEMBERS THEMSELVES.
Who knows if they read it, though.
TAP TAP TAP TAP TAP TAP
IT WON'T LET ME SEND IT...
CHARACTER LIMIT EXCEEDED
3,792 CHARS TOO LONG
I FORGOT TO MENTION: NO ESSAY-LENGTH POSTS.
OH...

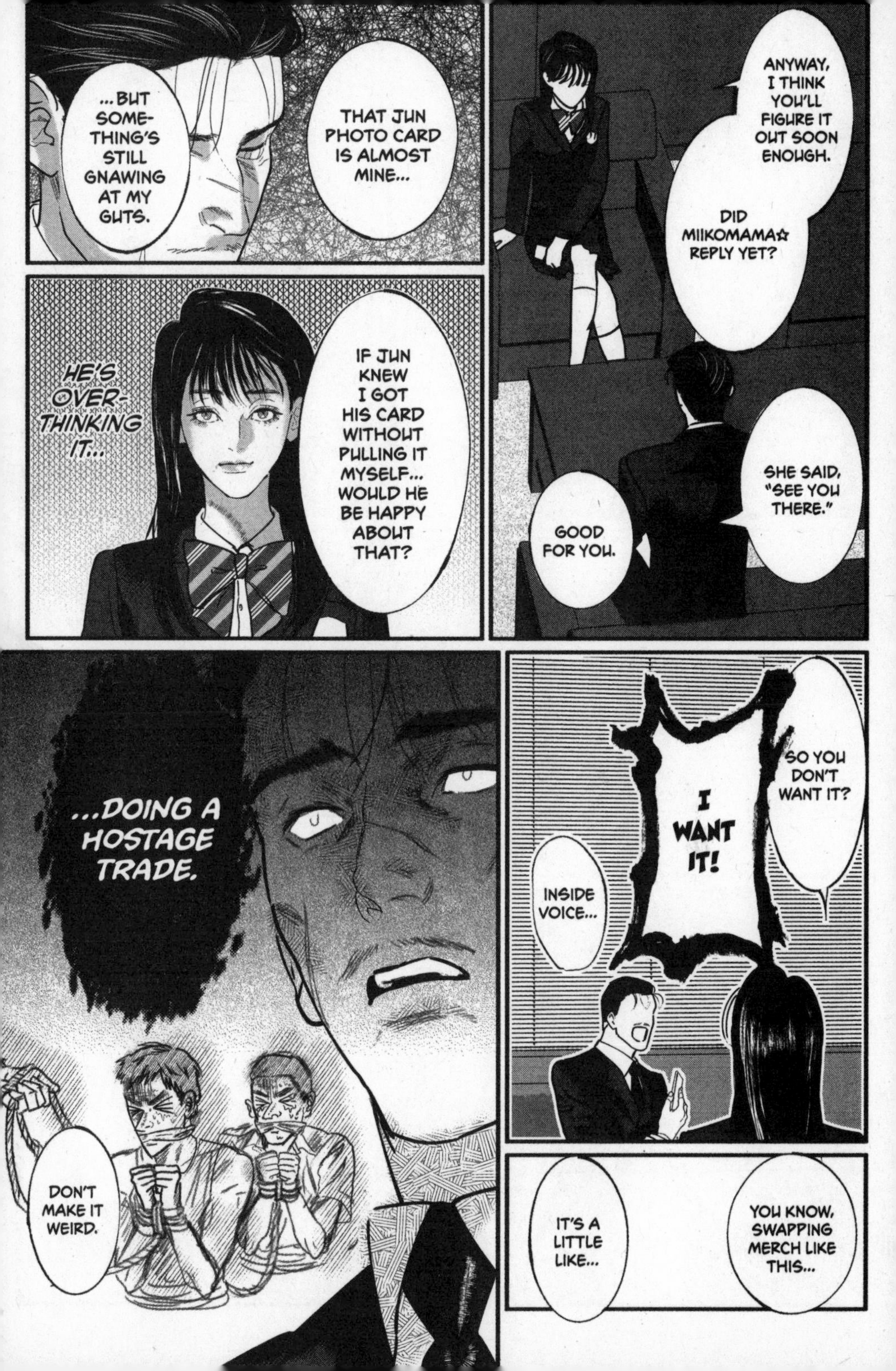
ANYWAY, I THINK YOU'LL FIGURE IT OUT SOON ENOUGH.
DID MIIKOMAMA☆ REPLY YET?
SHE SAID, "SEE YOU THERE."
GOOD FOR YOU.
THAT JUN PHOTO CARD IS ALMOST MINE...
...BUT SOME-THING'S STILL GNAWING AT MY GUTS.
IF JUN KNEW I GOT HIS CARD WITHOUT PULLING IT MYSELF... WOULD HE BE HAPPY ABOUT THAT?
HE'S OVER-THINKING IT...
SO YOU DON'T WANT IT?
I WANT IT!
INSIDE VOICE...
YOU KNOW, SWAPPING MERCH LIKE THIS...
IT'S A LITTLE LIKE...
...DOING A HOSTAGE TRADE.
DON'T MAKE IT WEIRD.

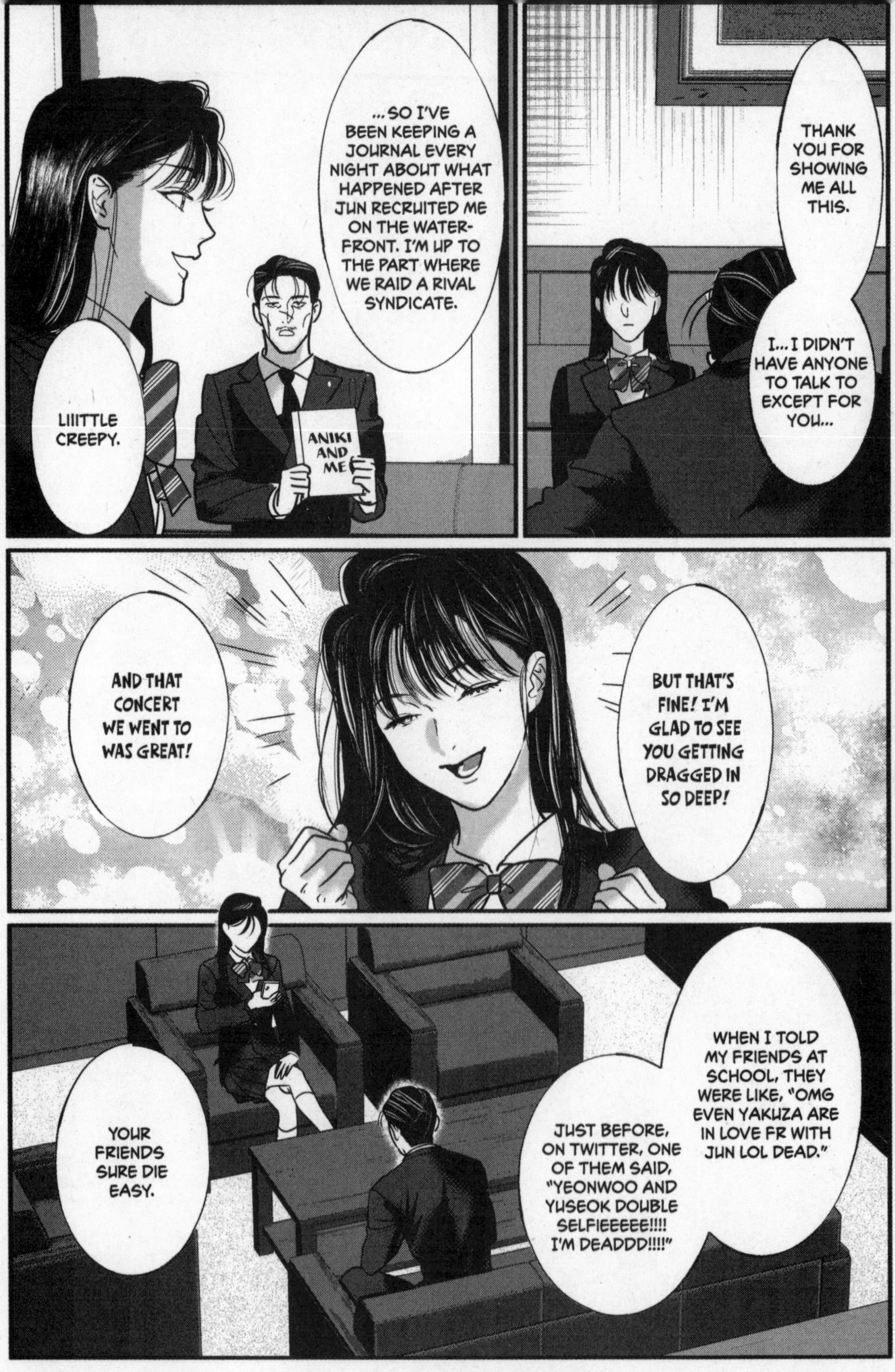
THANK YOU FOR SHOWING ME ALL THIS.
I... I DIDN'T HAVE ANYONE TO TALK TO EXCEPT FOR YOU...
...SO I'VE BEEN KEEPING A JOURNAL EVERY NIGHT ABOUT WHAT HAPPENED AFTER JUN RECRUITED ME ON THE WATER-FRONT. I'M UP TO THE PART WHERE WE RAID A RIVAL SYNDICATE.
ANIKI AND ME
LIIITTLE CREEPY.
BUT THAT'S FINE! I'M GLAD TO SEE YOU GETTING DRAGGED IN SO DEEP!
AND THAT CONCERT WE WENT TO WAS GREAT!
WHEN I TOLD MY FRIENDS AT SCHOOL, THEY WERE LIKE, "OMG EVEN YAKUZA ARE IN LOVE FR WITH JUN LOL DEAD."
JUST BEFORE, ON TWITTER, ONE OF THEM SAID, "YEONWOO AND YUSEOK DOUBLE SELFIEEEEE!!!! I'M DEADDD!!!!"
YOUR FRIENDS SURE DIE EASY.

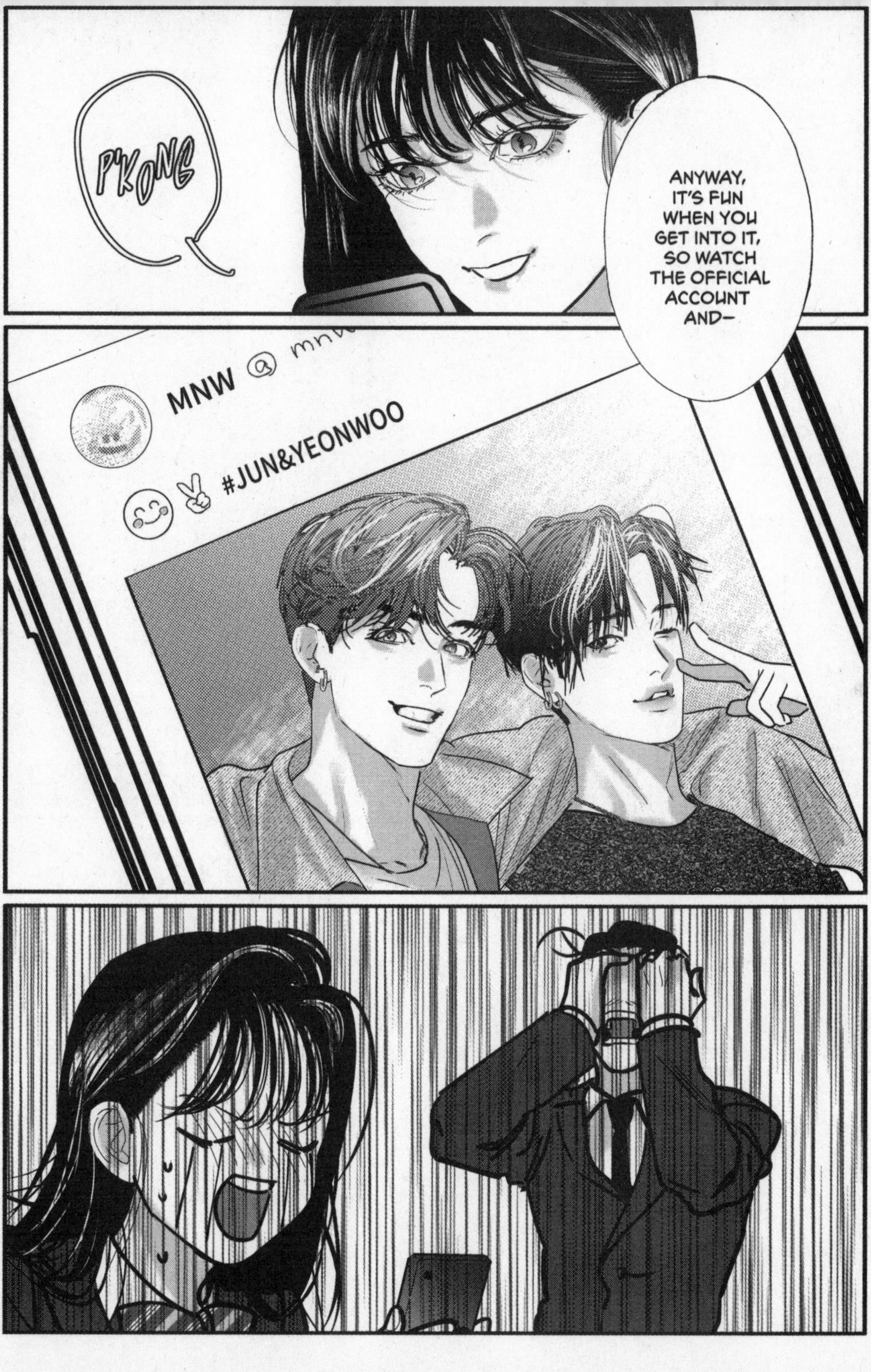
ANYWAY, IT'S FUN WHEN YOU GET INTO IT, SO WATCH THE OFFICIAL ACCOUNT AND–
P'KONG
MNW @ mnw
#JUN&YEONWOO

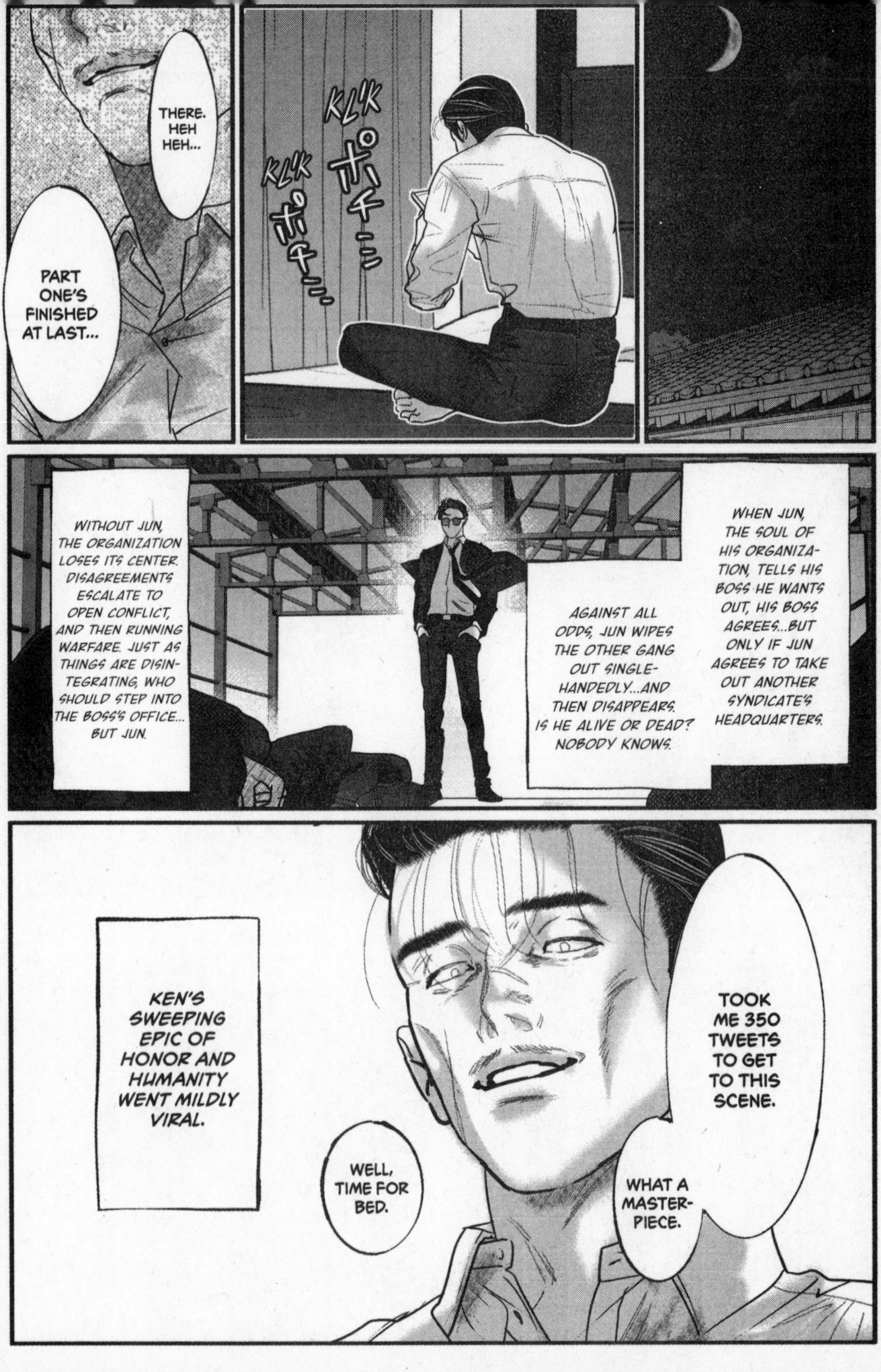
KLIK ポチーー
KLIK ポチーー
THERE. HEH HEH...
PART ONE'S FINISHED AT LAST...
WHEN JUN, THE SOUL OF HIS ORGANIZATION, TELLS HIS BOSS HE WANTS OUT, HIS BOSS AGREES...BUT ONLY IF JUN AGREES TO TAKE OUT ANOTHER SYNDICATE'S HEADQUARTERS.
AGAINST ALL ODDS, JUN WIPES THE OTHER GANG OUT SINGLE-HANDEDLY...AND THEN DISAPPEARS. IS HE ALIVE OR DEAD? NOBODY KNOWS.
WITHOUT JUN, THE ORGANIZATION LOSES ITS CENTER. DISAGREEMENTS ESCALATE TO OPEN CONFLICT, AND THEN RUNNING WARFARE. JUST AS THINGS ARE DISINTEGRATING, WHO SHOULD STEP INTO THE BOSS'S OFFICE... BUT JUN.
TOOK ME 350 TWEETS TO GET TO THIS SCENE.
WHAT A MASTERPIECE.
WELL, TIME FOR BED.
KEN'S SWEEPING EPIC OF HONOR AND HUMANITY WENT MILDLY VIRAL.

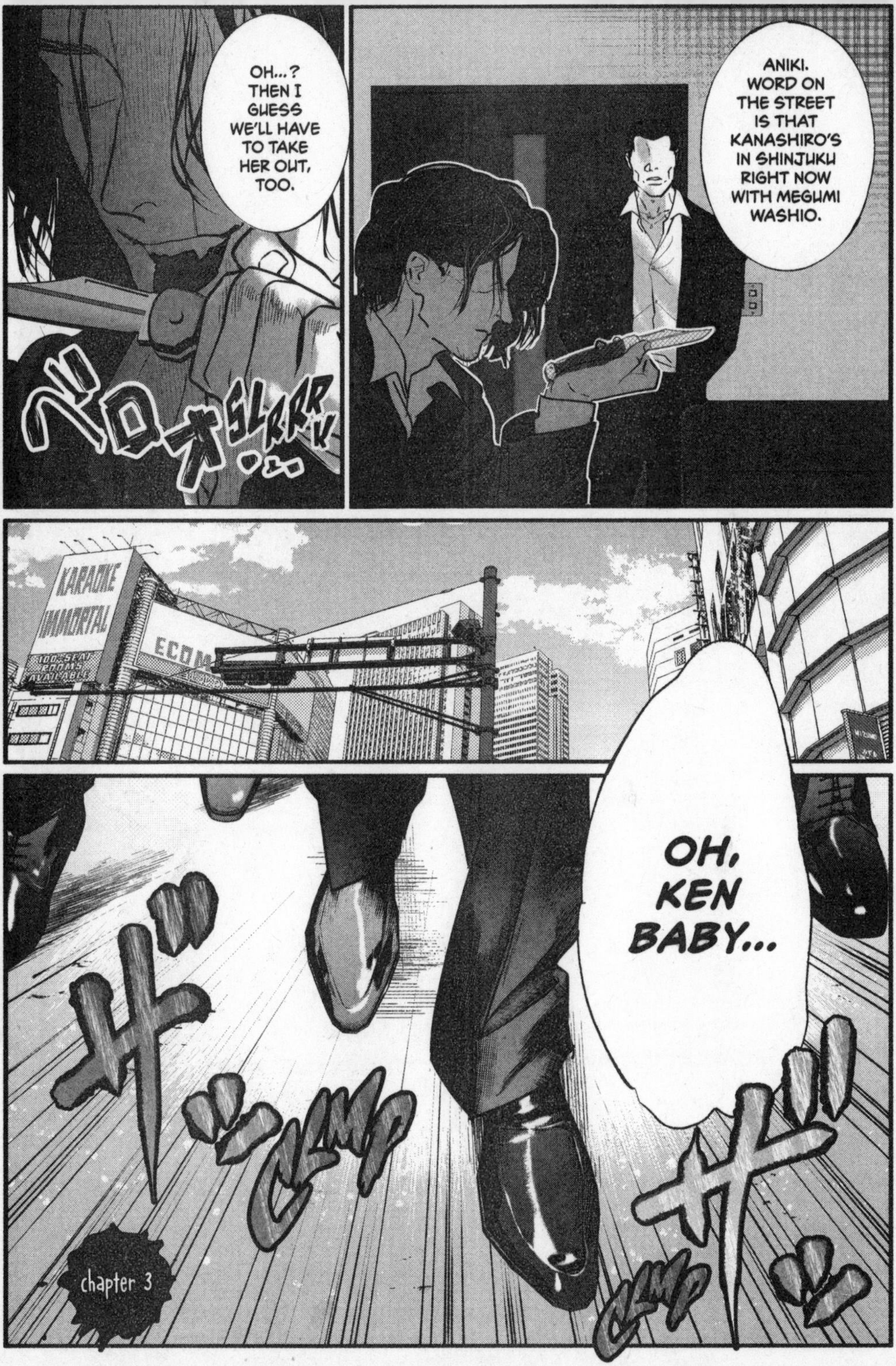
ANIKI. WORD ON THE STREET IS THAT KANASHIRO'S IN SHINJUKU RIGHT NOW WITH MEGUMI WASHIO.
OH...? THEN I GUESS WE'LL HAVE TO TAKE HER OUT, TOO.
SLRRRK
KARAOKE IMMORTAL
100-SEAT ROOMS AVAILABLE
ECOM
OH, KEN BABY...
CLMP
CLMP
chapter 3

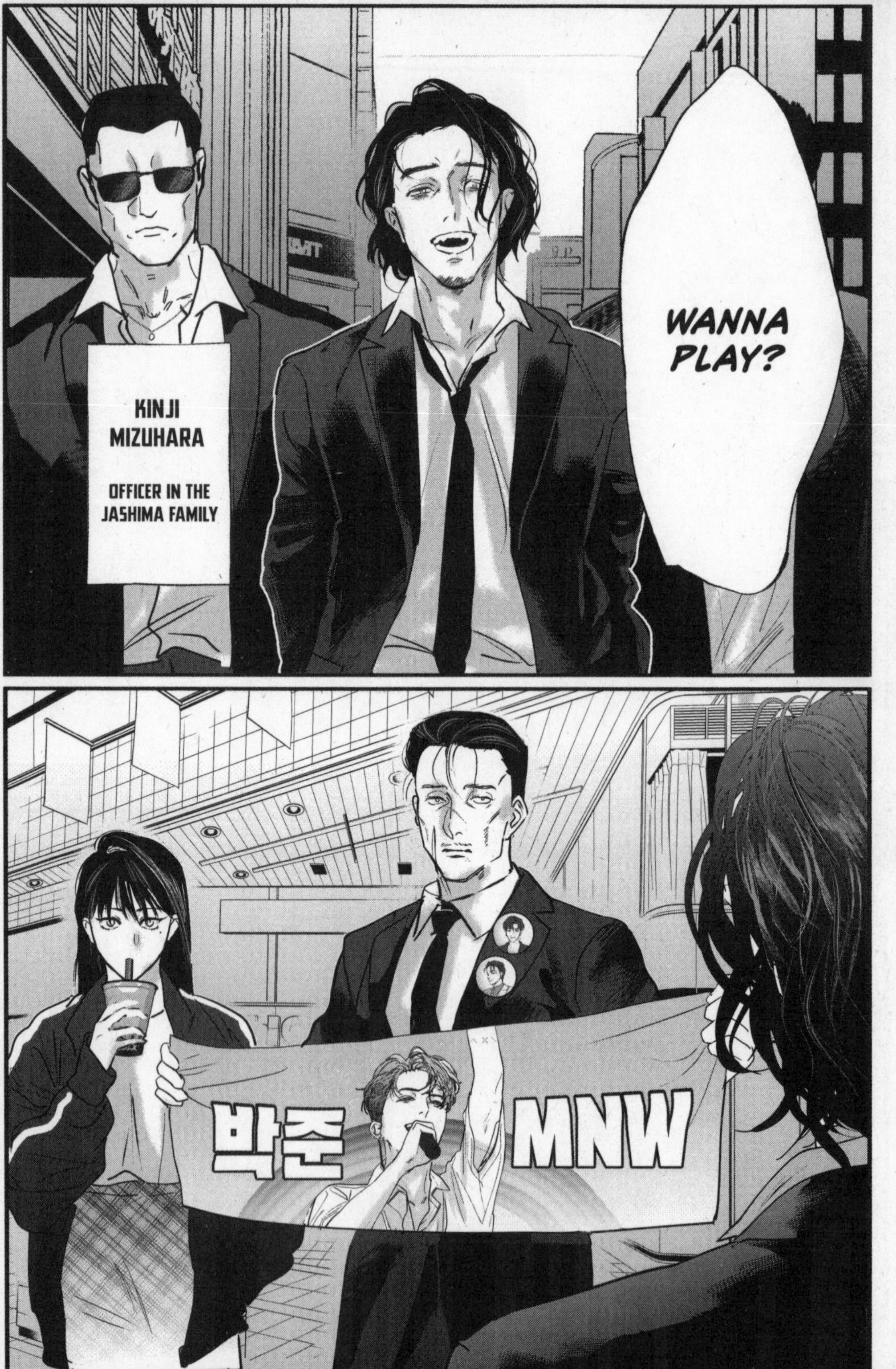
WANNA PLAY?
KINJI MIZUHARA
OFFICER IN THE JASHIMA FAMILY
박준 MNW

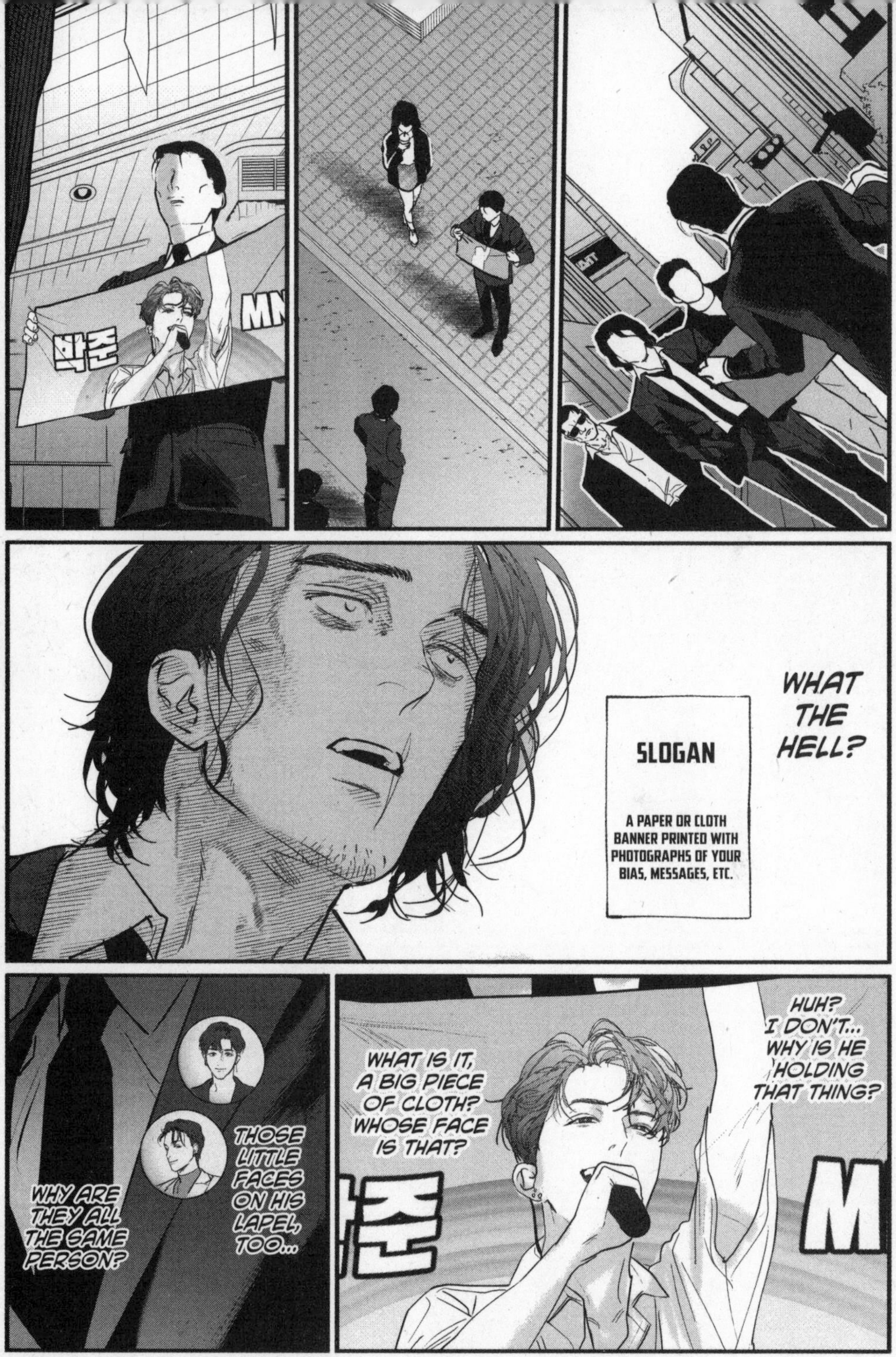
박준
MN
WHAT THE HELL?
SLOGAN
A PAPER OR CLOTH BANNER PRINTED WITH PHOTOGRAPHS OF YOUR BIAS, MESSAGES, ETC.
HUH? I DON'T... WHY IS HE HOLDING THAT THING?
WHAT IS IT, A BIG PIECE OF CLOTH? WHOSE FACE IS THAT?
M
THOSE LITTLE FACES ON HIS LAPEL, TOO...
WHY ARE THEY ALL THE SAME PERSON?

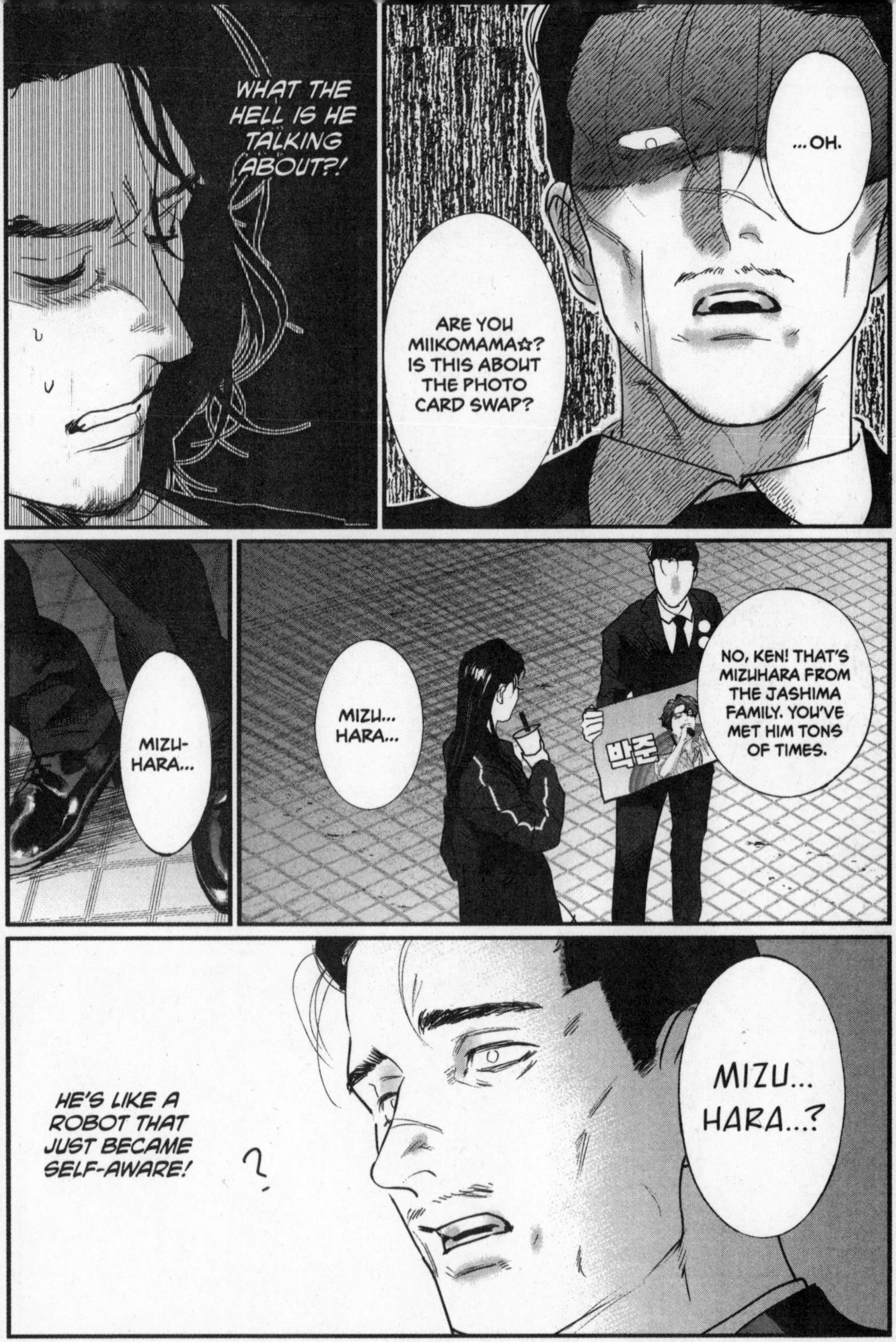
...OH.
ARE YOU MIIKOMAMA☆? IS THIS ABOUT THE PHOTO CARD SWAP?
WHAT THE HELL IS HE TALKING ABOUT?!
NO, KEN! THAT'S MIZUHARA FROM THE JASHIMA FAMILY. YOU'VE MET HIM TONS OF TIMES.
박준
MIZU... HARA...
MIZU-HARA...
MIZU... HARA...?
?
HE'S LIKE A ROBOT THAT JUST BECAME SELF-AWARE!

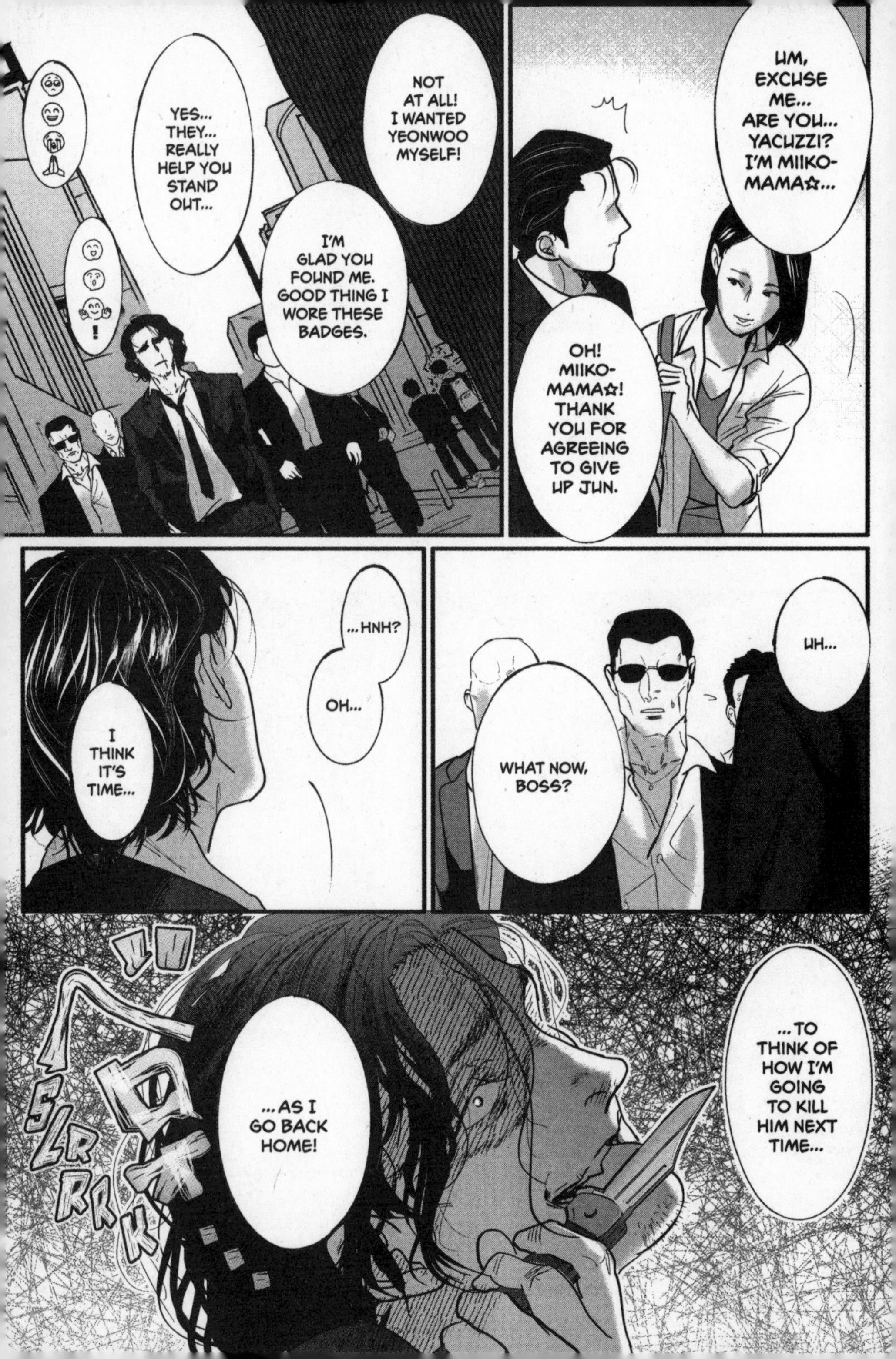
UM, EXCUSE ME... ARE YOU... YACUZZI? I'M MIIKO-MAMA☆...
OH! MIIKO-MAMA☆! THANK YOU FOR AGREEING TO GIVE UP JUN.
NOT AT ALL! I WANTED YEONWOO MYSELF!
I'M GLAD YOU FOUND ME. GOOD THING I WORE THESE BADGES.
YES... THEY... REALLY HELP YOU STAND OUT...
!
UH...
WHAT NOW, BOSS?
...HNH?
OH...
I THINK IT'S TIME...
...TO THINK OF HOW I'M GOING TO KILL HIM NEXT TIME...
...AS I GO BACK HOME!
SLRRRK

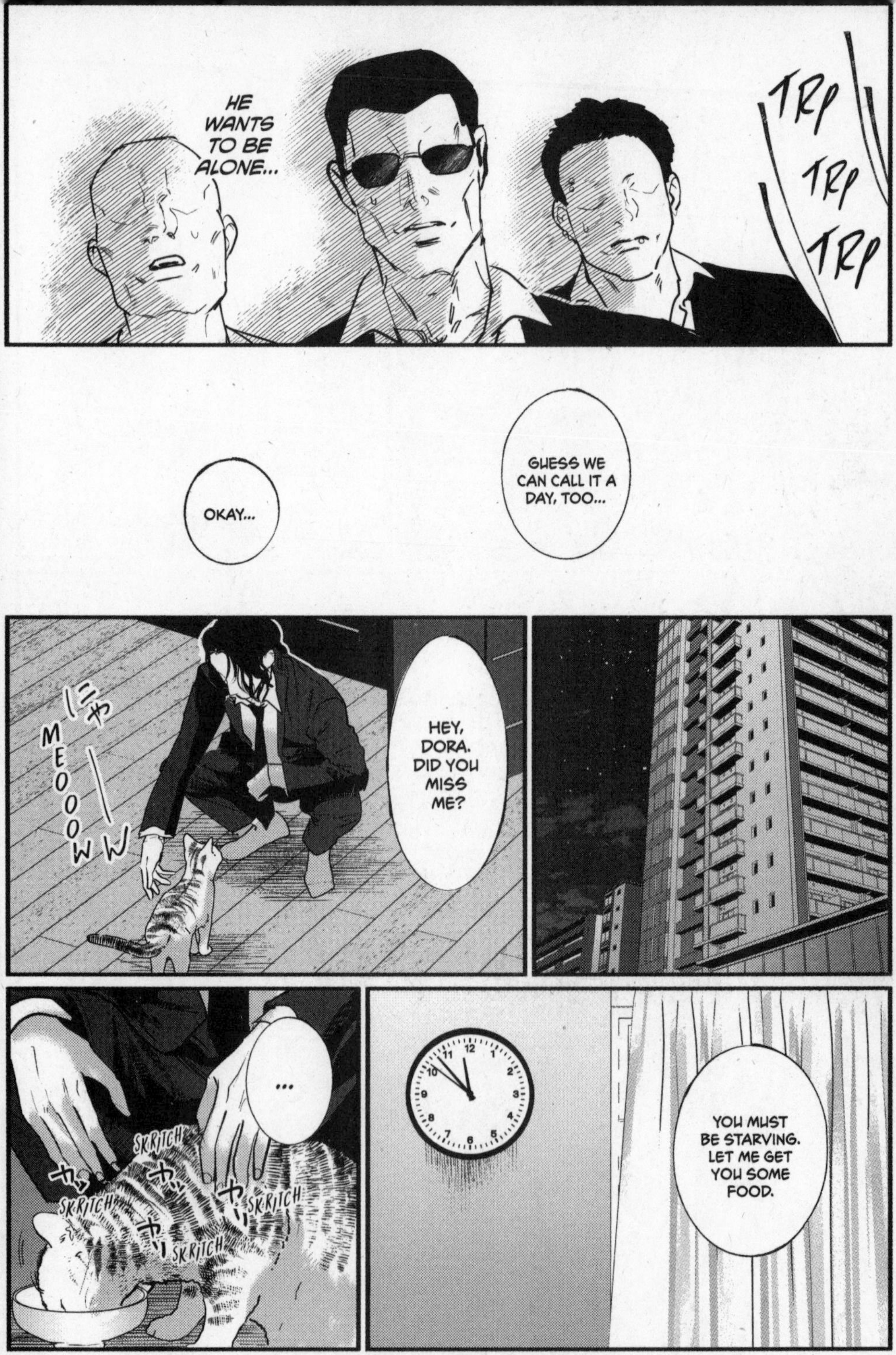
TRP TRP TRP
HE WANTS TO BE ALONE...
GUESS WE CAN CALL IT A DAY, TOO...
OKAY...
HEY, DORA. DID YOU MISS ME?
にゃー
MEOOOOW
YOU MUST BE STARVING. LET ME GET YOU SOME FOOD.
...
SKRITCH
SKRITCH
SKRITCH
SKRITCH

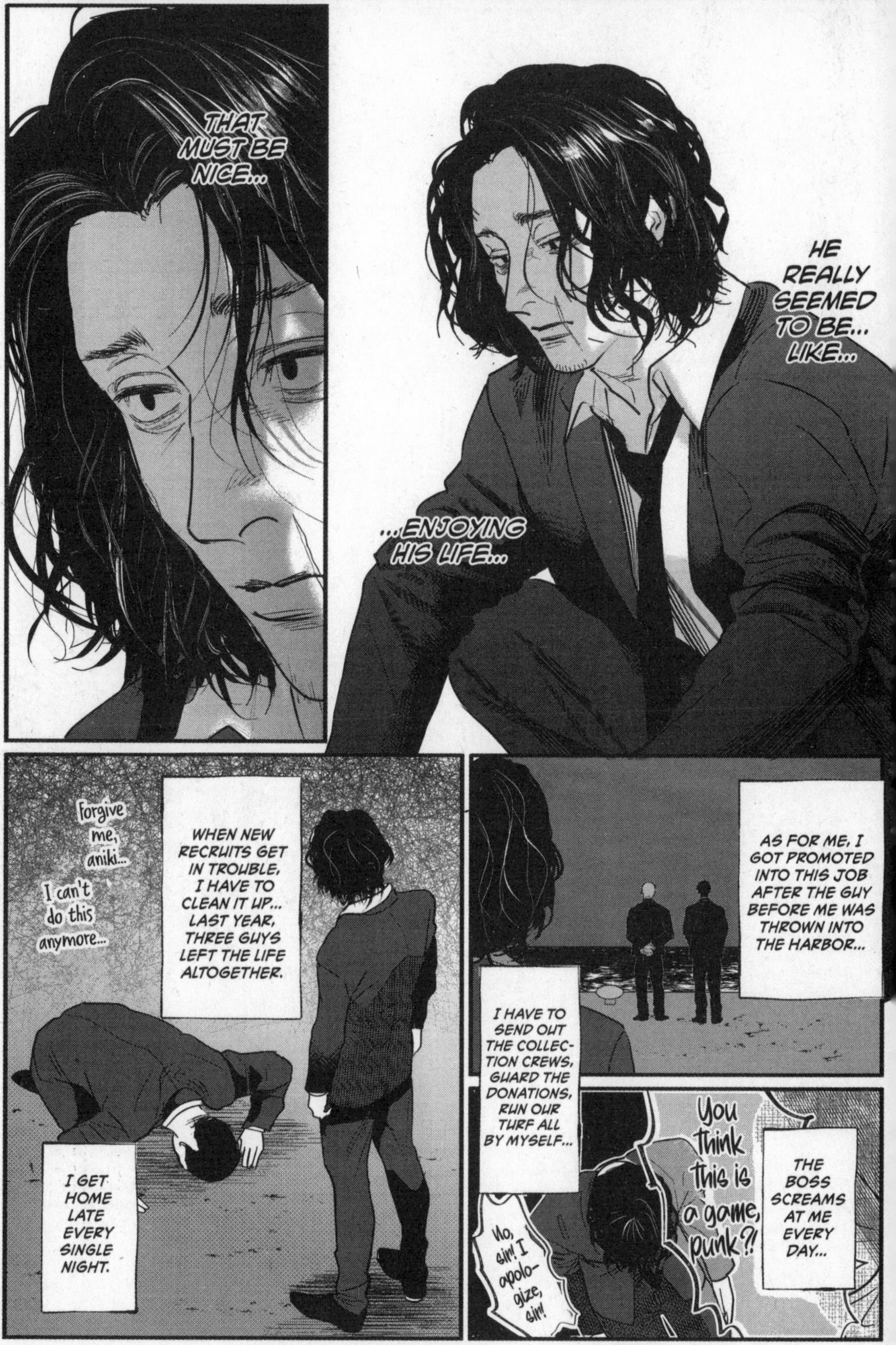
HE REALLY SEEMED TO BE... LIKE...
...ENJOYING HIS LIFE...
THAT MUST BE NICE...
AS FOR ME, I GOT PROMOTED INTO THIS JOB AFTER THE GUY BEFORE ME WAS THROWN INTO THE HARBOR...
I HAVE TO SEND OUT THE COLLECTION CREWS, GUARD THE DONATIONS, RUN OUR TURF ALL BY MYSELF...
THE BOSS SCREAMS AT ME EVERY DAY...
You think this is a game, punk?!
No, sir! I apologize, sir!
WHEN NEW RECRUITS GET IN TROUBLE, I HAVE TO CLEAN IT UP... LAST YEAR, THREE GUYS LEFT THE LIFE ALTOGETHER.
forgive me, aniki...
I can't do this anymore...
I GET HOME LATE EVERY SINGLE NIGHT.

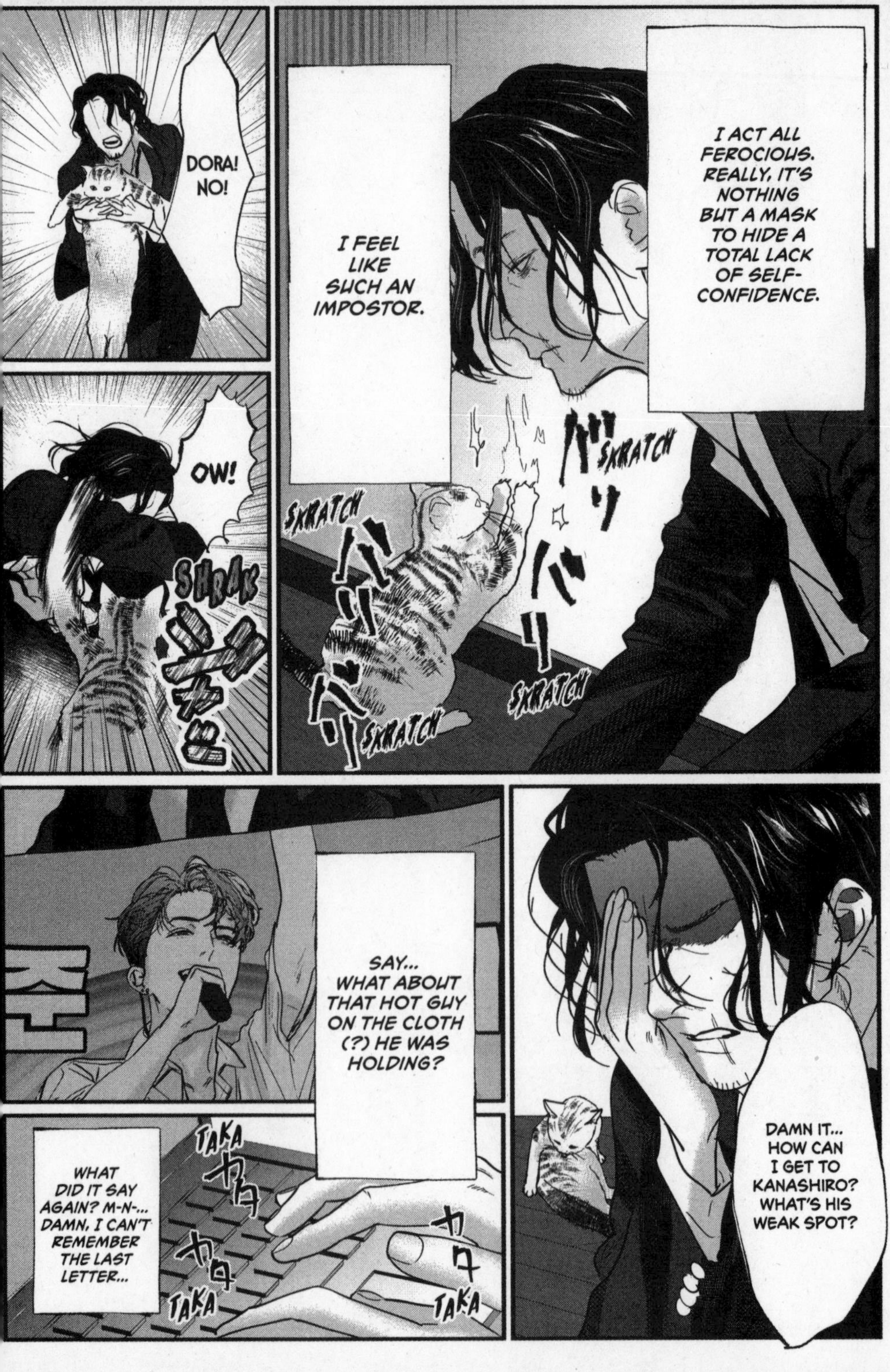

I ACT ALL FEROCIOUS. REALLY, IT'S NOTHING BUT A MASK TO HIDE A TOTAL LACK OF SELF-CONFIDENCE.
I FEEL LIKE SUCH AN IMPOSTOR.
SKRATCH
SKRATCH
SKRATCH
SKRATCH
DORA! NO!
OW!
SHRAK
DAMN IT... HOW CAN I GET TO KANASHIRO? WHAT'S HIS WEAK SPOT?
SAY... WHAT ABOUT THAT HOT GUY ON THE CLOTH (?) HE WAS HOLDING?
TAKA
TAKA
WHAT DID IT SAY AGAIN? M-N-... DAMN, I CAN'T REMEMBER THE LAST LETTER...
TAKA
TAKA

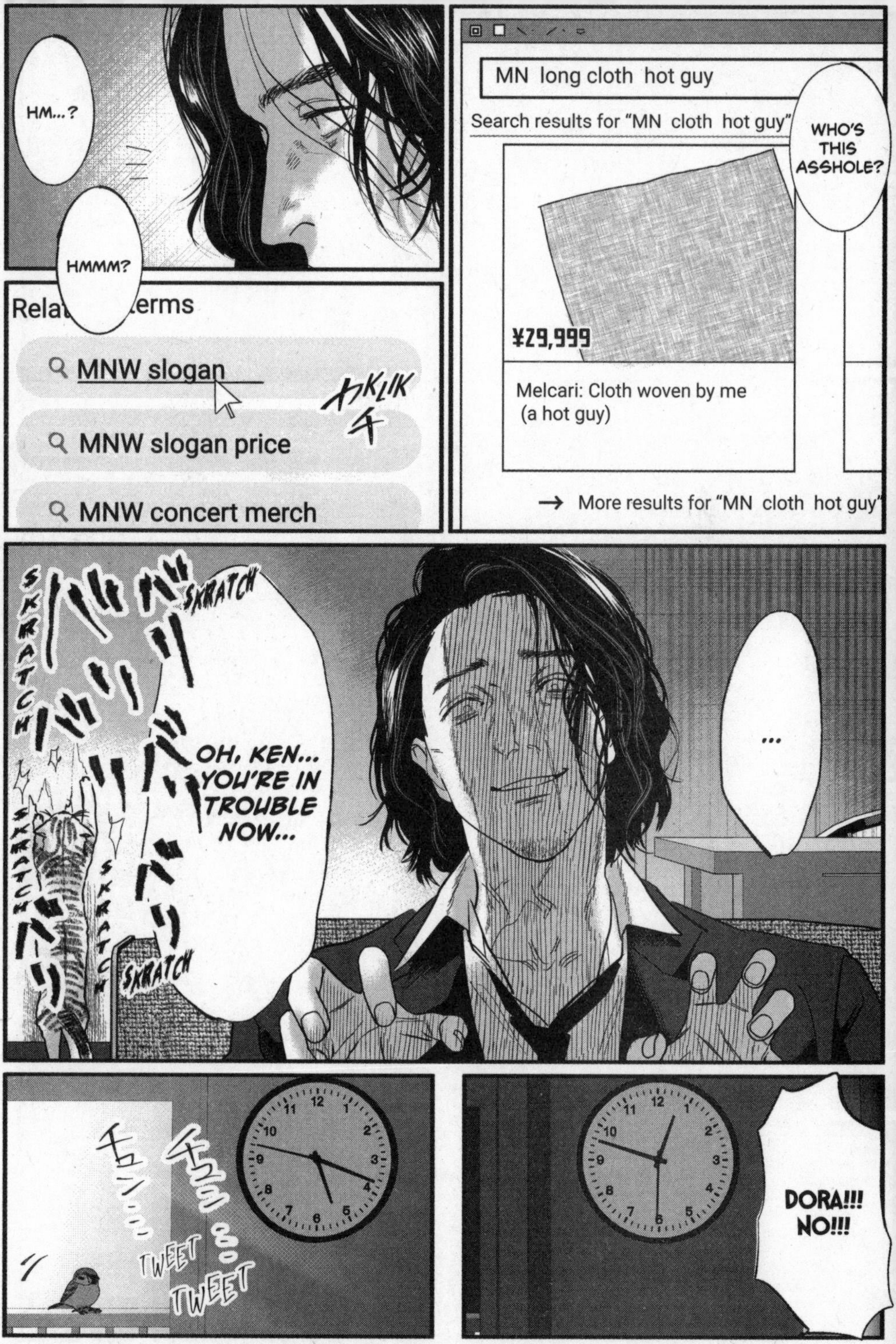

MN long cloth hot guy
Search results for "MN cloth hot guy"
WHO'S THIS ASSHOLE?
¥29,999
Melcari: Cloth woven by me (a hot guy)
→ More results for "MN cloth hot guy"
HM...?
HMMM?
Relat terms
MNW slogan
KLIK
MNW slogan price
MNW concert merch
...
OH, KEN... YOU'RE IN TROUBLE NOW...
SKRATCH
SKRATCH
SKRATCH
SKRATCH
SKRATCH
DORA!!! NO!!!
TWEET
TWEET

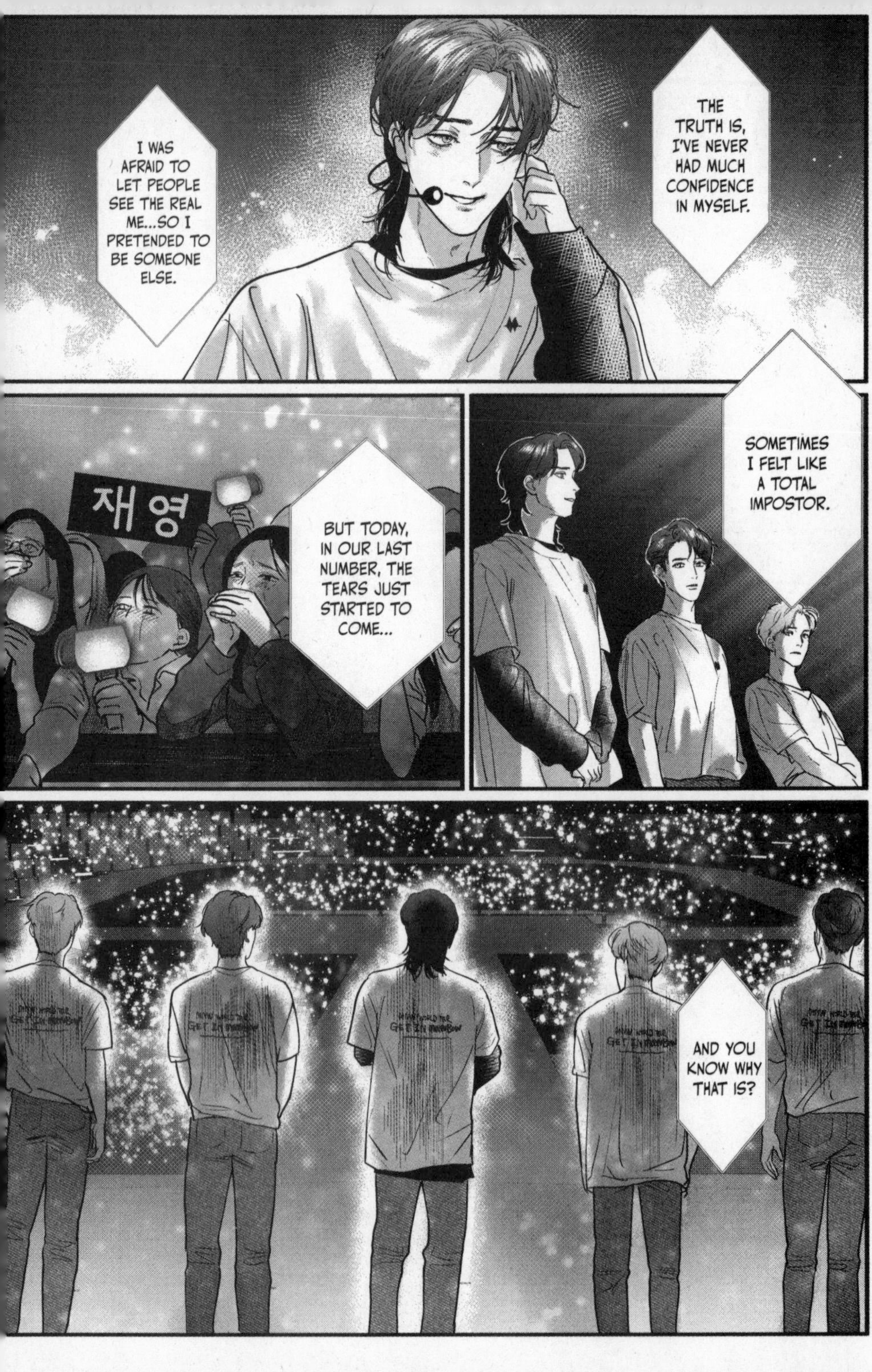
THE TRUTH IS, I'VE NEVER HAD MUCH CONFIDENCE IN MYSELF.
I WAS AFRAID TO LET PEOPLE SEE THE REAL ME...SO I PRETENDED TO BE SOMEONE ELSE.
SOMETIMES I FELT LIKE A TOTAL IMPOSTOR.
재영
BUT TODAY, IN OUR LAST NUMBER, THE TEARS JUST STARTED TO COME...
AND YOU KNOW WHY THAT IS?

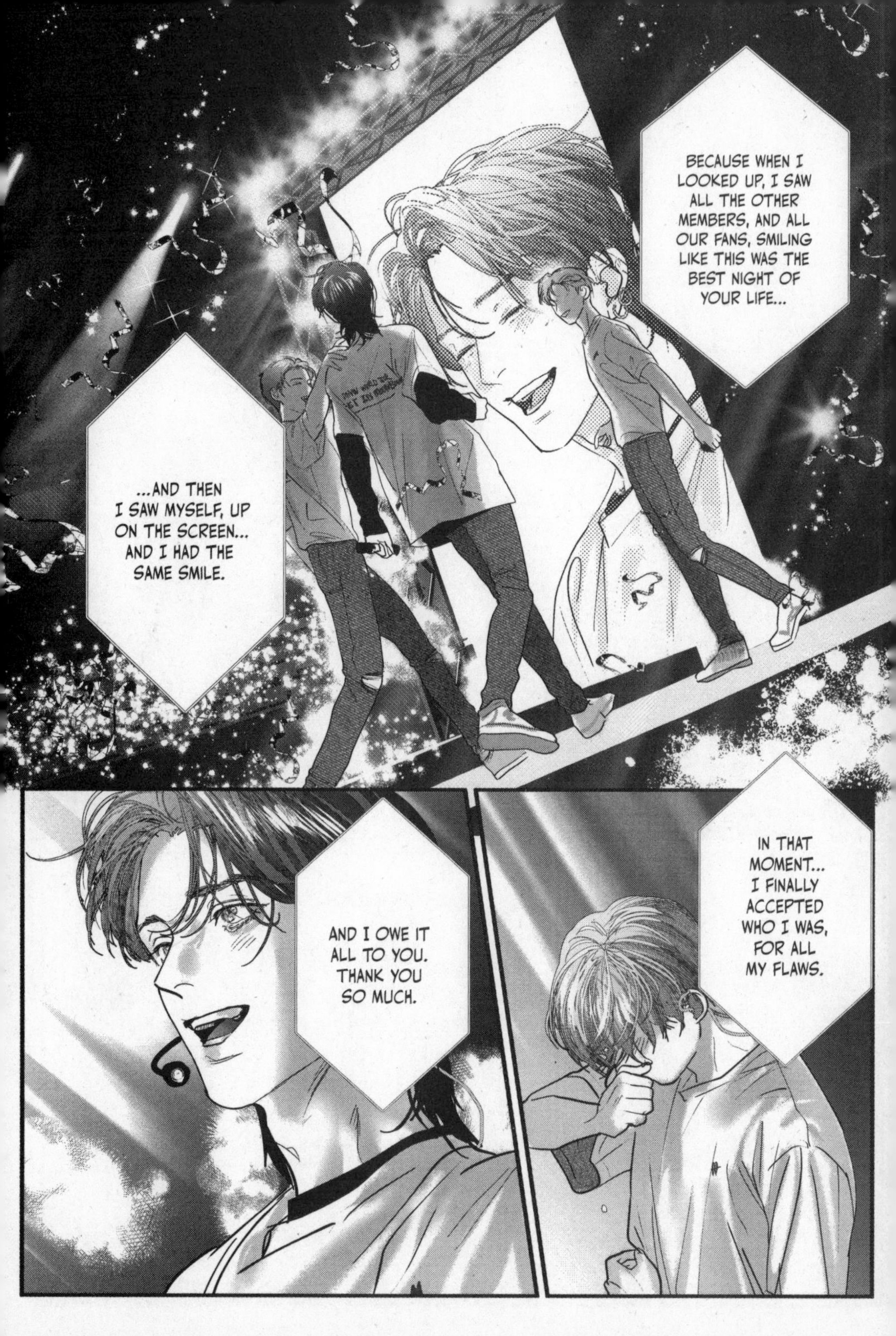
BECAUSE WHEN I LOOKED UP, I SAW ALL THE OTHER MEMBERS, AND ALL OUR FANS, SMILING LIKE THIS WAS THE BEST NIGHT OF YOUR LIFE...
...AND THEN I SAW MYSELF, UP ON THE SCREEN... AND I HAD THE SAME SMILE.
IN THAT MOMENT... I FINALLY ACCEPTED WHO I WAS, FOR ALL MY FLAWS.
AND I OWE IT ALL TO YOU. THANK YOU SO MUCH.

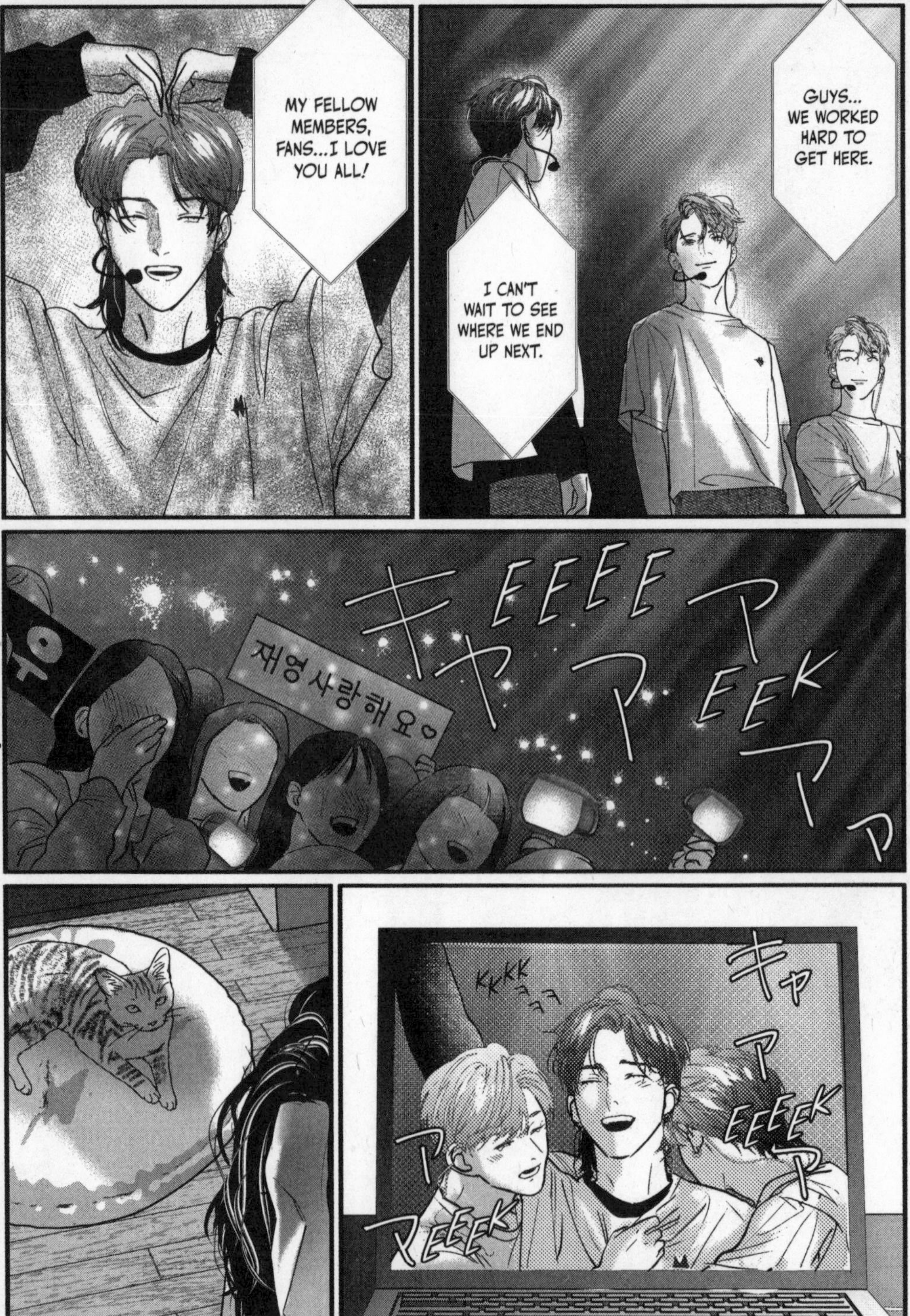
GUYS... WE WORKED HARD TO GET HERE.
I CAN'T WAIT TO SEE WHERE WE END UP NEXT.
MY FELLOW MEMBERS, FANS...I LOVE YOU ALL!
キャアアァ
EEEE
EEK
재영사랑해요♡
KKKK
ㅋㅋㅋ
キャア
EEEEK
ア
EEEEK

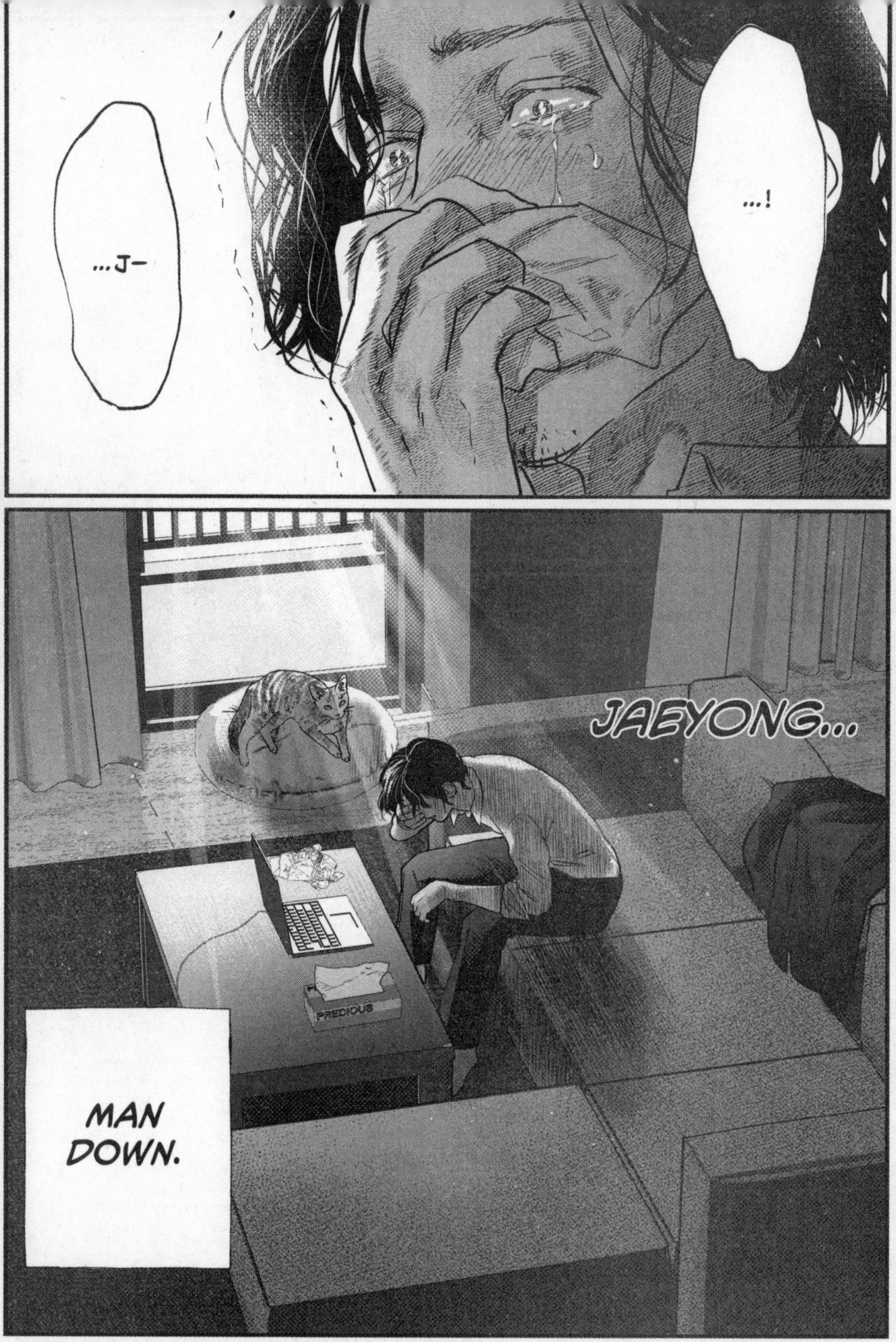
...!
...J-
JAEYONG...
PRECIOUS
MAN DOWN.

THE YAKUZA'S Bias

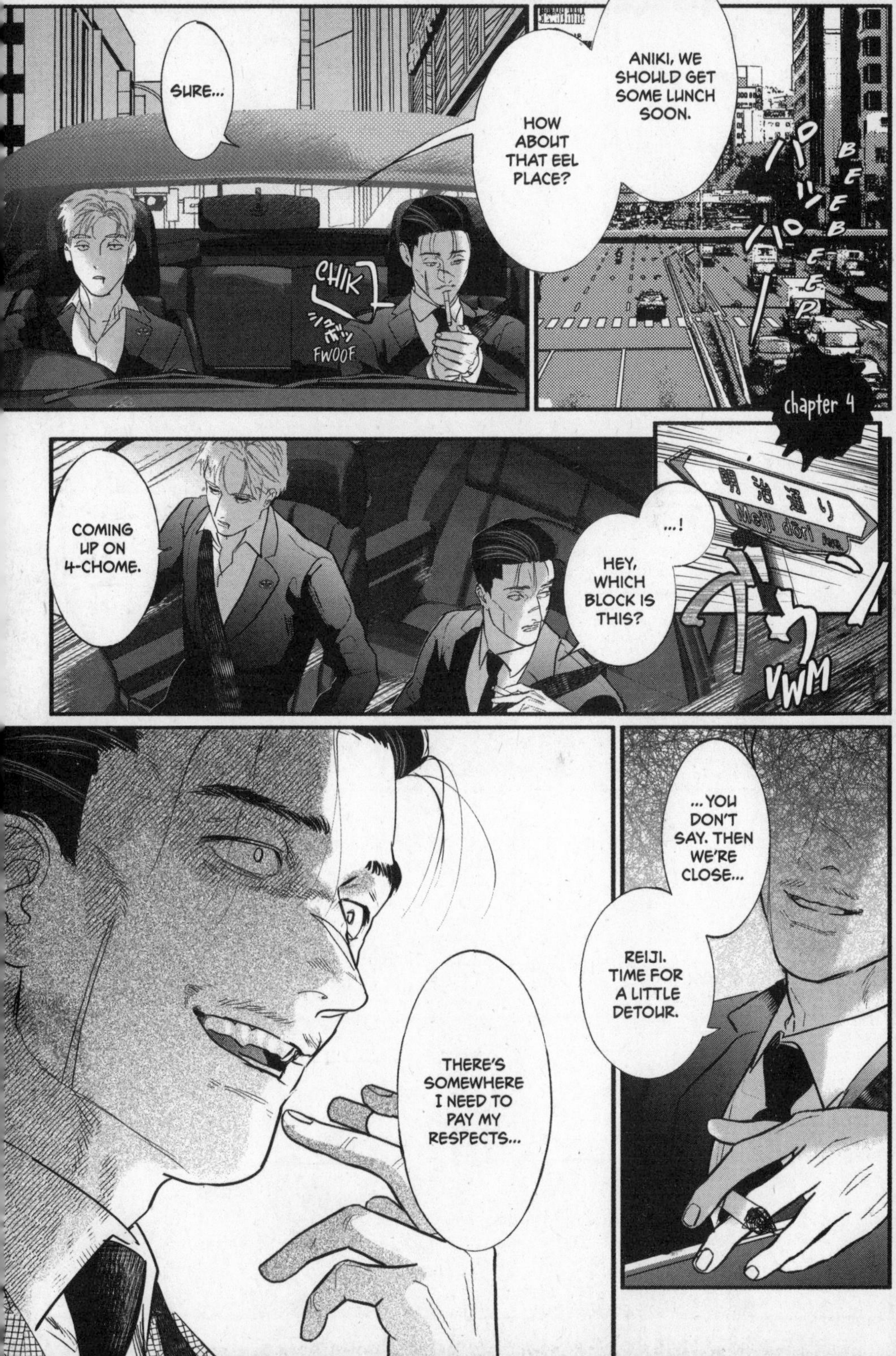
BEEBEEP
ANIKI, WE SHOULD GET SOME LUNCH SOON.
HOW ABOUT THAT EEL PLACE?
SURE...
CHIK
FWOOF
chapter 4
明治通り
Meiji dōri
VWM
...!
HEY, WHICH BLOCK IS THIS?
COMING UP ON 4-CHOME.
...YOU DON'T SAY. THEN WE'RE CLOSE...
REIJI. TIME FOR A LITTLE DETOUR.
THERE'S SOMEWHERE I NEED TO PAY MY RESPECTS...

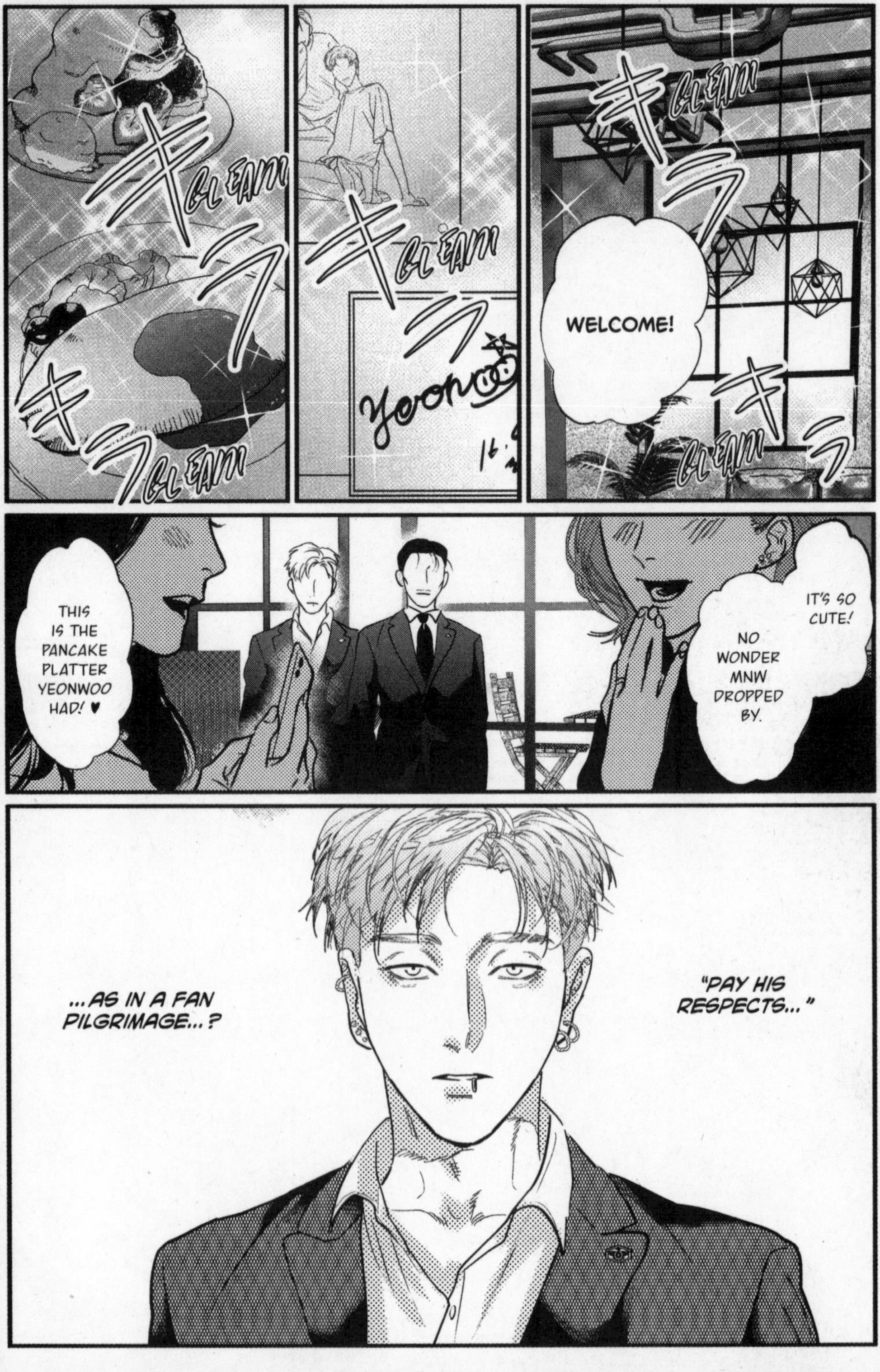
キラ
GLEAM
WELCOME!
キラ
GLEAM
キラ
GLEAM
キラ
GLEAM
キラ
GLEAM
IT'S SO CUTE!
NO WONDER MNW DROPPED BY.
THIS IS THE PANCAKE PLATTER YEONWOO HAD! ♥
"PAY HIS RESPECTS..."
...AS IN A FAN PILGRIMAGE...?

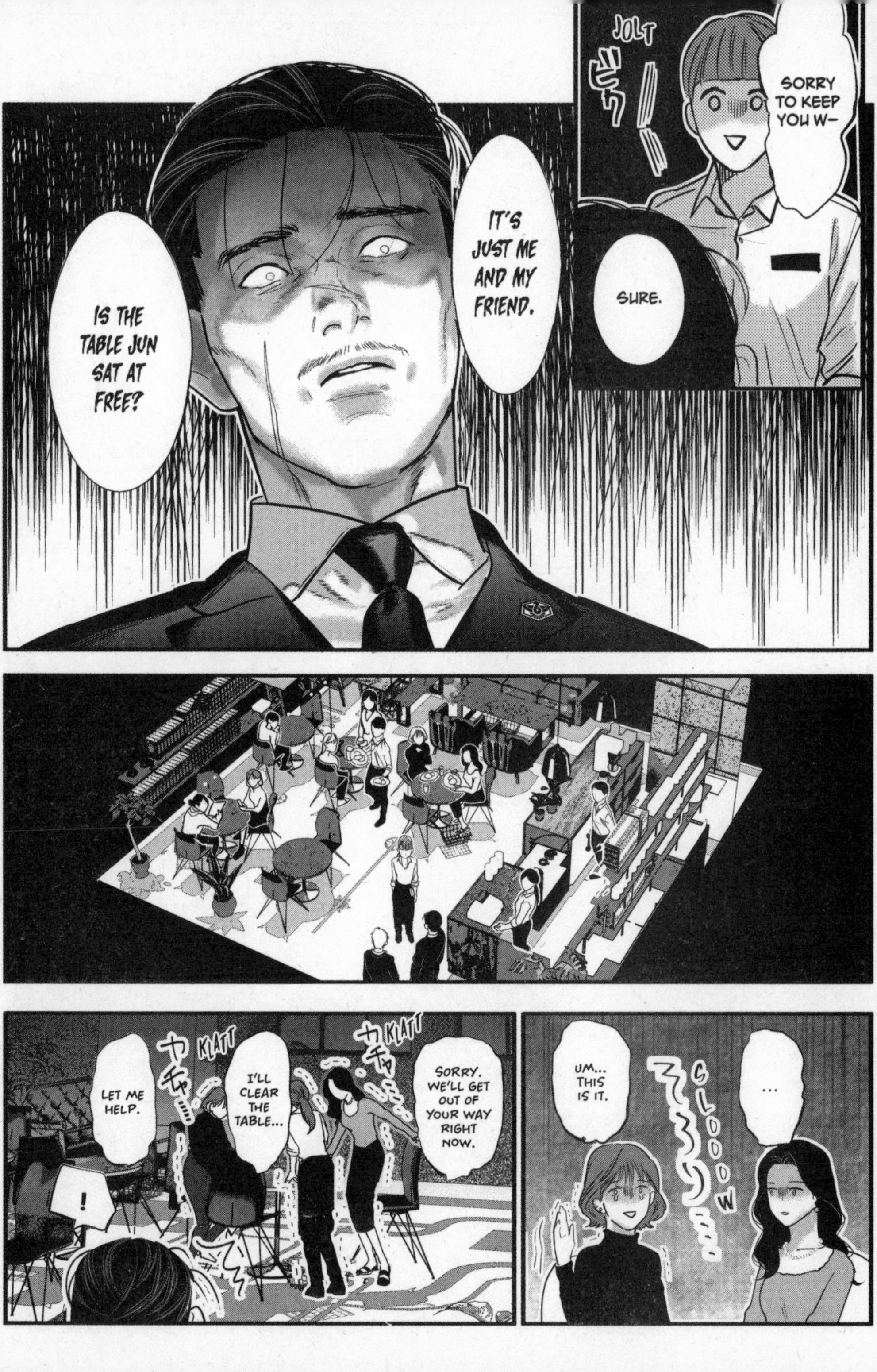
SORRY TO KEEP YOU W–
JOLT
SURE.
IT'S JUST ME AND MY FRIEND.
IS THE TABLE JUN SAT AT FREE?
...
SLOOOOW
UM... THIS IS IT.
SORRY. WE'LL GET OUT OF YOUR WAY RIGHT NOW.
KLATT
I'LL CLEAR THE TABLE...
KLATT
LET ME HELP.
!

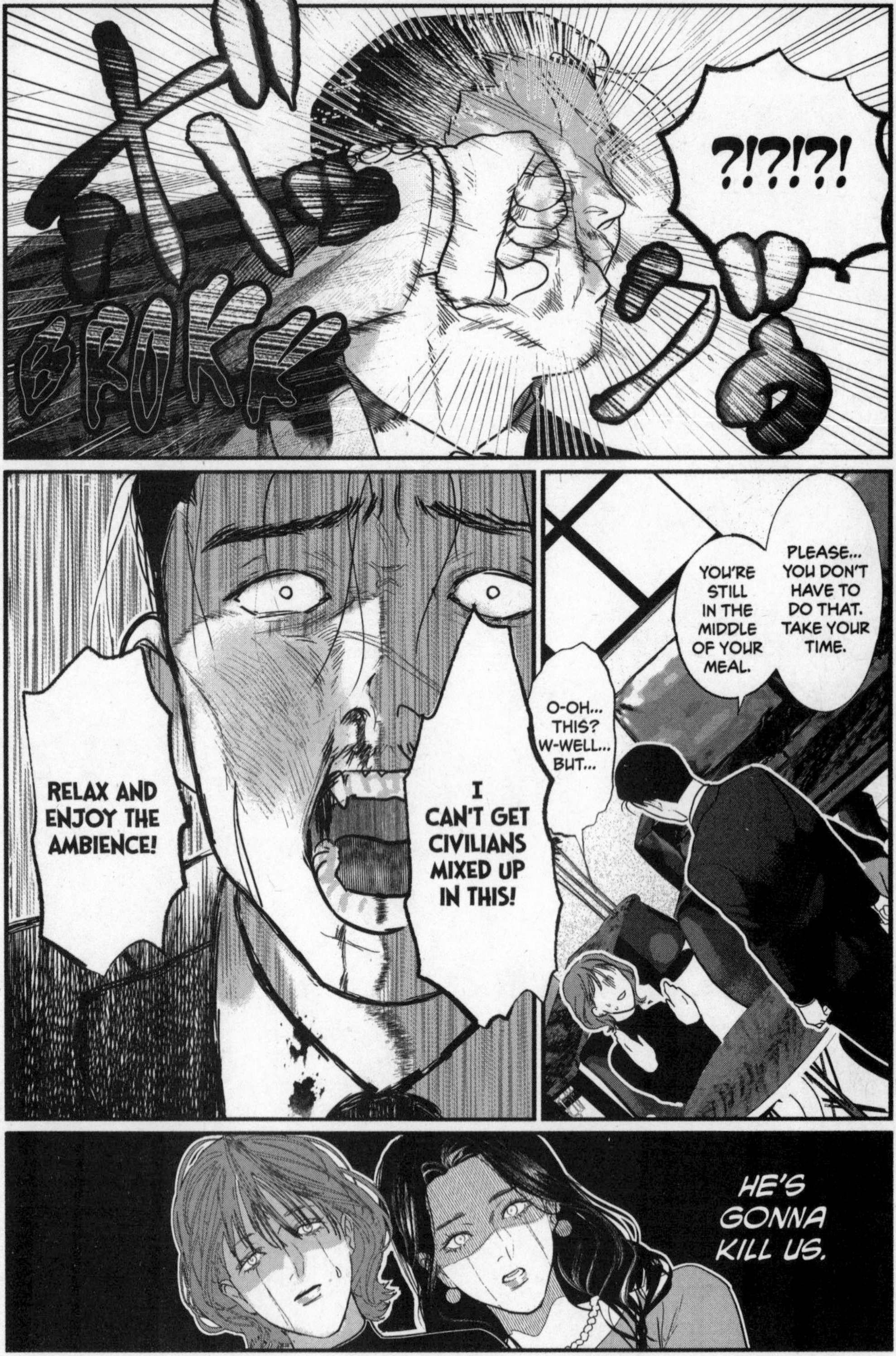
?!?!?!
BROKK
PLEASE... YOU DON'T HAVE TO DO THAT. TAKE YOUR TIME.
YOU'RE STILL IN THE MIDDLE OF YOUR MEAL.
O-OH... THIS? W-WELL... BUT...
I CAN'T GET CIVILIANS MIXED UP IN THIS!
RELAX AND ENJOY THE AMBIENCE!
HE'S GONNA KILL US.

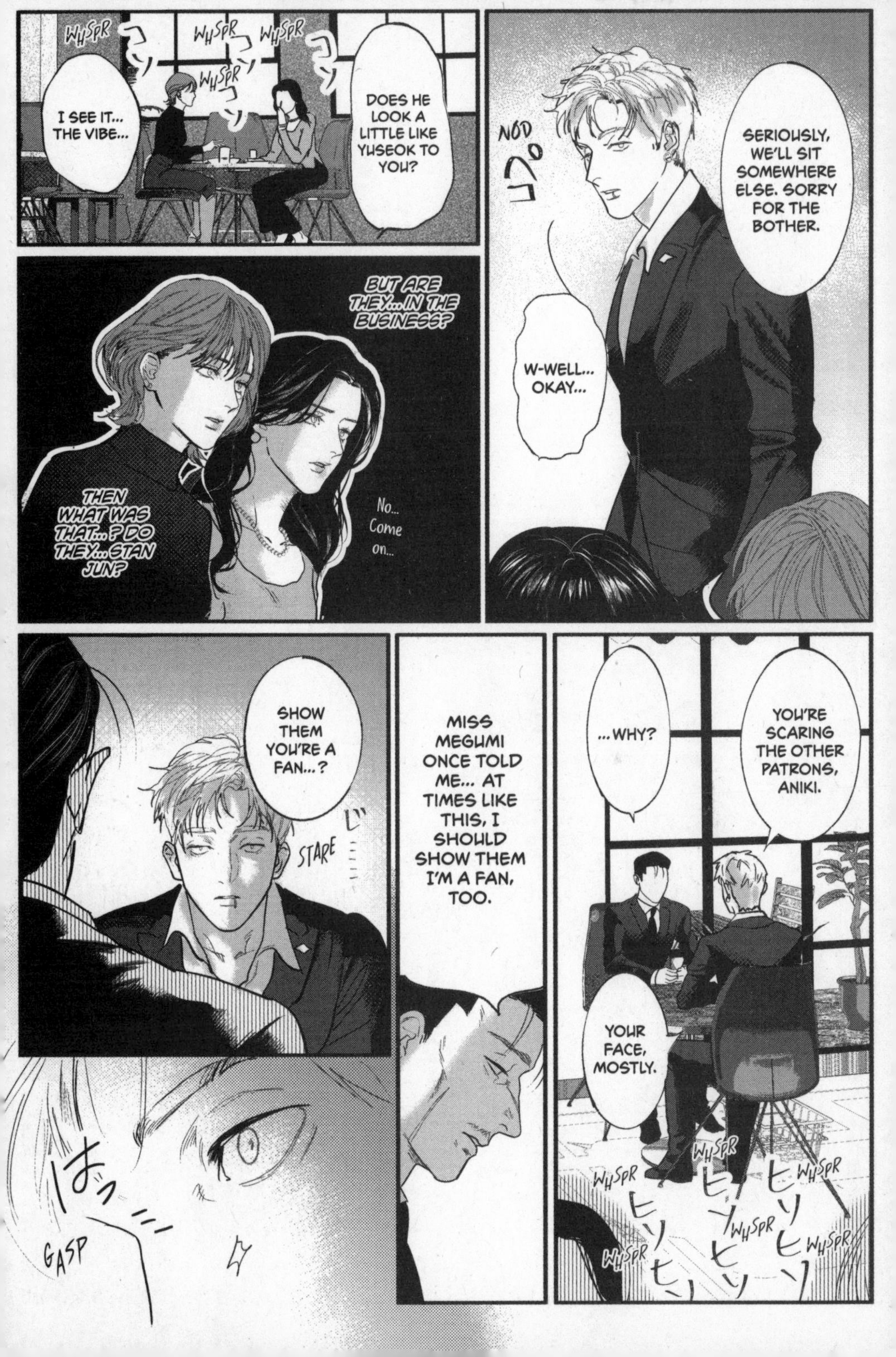
SERIOUSLY, WE'LL SIT SOMEWHERE ELSE. SORRY FOR THE BOTHER.
NOD
W-WELL... OKAY...
WHSPR WHSPR WHSPR WHSPR
DOES HE LOOK A LITTLE LIKE YUSEOK TO YOU?
I SEE IT... THE VIBE...
BUT ARE THEY... IN THE BUSINESS?
No... Come on...
THEN WHAT WAS THAT...? DO THEY... STAN JUN?
YOU'RE SCARING THE OTHER PATRONS, ANIKI.
...WHY?
YOUR FACE, MOSTLY.
WHSPR WHSPR WHSPR WHSPR WHSPR WHSPR
MISS MEGUMI ONCE TOLD ME... AT TIMES LIKE THIS, I SHOULD SHOW THEM I'M A FAN, TOO.
SHOW THEM YOU'RE A FAN...?
STARE
GASP

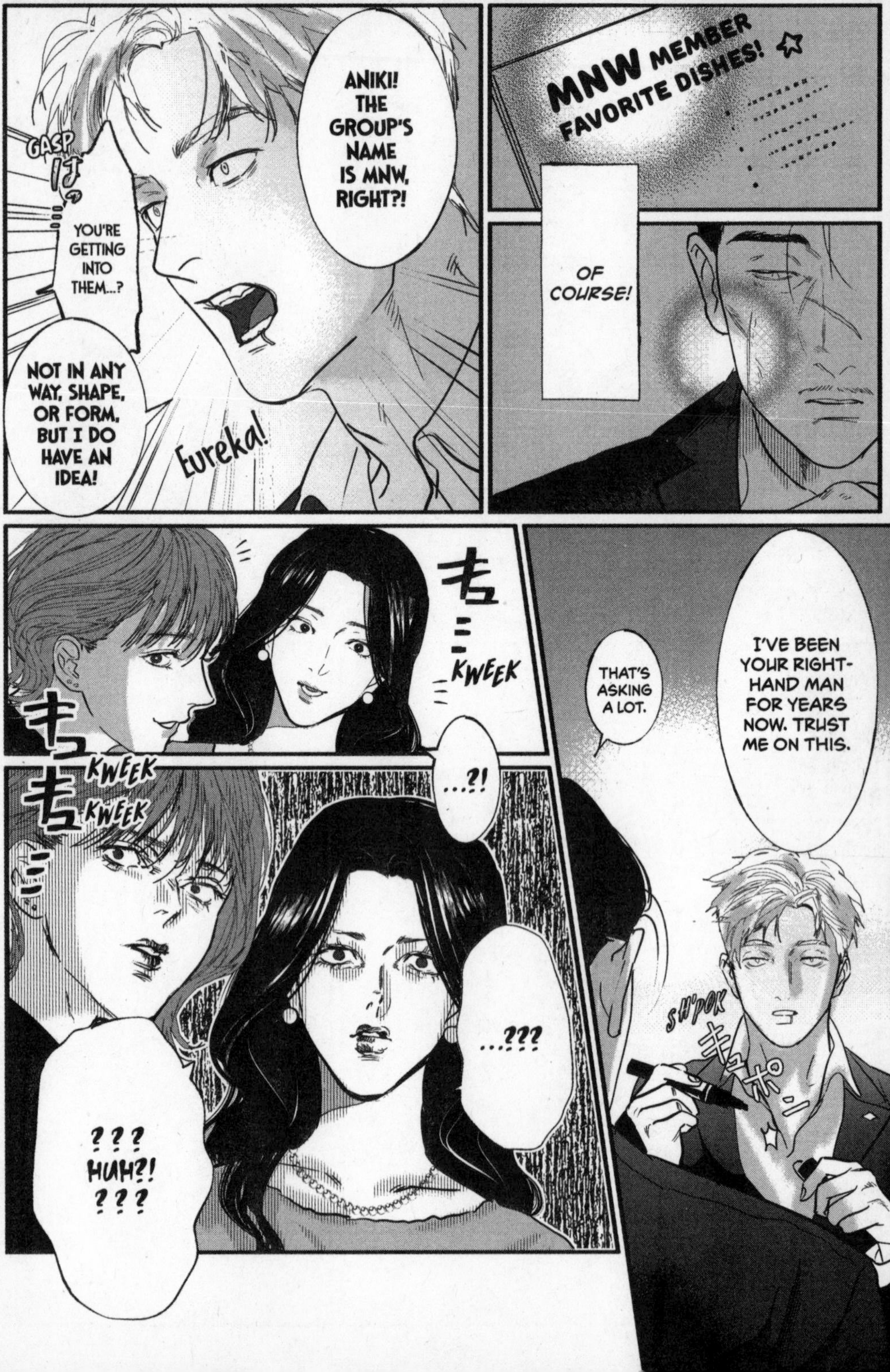
MNW MEMBER FAVORITE DISHES!
OF COURSE!
ANIKI! THE GROUP'S NAME IS MNW, RIGHT?!
GASP
YOU'RE GETTING INTO THEM...?
NOT IN ANY WAY, SHAPE, OR FORM, BUT I DO HAVE AN IDEA!
Eureka!
I'VE BEEN YOUR RIGHT-HAND MAN FOR YEARS NOW. TRUST ME ON THIS.
THAT'S ASKING A LOT.
SH'POK
KWEEK
...?!
KWEEK
KWEEK
...???
??? HUH?! ???

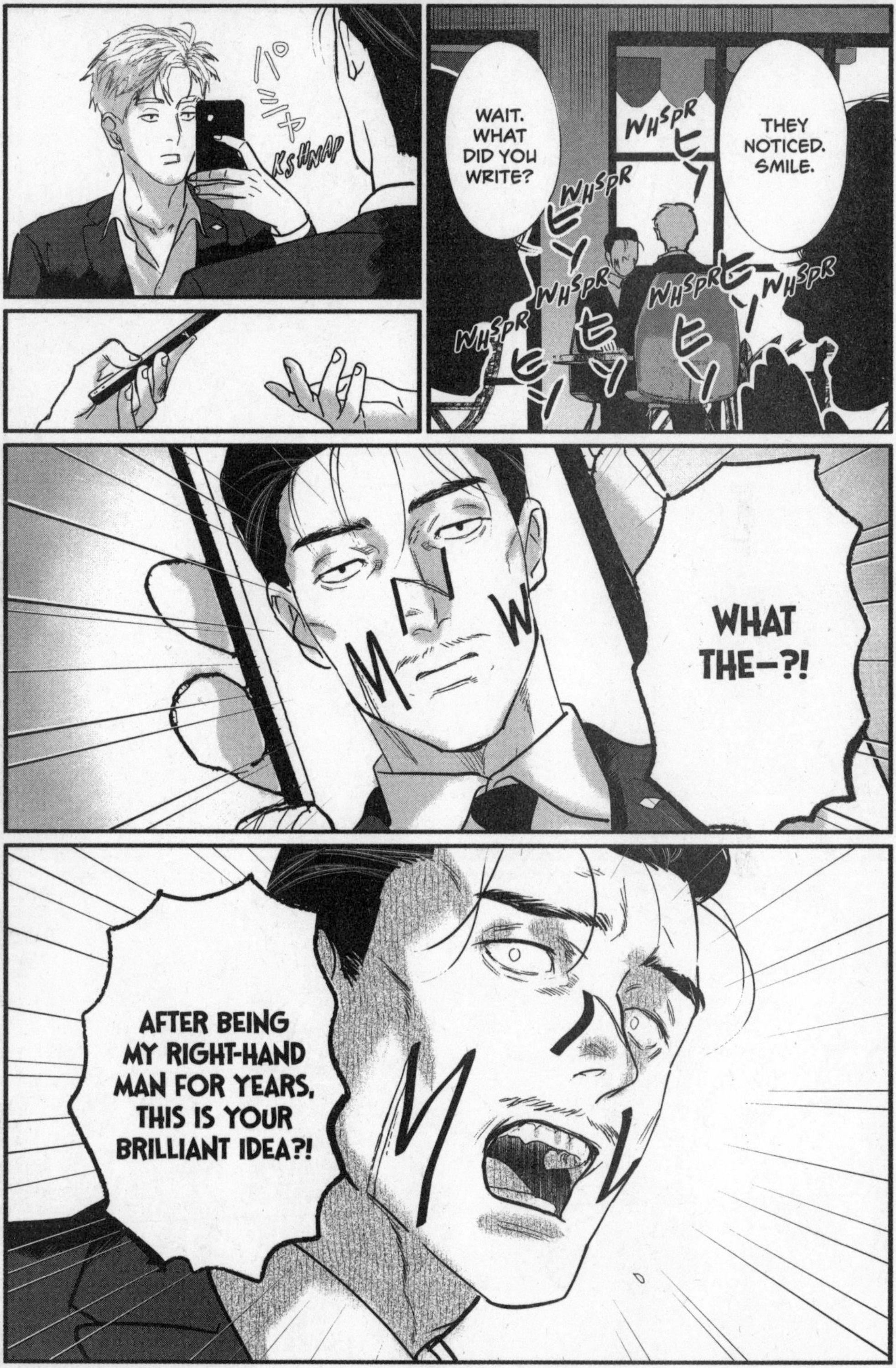
THEY NOTICED. SMILE.
WAIT. WHAT DID YOU WRITE?
WHSPR
WHSPR
WHSPR
WHSPR
WHSPR
WHSPR
パシャ
KSHNAP
WHAT THE-?!
AFTER BEING MY RIGHT-HAND MAN FOR YEARS, THIS IS YOUR BRILLIANT IDEA?!

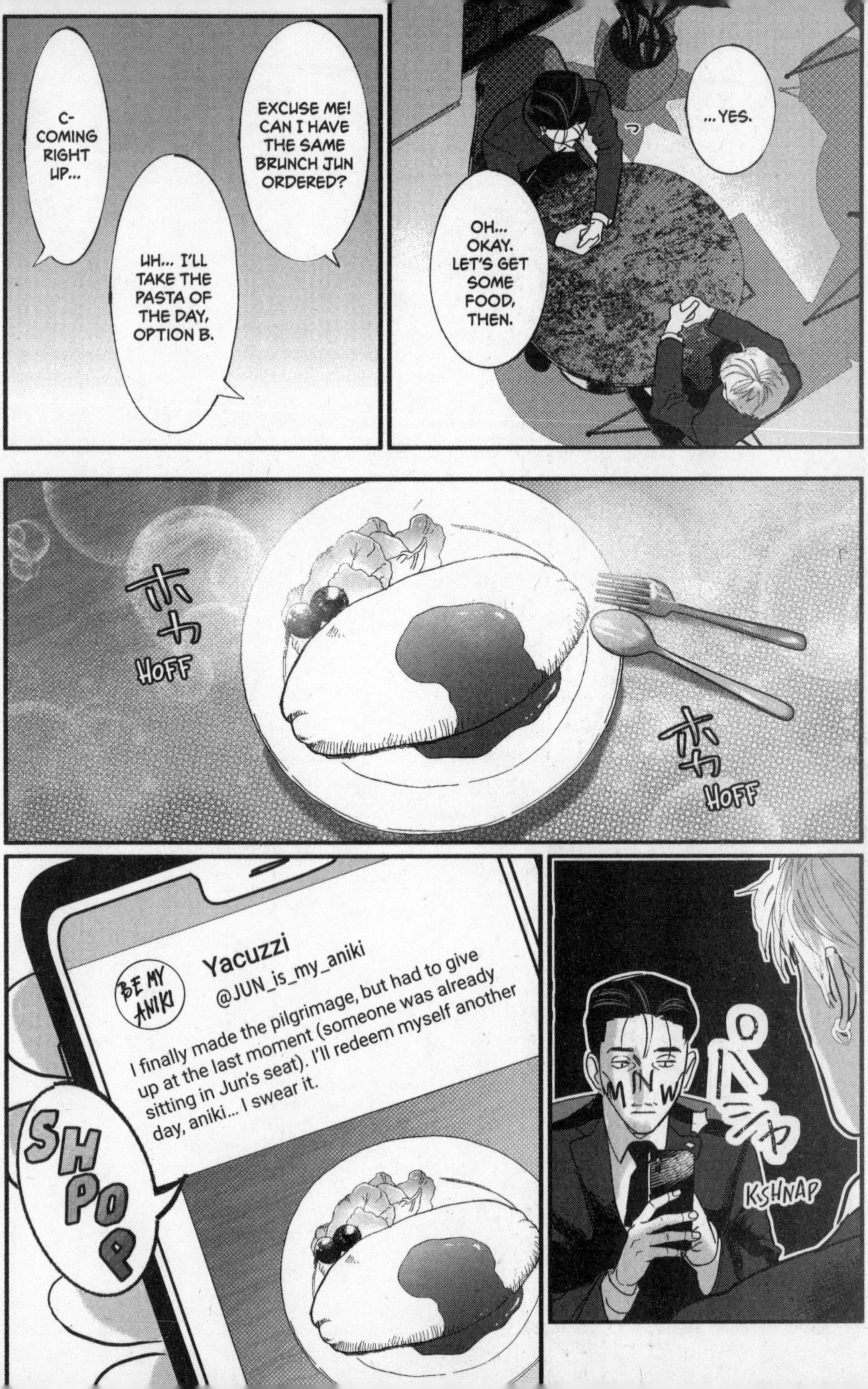
...YES.
OH... OKAY. LET'S GET SOME FOOD, THEN.
EXCUSE ME! CAN I HAVE THE SAME BRUNCH JUN ORDERED?
UH... I'LL TAKE THE PASTA OF THE DAY, OPTION B.
C-COMING RIGHT UP...
HOFF
HOFF
KSHNAP
Yacuzzi
@JUN_is_my_aniki
BE MY ANIKI
I finally made the pilgrimage, but had to give up at the last moment (someone was already sitting in Jun's seat). I'll redeem myself another day, aniki... I swear it.
SHPOP

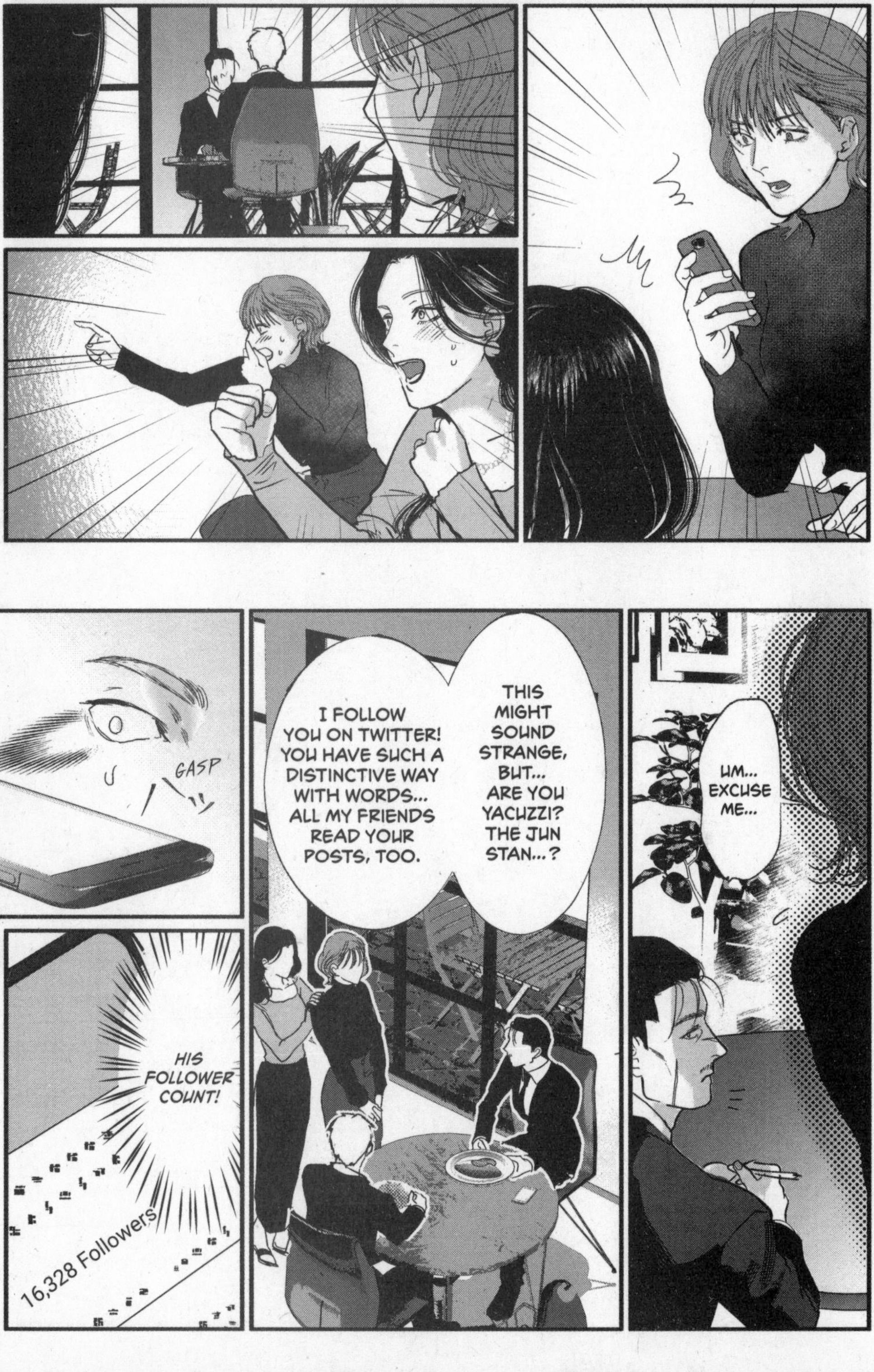
UM... EXCUSE ME...
THIS MIGHT SOUND STRANGE, BUT... ARE YOU YACUZZI? THE JUN STAN...?
I FOLLOW YOU ON TWITTER! YOU HAVE SUCH A DISTINCTIVE WAY WITH WORDS... ALL MY FRIENDS READ YOUR POSTS, TOO.
GASP
HIS FOLLOWER COUNT!
16,328 Followers

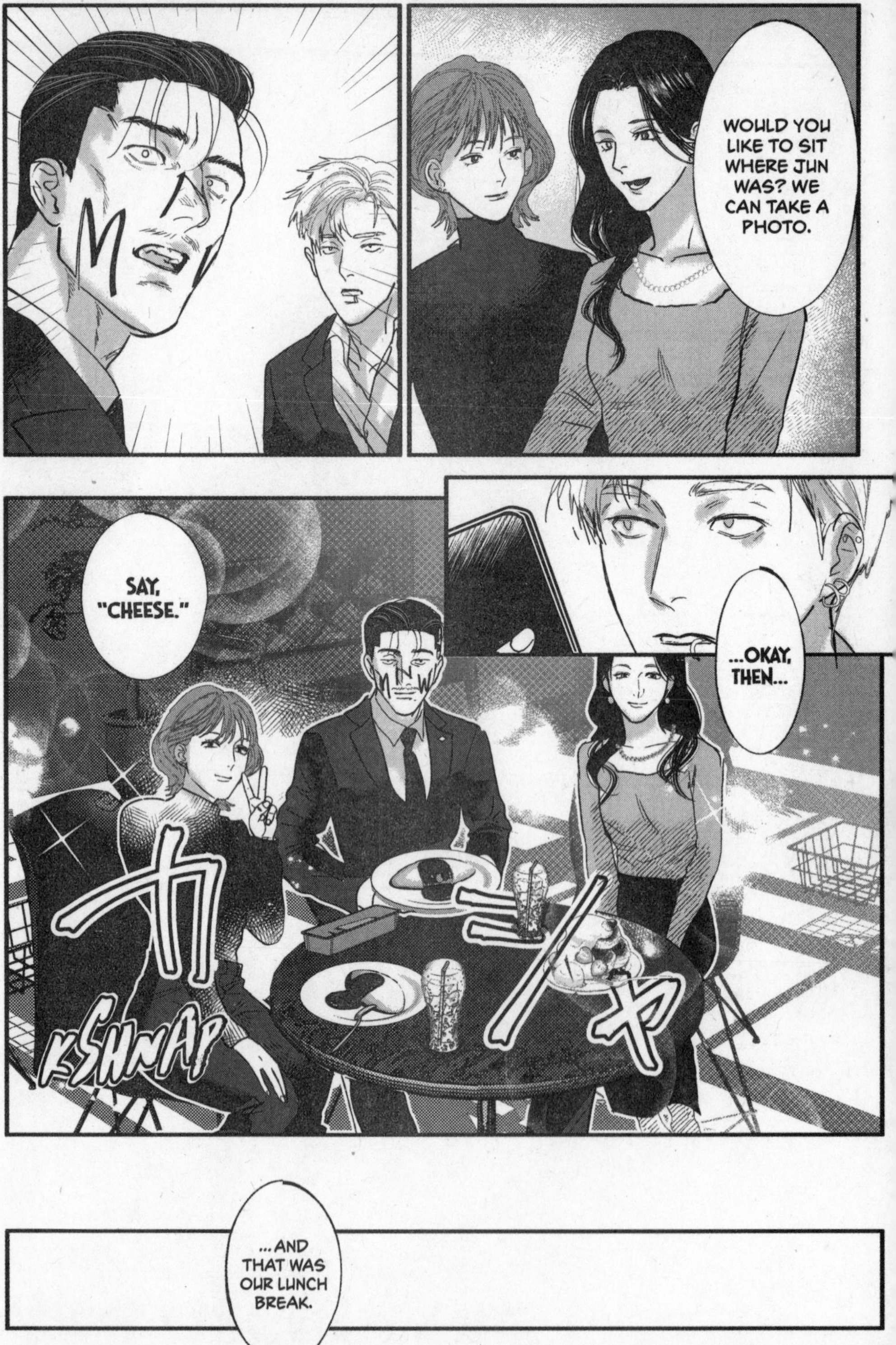
WOULD YOU LIKE TO SIT WHERE JUN WAS? WE CAN TAKE A PHOTO.
...OKAY, THEN...
SAY, "CHEESE."
KSHNAP
...AND THAT WAS OUR LUNCH BREAK.

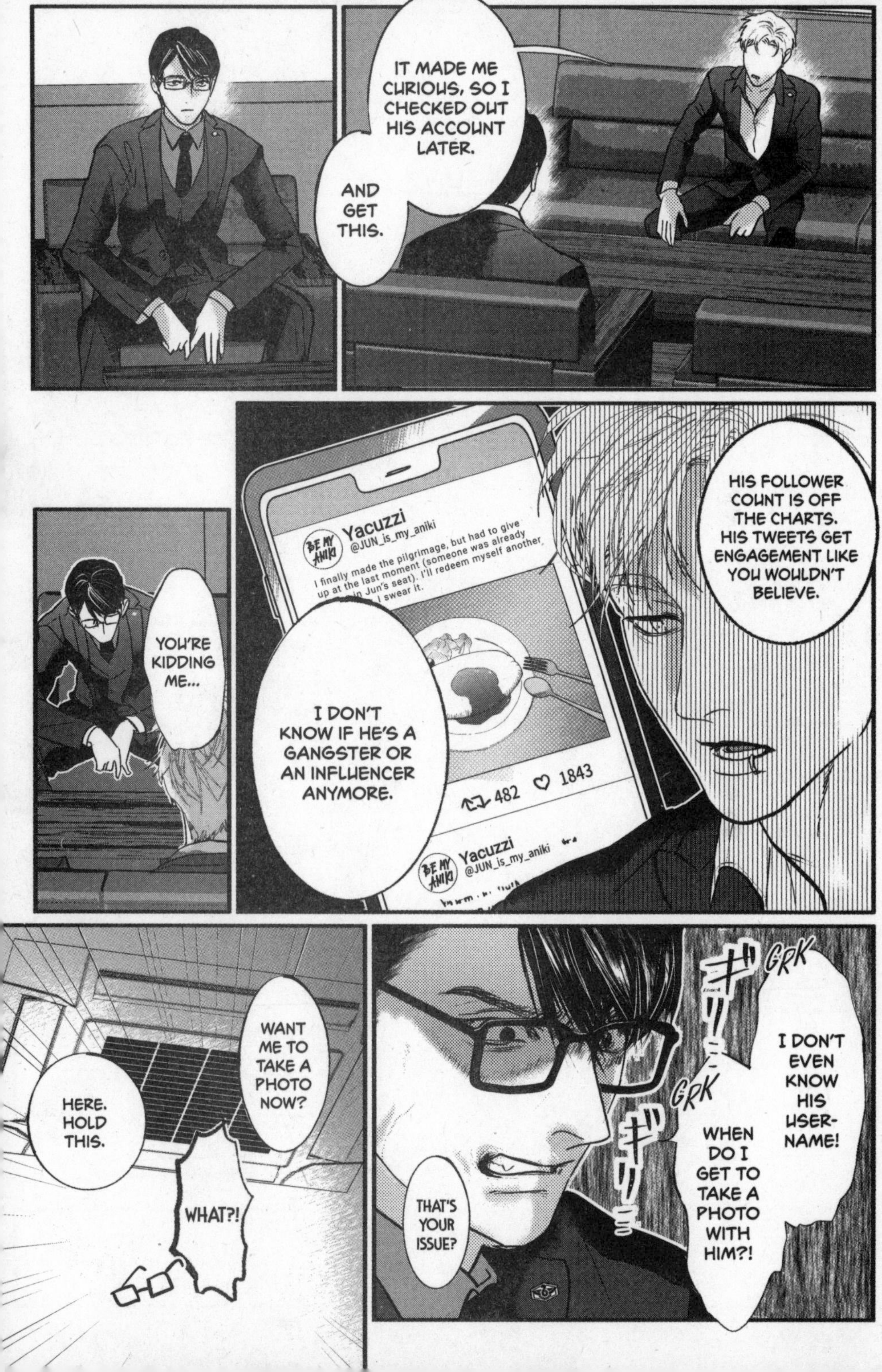
IT MADE ME CURIOUS, SO I CHECKED OUT HIS ACCOUNT LATER.
AND GET THIS.
HIS FOLLOWER COUNT IS OFF THE CHARTS. HIS TWEETS GET ENGAGEMENT LIKE YOU WOULDN'T BELIEVE.
BE MY ANIKI
Yacuzzi
@JUN_is_my_aniki
I finally made the pilgrimage, but had to give up at the last moment (someone was already
in Jun's seat). I'll redeem myself another
I swear it.
482
1843
BE MY ANIKI
Yacuzzi
@JUN_is_my_aniki
I DON'T KNOW IF HE'S A GANGSTER OR AN INFLUENCER ANYMORE.
YOU'RE KIDDING ME...
GRK
GRK
I DON'T EVEN KNOW HIS USER-NAME!
WHEN DO I GET TO TAKE A PHOTO WITH HIM?!
THAT'S YOUR ISSUE?
WANT ME TO TAKE A PHOTO NOW?
HERE. HOLD THIS.
WHAT?!

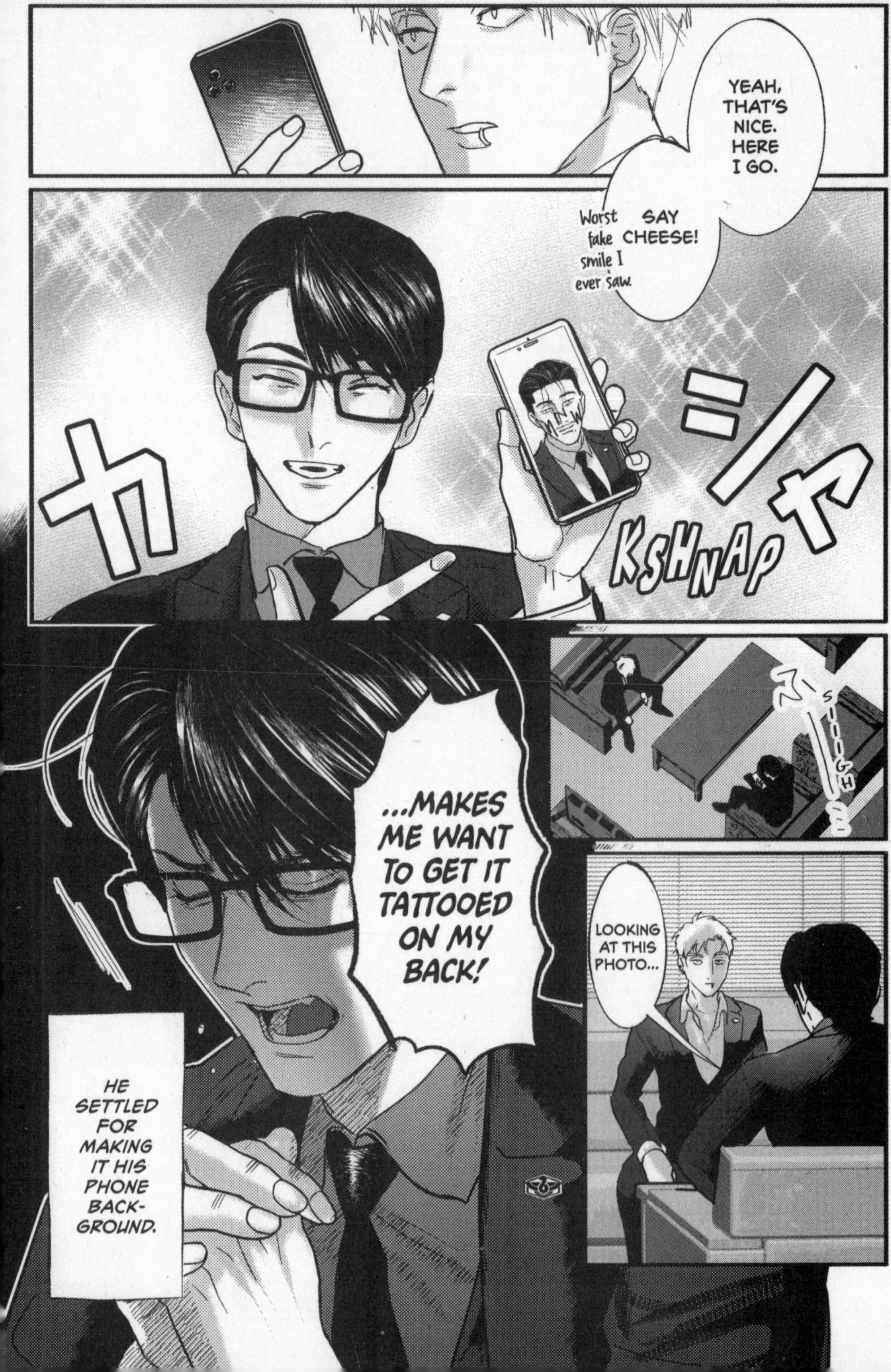

YEAH, THAT'S NICE. HERE I GO.
SAY CHEESE!
Worst fake smile I ever saw.
カシャ
KSHNAP
S-I-I-I-GH...
LOOKING AT THIS PHOTO...
...MAKES ME WANT TO GET IT TATTOOED ON MY BACK!
HE SETTLED FOR MAKING IT HIS PHONE BACK-GROUND.

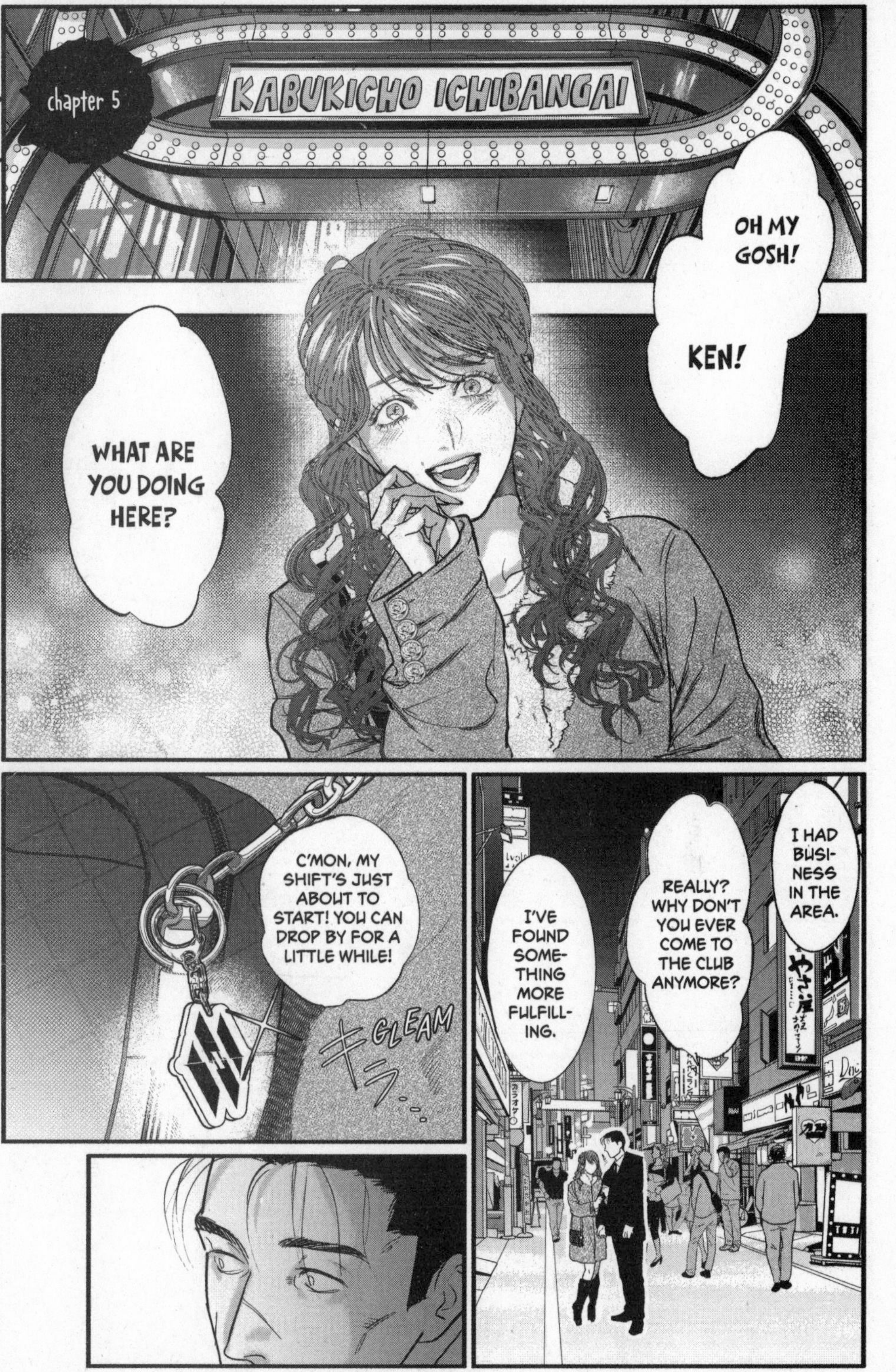
chapter 5
KABUKICHO ICHIBANGAI
OH MY GOSH!
KEN!
WHAT ARE YOU DOING HERE?
I HAD BUSI-NESS IN THE AREA.
REALLY? WHY DON'T YOU EVER COME TO THE CLUB ANYMORE?
I'VE FOUND SOME-THING MORE FULFILL-ING.
C'MON, MY SHIFT'S JUST ABOUT TO START! YOU CAN DROP BY FOR A LITTLE WHILE!
キラ GLEAM

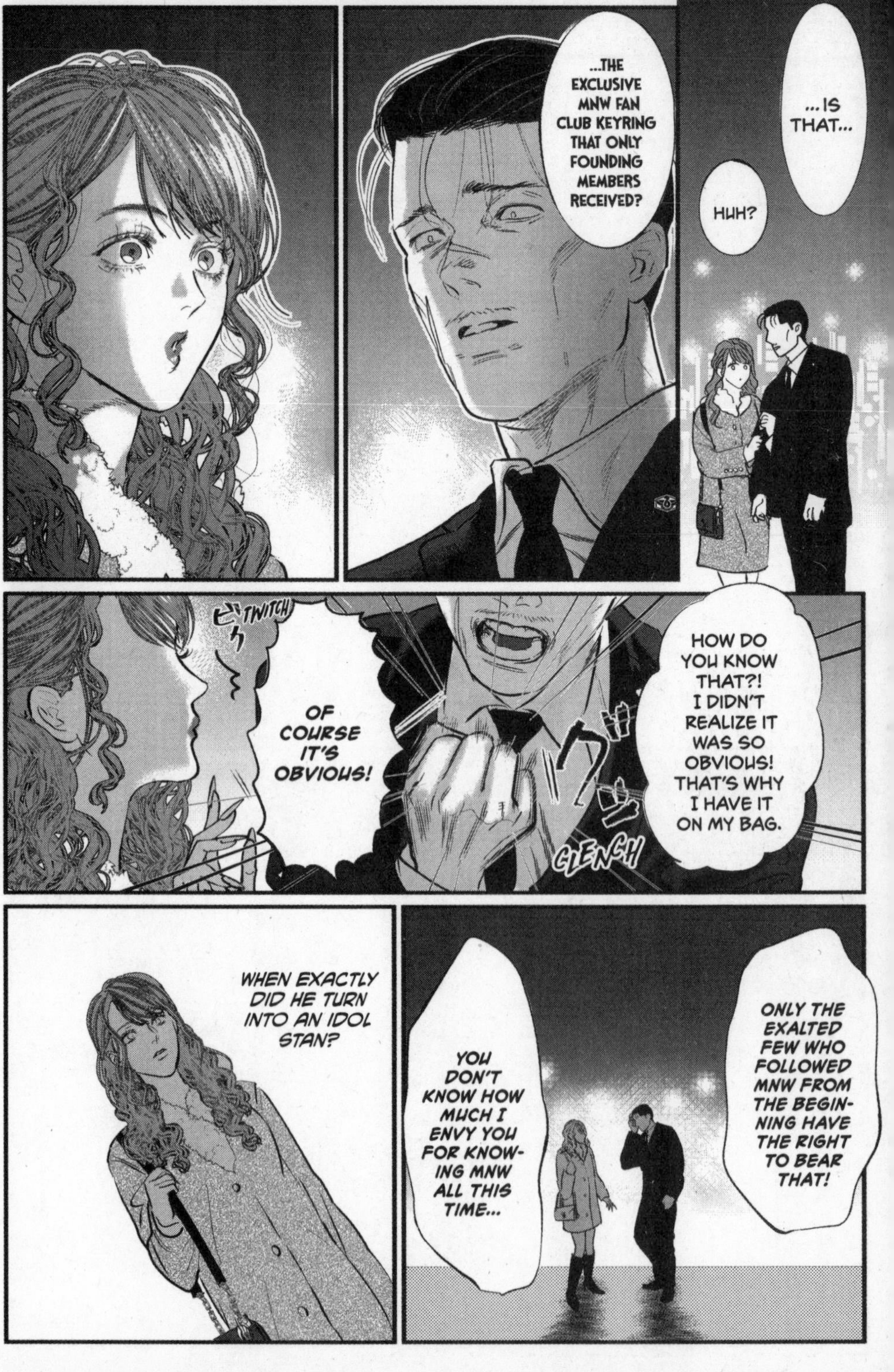
...IS THAT...
HUH?
...THE EXCLUSIVE MNW FAN CLUB KEYRING THAT ONLY FOUNDING MEMBERS RECEIVED?
HOW DO YOU KNOW THAT?! I DIDN'T REALIZE IT WAS SO OBVIOUS! THAT'S WHY I HAVE IT ON MY BAG.
CLENCH
TWITCH
OF COURSE IT'S OBVIOUS!
ONLY THE EXALTED FEW WHO FOLLOWED MNW FROM THE BEGIN-NING HAVE THE RIGHT TO BEAR THAT!
YOU DON'T KNOW HOW MUCH I ENVY YOU FOR KNOW-ING MNW ALL THIS TIME...
WHEN EXACTLY DID HE TURN INTO AN IDOL STAN?

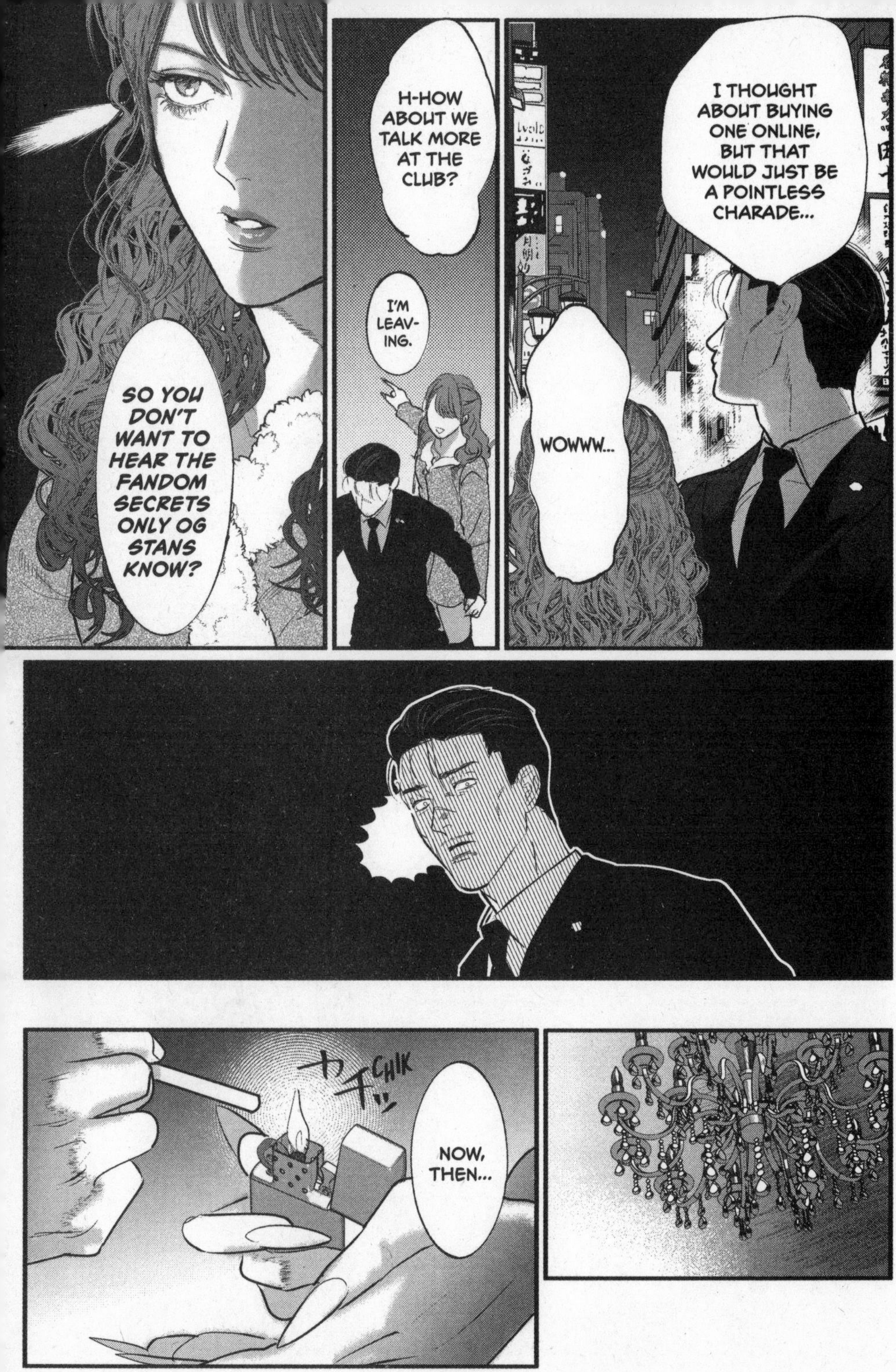
I THOUGHT ABOUT BUYING ONE ONLINE, BUT THAT WOULD JUST BE A POINTLESS CHARADE...
WOWWW...
H-HOW ABOUT WE TALK MORE AT THE CLUB?
I'M LEAVING.
SO YOU DON'T WANT TO HEAR THE FANDOM SECRETS ONLY OG STANS KNOW?
カチッ
CHIK
NOW, THEN...

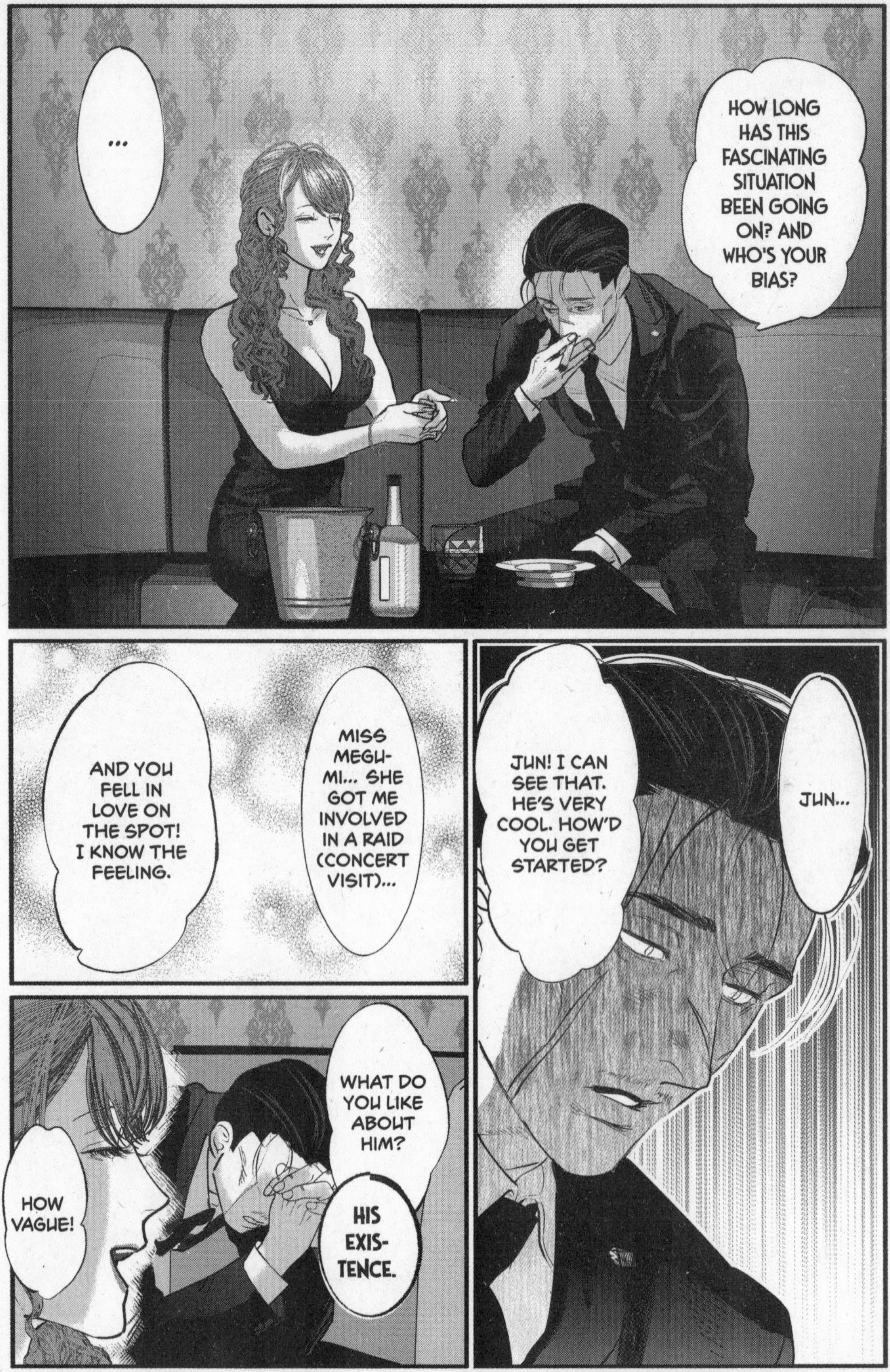
HOW LONG HAS THIS FASCINATING SITUATION BEEN GOING ON? AND WHO'S YOUR BIAS?
...
JUN...
JUN! I CAN SEE THAT. HE'S VERY COOL. HOW'D YOU GET STARTED?
MISS MEGU-MI... SHE GOT ME INVOLVED IN A RAID (CONCERT VISIT)...
AND YOU FELL IN LOVE ON THE SPOT! I KNOW THE FEELING.
WHAT DO YOU LIKE ABOUT HIM?
HIS EXIS-TENCE.
HOW VAGUE!

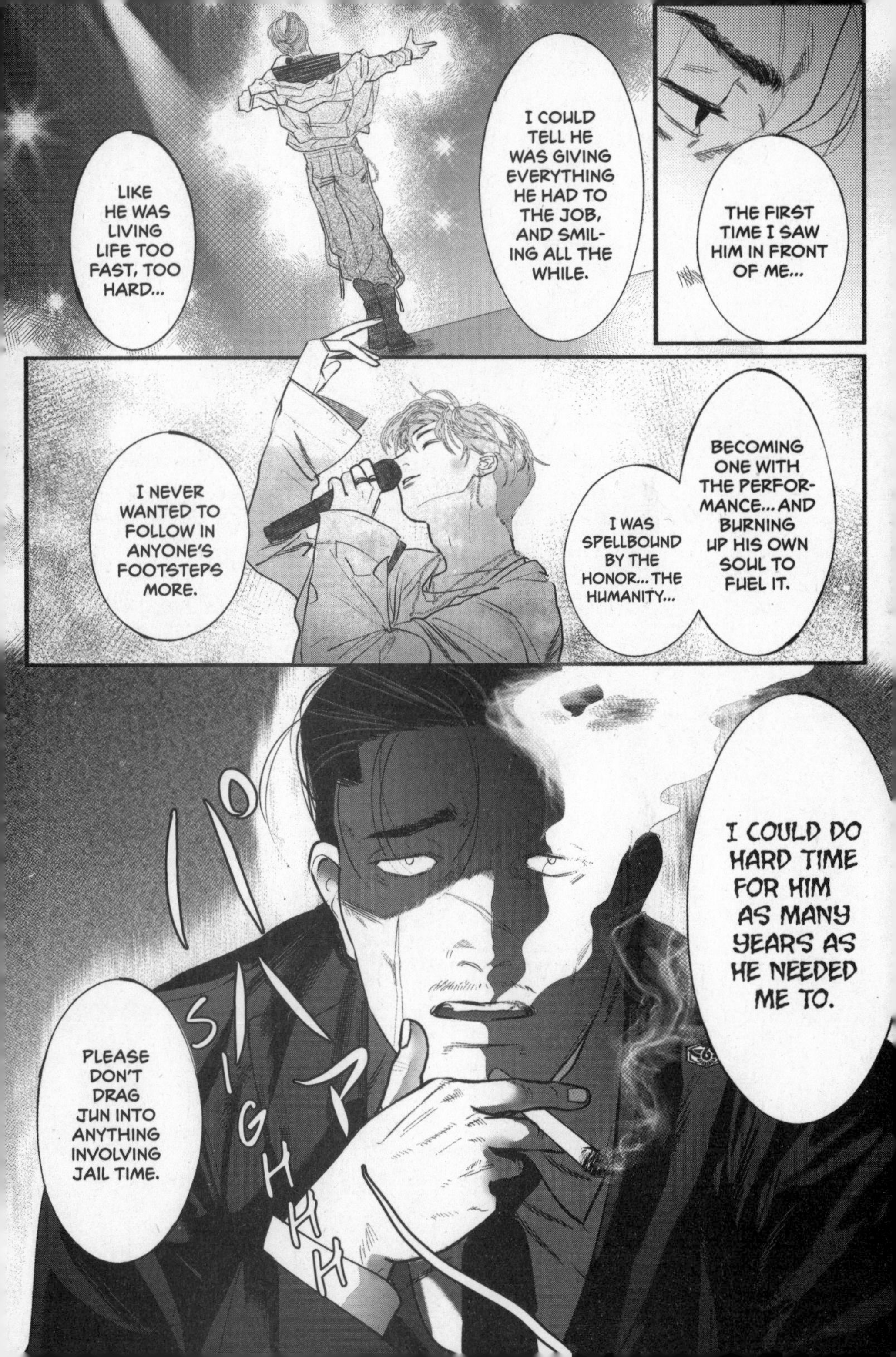
THE FIRST TIME I SAW HIM IN FRONT OF ME...
I COULD TELL HE WAS GIVING EVERYTHING HE HAD TO THE JOB, AND SMIL-ING ALL THE WHILE.
LIKE HE WAS LIVING LIFE TOO FAST, TOO HARD...
BECOMING ONE WITH THE PERFOR-MANCE... AND BURNING UP HIS OWN SOUL TO FUEL IT.
I WAS SPELLBOUND BY THE HONOR... THE HUMANITY...
I NEVER WANTED TO FOLLOW IN ANYONE'S FOOTSTEPS MORE.
I COULD DO HARD TIME FOR HIM AS MANY YEARS AS HE NEEDED ME TO.
SIGHHH
PLEASE DON'T DRAG JUN INTO ANYTHING INVOLVING JAIL TIME.

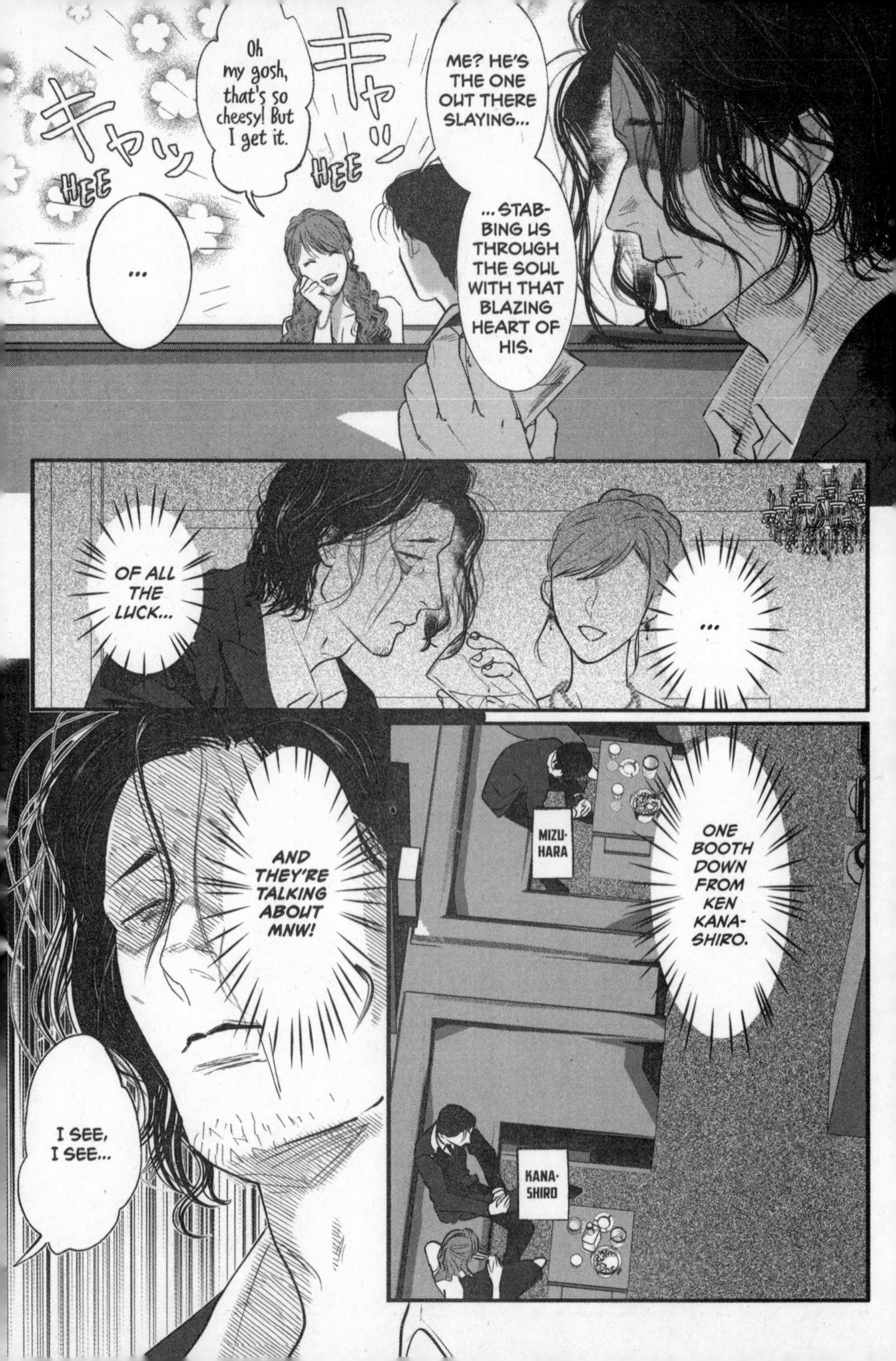
ME? HE'S THE ONE OUT THERE SLAYING...
...STABBING US THROUGH THE SOUL WITH THAT BLAZING HEART OF HIS.
キャ
HEE
Oh my gosh, that's so cheesy! But I get it.
キャッ
HEE
...
...
OF ALL THE LUCK...
ONE BOOTH DOWN FROM KEN KANASHIRO.
MIZUHARA
KANASHIRO
AND THEY'RE TALKING ABOUT MNW!
I SEE, I SEE...

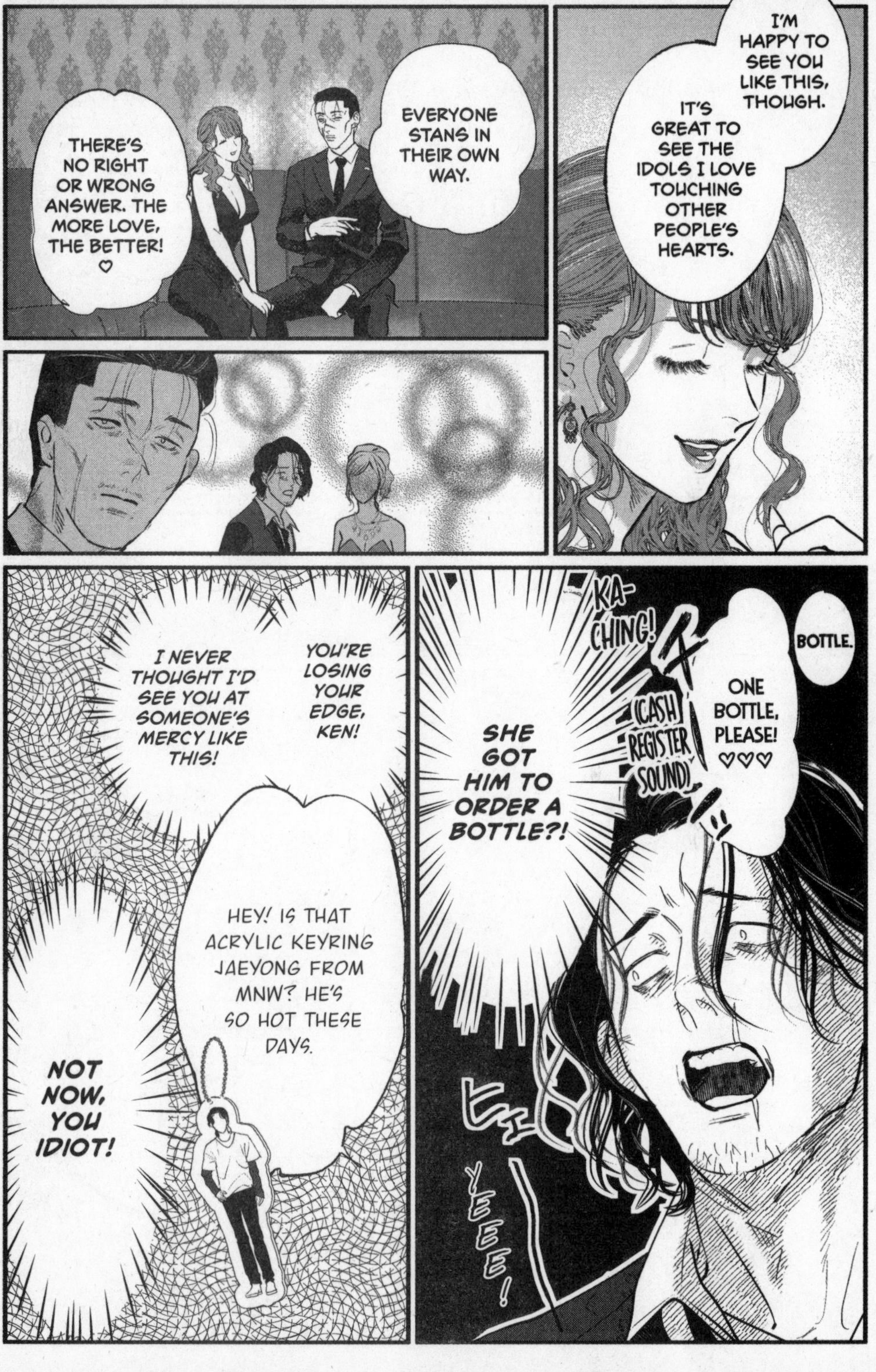
I'M HAPPY TO SEE YOU LIKE THIS, THOUGH.
IT'S GREAT TO SEE THE IDOLS I LOVE TOUCHING OTHER PEOPLE'S HEARTS.
EVERYONE STANS IN THEIR OWN WAY.
THERE'S NO RIGHT OR WRONG ANSWER. THE MORE LOVE, THE BETTER! ♡
BOTTLE.
KA-CHING!
ONE BOTTLE, PLEASE! ♡♡♡
(CASH REGISTER SOUND)
SHE GOT HIM TO ORDER A BOTTLE?!
ヒィ
YEEEE!
YOU'RE LOSING YOUR EDGE, KEN!
I NEVER THOUGHT I'D SEE YOU AT SOMEONE'S MERCY LIKE THIS!
HEY! IS THAT ACRYLIC KEYRING JAEYONG FROM MNW? HE'S SO HOT THESE DAYS.
NOT NOW, YOU IDIOT!

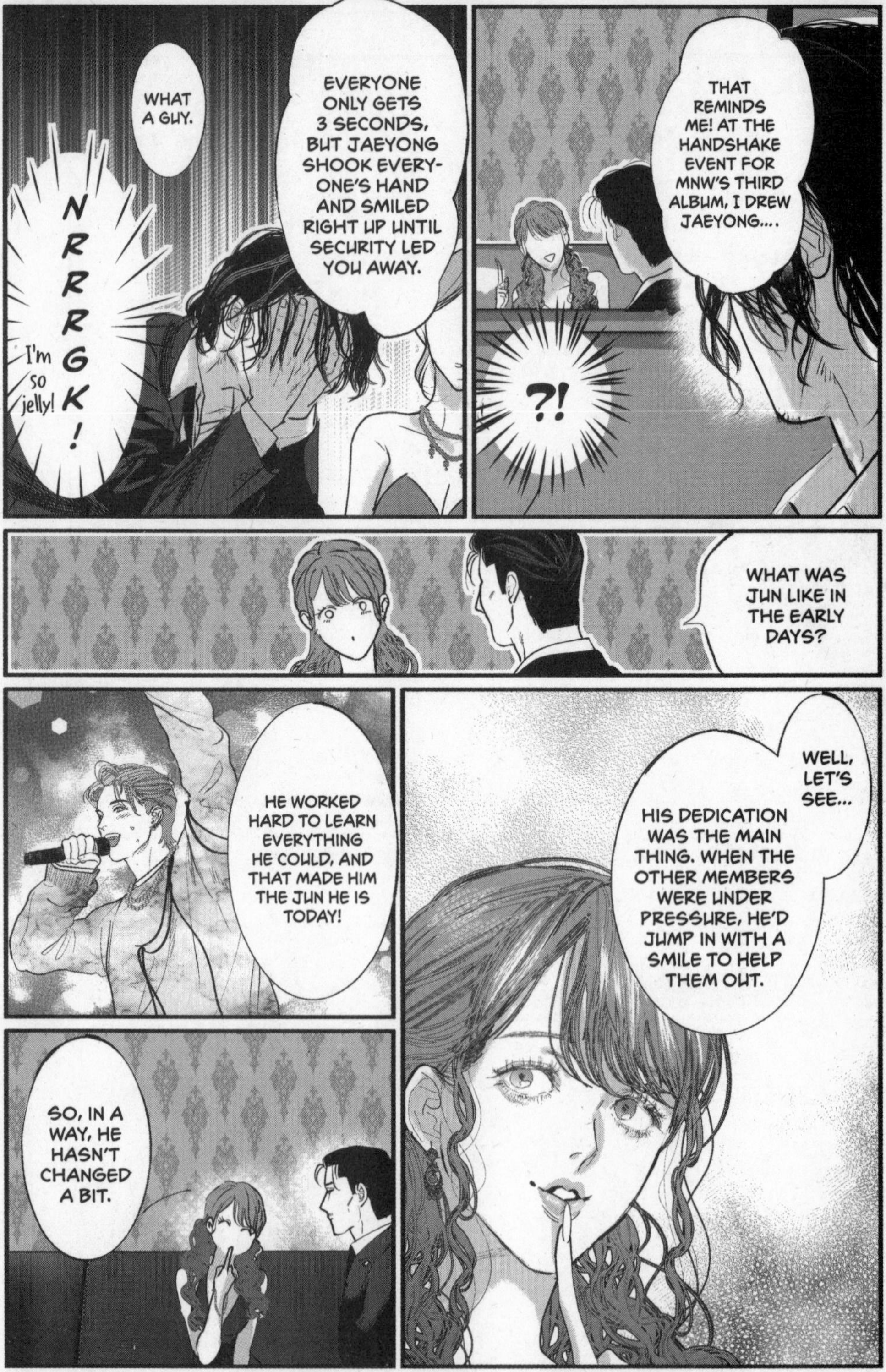
THAT REMINDS ME! AT THE HANDSHAKE EVENT FOR MNW'S THIRD ALBUM, I DREW JAEYONG....
?!
EVERYONE ONLY GETS 3 SECONDS, BUT JAEYONG SHOOK EVERY-ONE'S HAND AND SMILED RIGHT UP UNTIL SECURITY LED YOU AWAY.
WHAT A GUY.
NRRRGK!
I'm so jelly!
WHAT WAS JUN LIKE IN THE EARLY DAYS?
WELL, LET'S SEE...
HIS DEDICATION WAS THE MAIN THING. WHEN THE OTHER MEMBERS WERE UNDER PRESSURE, HE'D JUMP IN WITH A SMILE TO HELP THEM OUT.
HE WORKED HARD TO LEARN EVERYTHING HE COULD, AND THAT MADE HIM THE JUN HE IS TODAY!
SO, IN A WAY, HE HASN'T CHANGED A BIT.

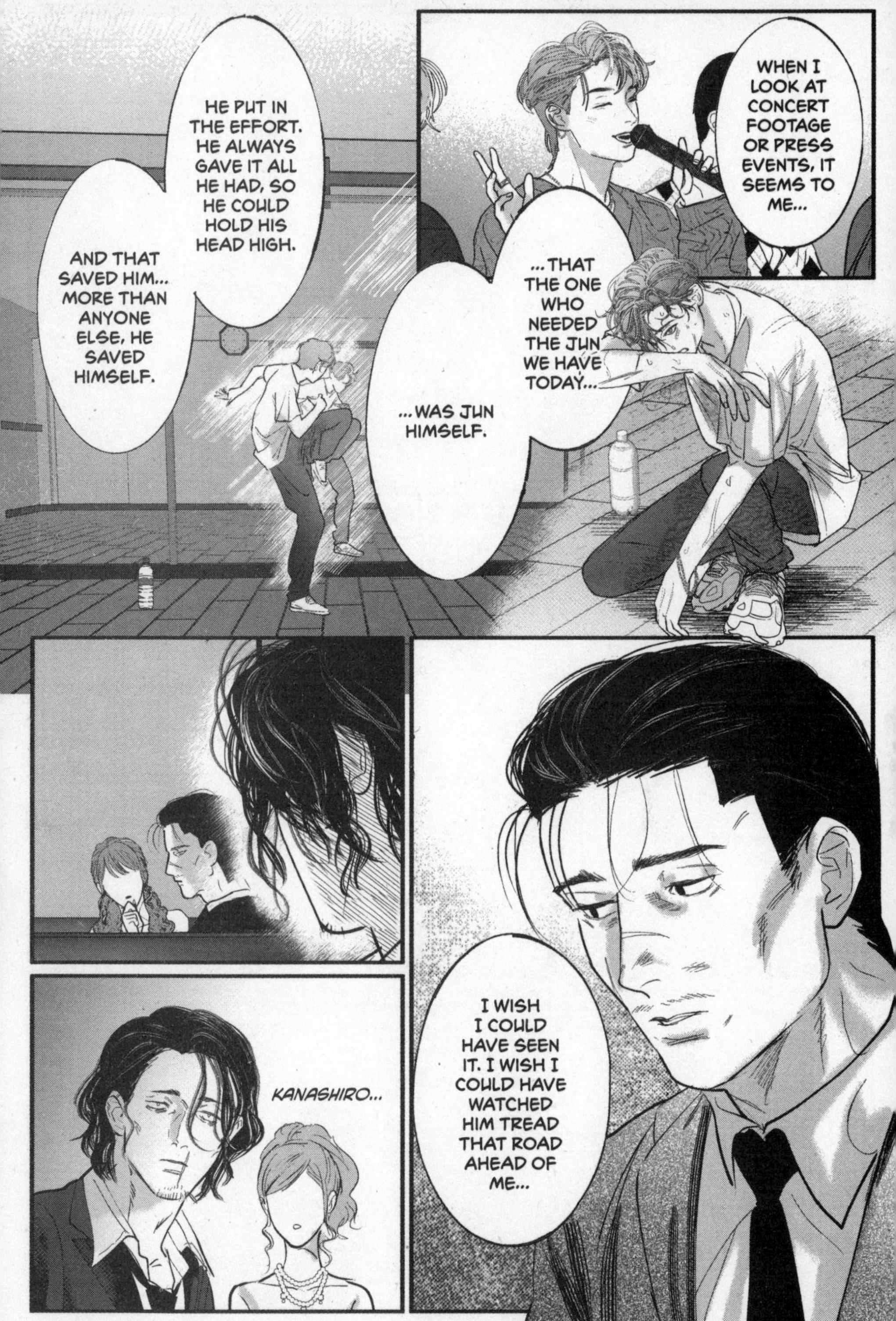
WHEN I LOOK AT CONCERT FOOTAGE OR PRESS EVENTS, IT SEEMS TO ME...
...THAT THE ONE WHO NEEDED THE JUN WE HAVE TODAY...
...WAS JUN HIMSELF.
HE PUT IN THE EFFORT. HE ALWAYS GAVE IT ALL HE HAD, SO HE COULD HOLD HIS HEAD HIGH.
AND THAT SAVED HIM... MORE THAN ANYONE ELSE, HE SAVED HIMSELF.
I WISH I COULD HAVE SEEN IT. I WISH I COULD HAVE WATCHED HIM TREAD THAT ROAD AHEAD OF ME...
KANASHIRO...

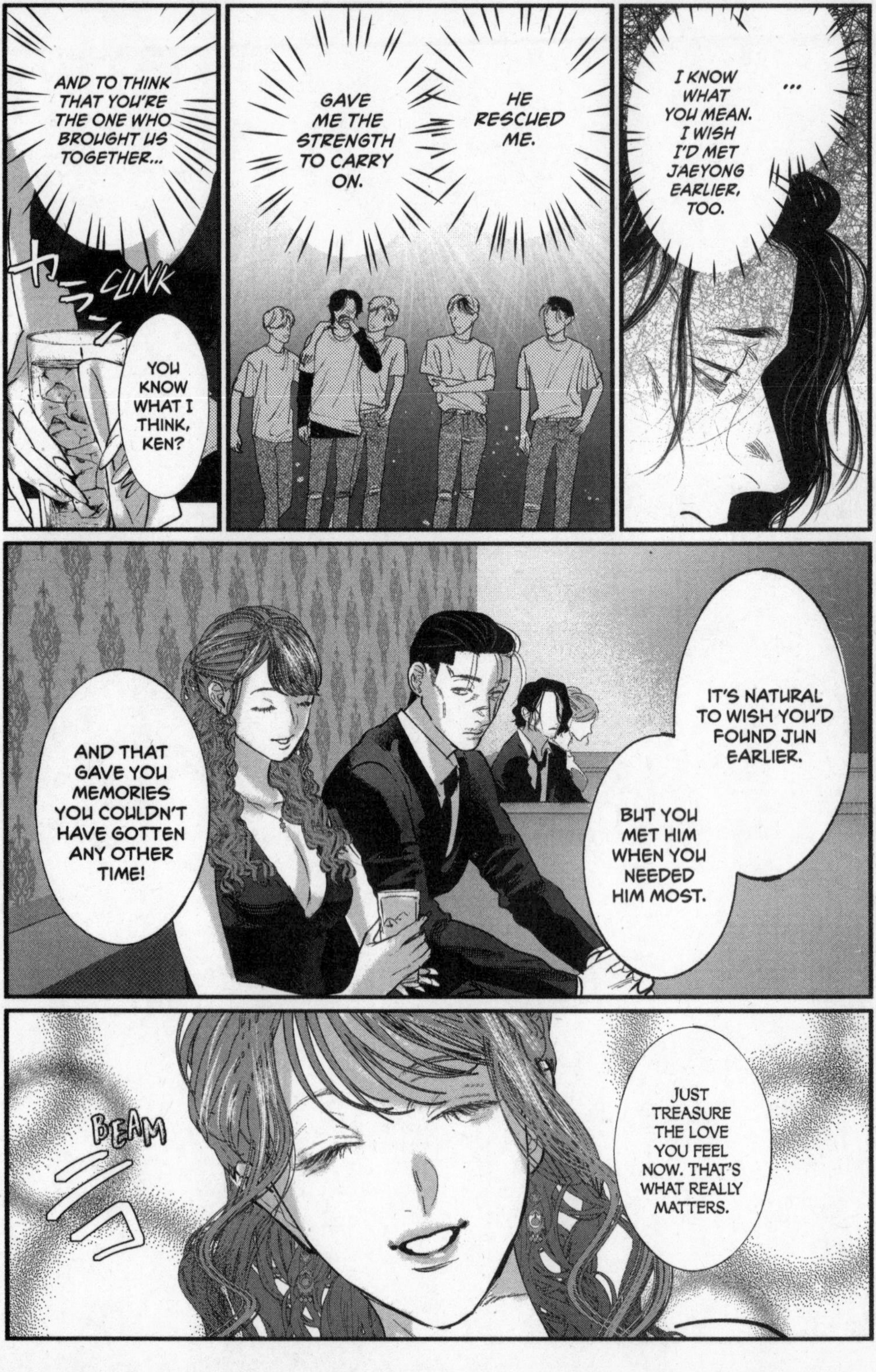
...
I KNOW WHAT YOU MEAN. I WISH I'D MET JAEYONG EARLIER, TOO.
HE RESCUED ME.
GAVE ME THE STRENGTH TO CARRY ON.
AND TO THINK THAT YOU'RE THE ONE WHO BROUGHT US TOGETHER...
CLINK
YOU KNOW WHAT I THINK, KEN?
IT'S NATURAL TO WISH YOU'D FOUND JUN EARLIER.
BUT YOU MET HIM WHEN YOU NEEDED HIM MOST.
AND THAT GAVE YOU MEMORIES YOU COULDN'T HAVE GOTTEN ANY OTHER TIME!
JUST TREASURE THE LOVE YOU FEEL NOW. THAT'S WHAT REALLY MATTERS.
BEAM

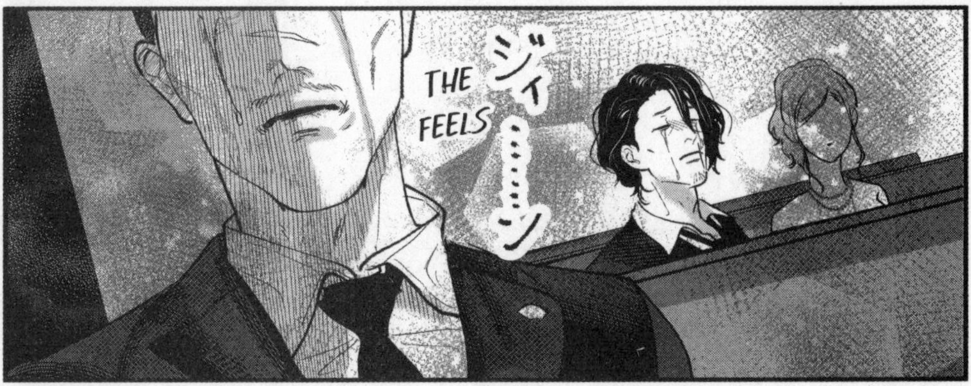
THE FEELS
ジィ……ン

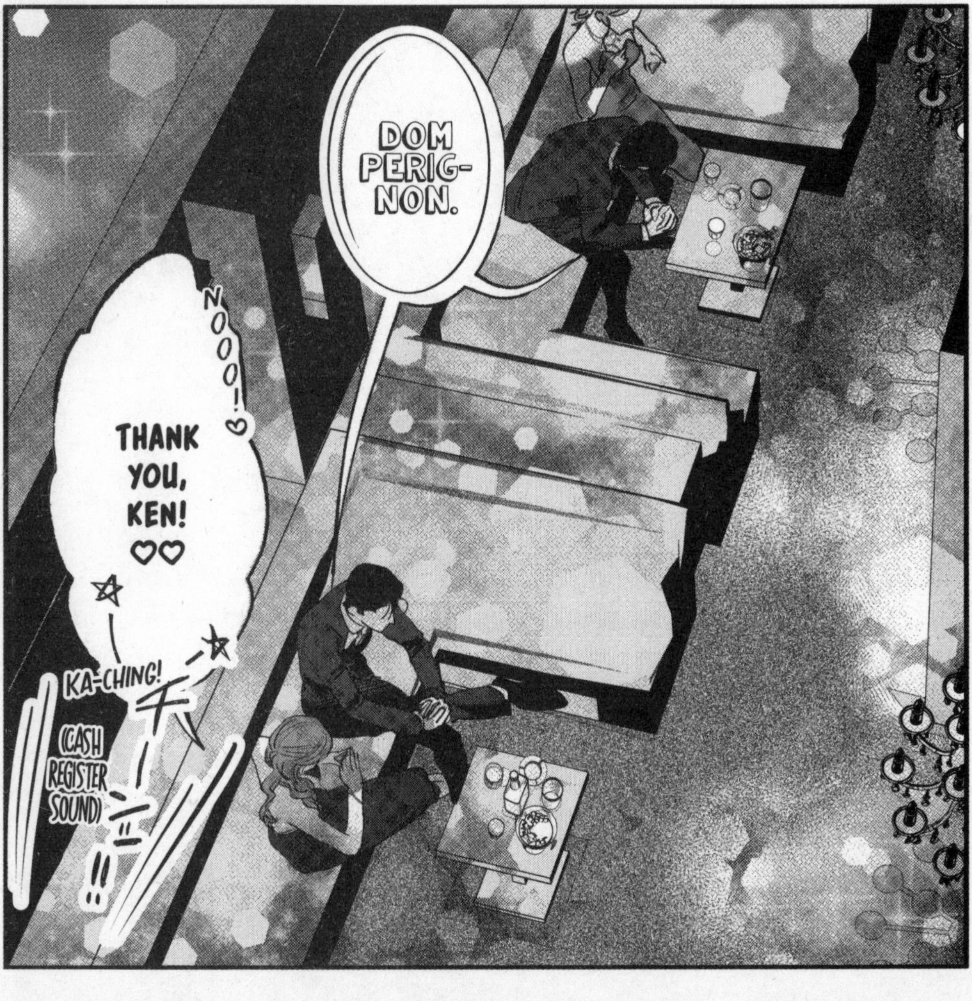
DOM PERIG-NON.
NOOOO!♡
THANK YOU, KEN! ♡♡
KA-CHING!
(CASH REGISTER SOUND)
チーン!!

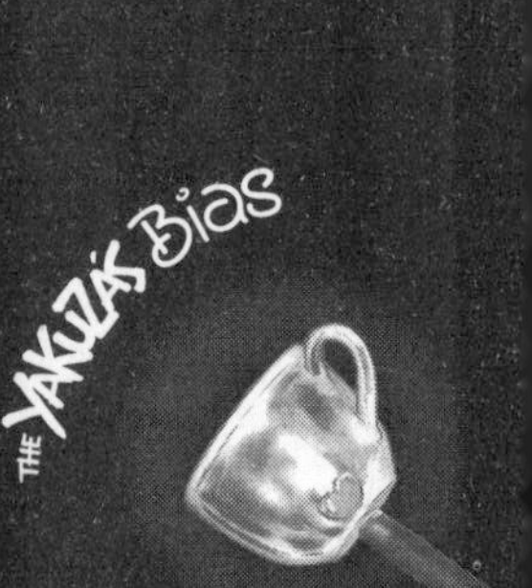
THE YAKUZA'S Bias

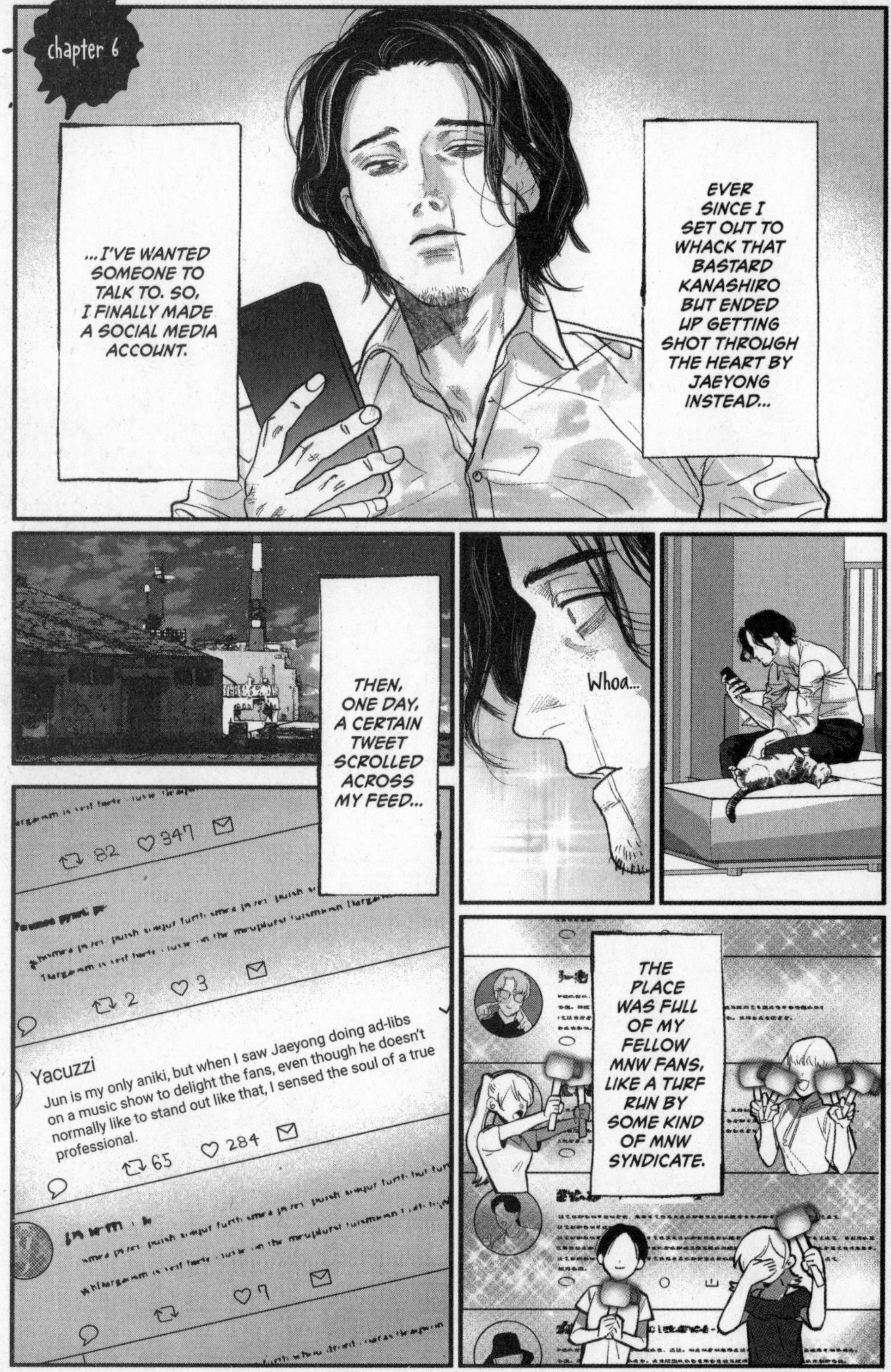
chapter 6
EVER SINCE I SET OUT TO WHACK THAT BASTARD KANASHIRO BUT ENDED UP GETTING SHOT THROUGH THE HEART BY JAEYONG INSTEAD...
...I'VE WANTED SOMEONE TO TALK TO. SO, I FINALLY MADE A SOCIAL MEDIA ACCOUNT.
Whoa...
THEN, ONE DAY, A CERTAIN TWEET SCROLLED ACROSS MY FEED...
THE PLACE WAS FULL OF MY FELLOW MNW FANS, LIKE A TURF RUN BY SOME KIND OF MNW SYNDICATE.
82 347
2 3
Yacuzzi
Jun is my only aniki, but when I saw Jaeyong doing ad-libs on a music show to delight the fans, even though he doesn't normally like to stand out like that, I sensed the soul of a true professional.
65 284
7

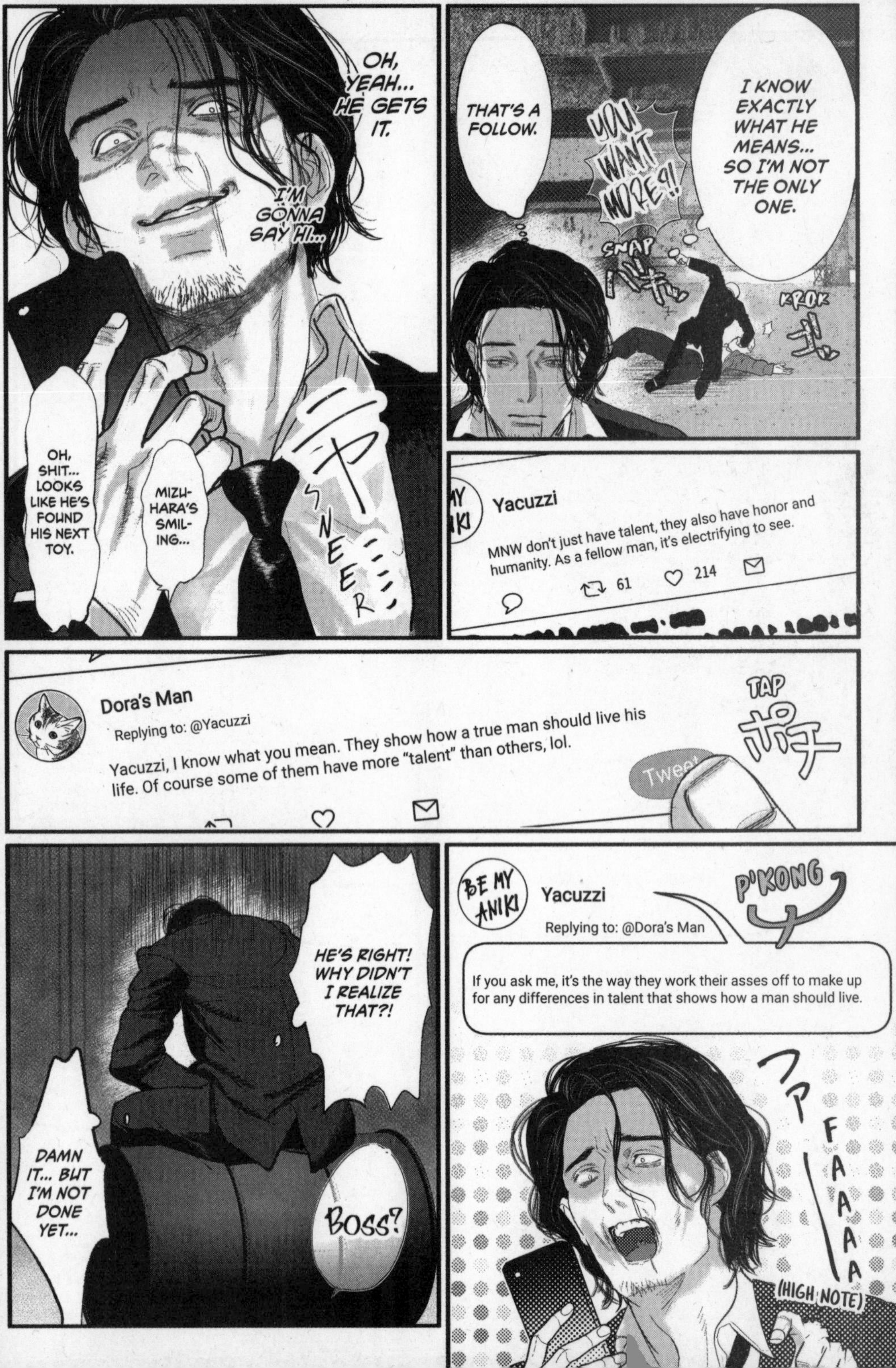
I KNOW EXACTLY WHAT HE MEANS... SO I'M NOT THE ONLY ONE.
YOU WANT MORE?!
THAT'S A FOLLOW.
SNAP
KROK
BE MY ANIKI
Yacuzzi
MNW don't just have talent, they also have honor and humanity. As a fellow man, it's electrifying to see.
61
214
OH, YEAH... HE GETS IT.
I'M GONNA SAY HI...
SNEER
MIZUHARA'S SMILING...
OH, SHIT... LOOKS LIKE HE'S FOUND HIS NEXT TOY.
TAP
Dora's Man
Replying to: @Yacuzzi
Yacuzzi, I know what you mean. They show how a true man should live his life. Of course some of them have more "talent" than others, lol.
Tweet
BE MY ANIKI
Yacuzzi
Replying to: @Dora's Man
P'KONG
If you ask me, it's the way they work their asses off to make up for any differences in talent that shows how a man should live.
FAAAAA
(HIGH NOTE)
HE'S RIGHT! WHY DIDN'T I REALIZE THAT?!
BOSS?
DAMN IT... BUT I'M NOT DONE YET...

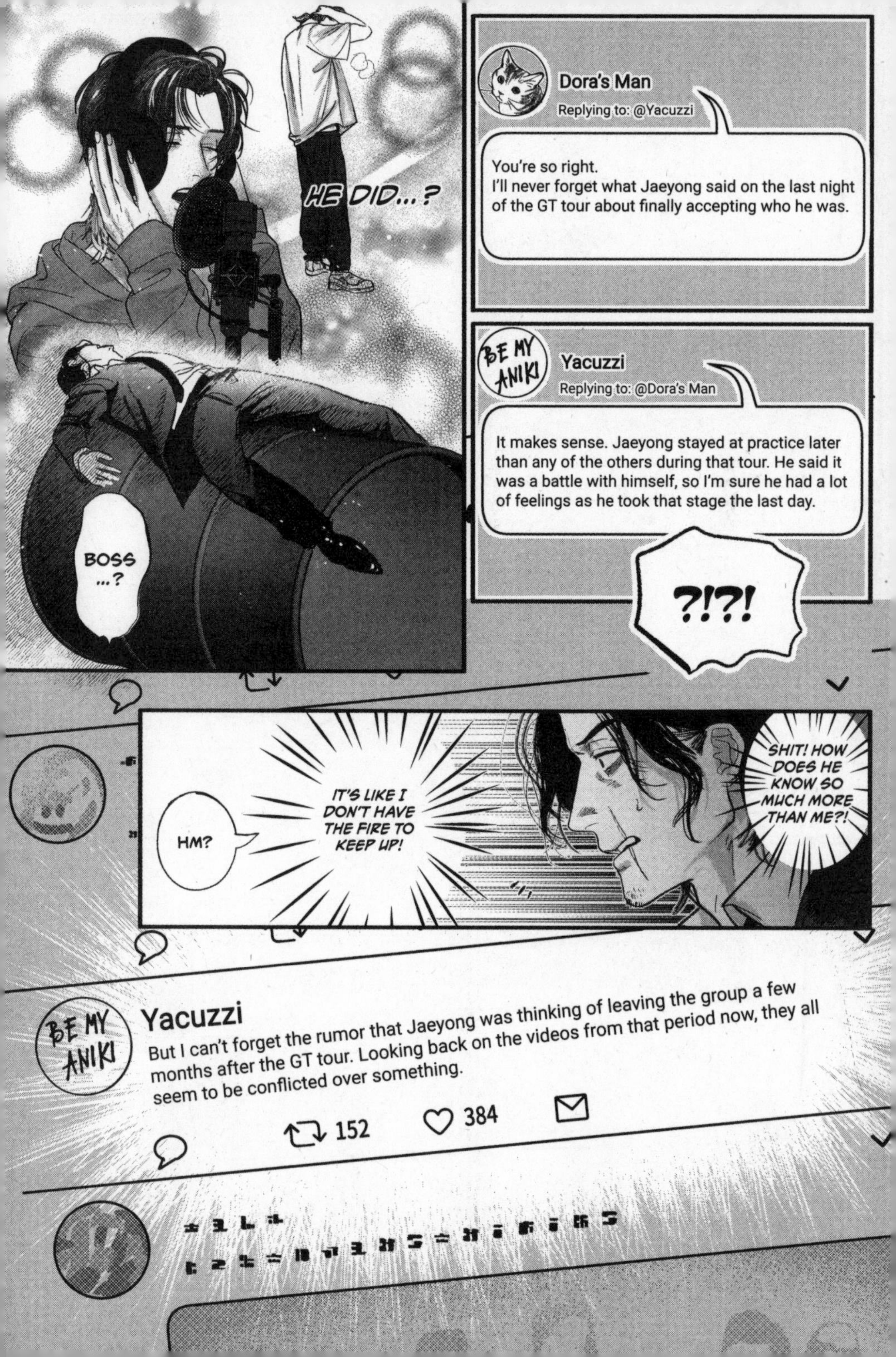
Dora's Man
Replying to: @Yacuzzi
You're so right.
I'll never forget what Jaeyong said on the last night of the GT tour about finally accepting who he was.
Yacuzzi
Replying to: @Dora's Man
It makes sense. Jaeyong stayed at practice later than any of the others during that tour. He said it was a battle with himself, so I'm sure he had a lot of feelings as he took that stage the last day.
?!?!
HE DID...?
BOSS ...?
SHIT! HOW DOES HE KNOW SO MUCH MORE THAN ME?!
IT'S LIKE I DON'T HAVE THE FIRE TO KEEP UP!
HM?
Yacuzzi
But I can't forget the rumor that Jaeyong was thinking of leaving the group a few months after the GT tour. Looking back on the videos from that period now, they all seem to be conflicted over something.
152
384

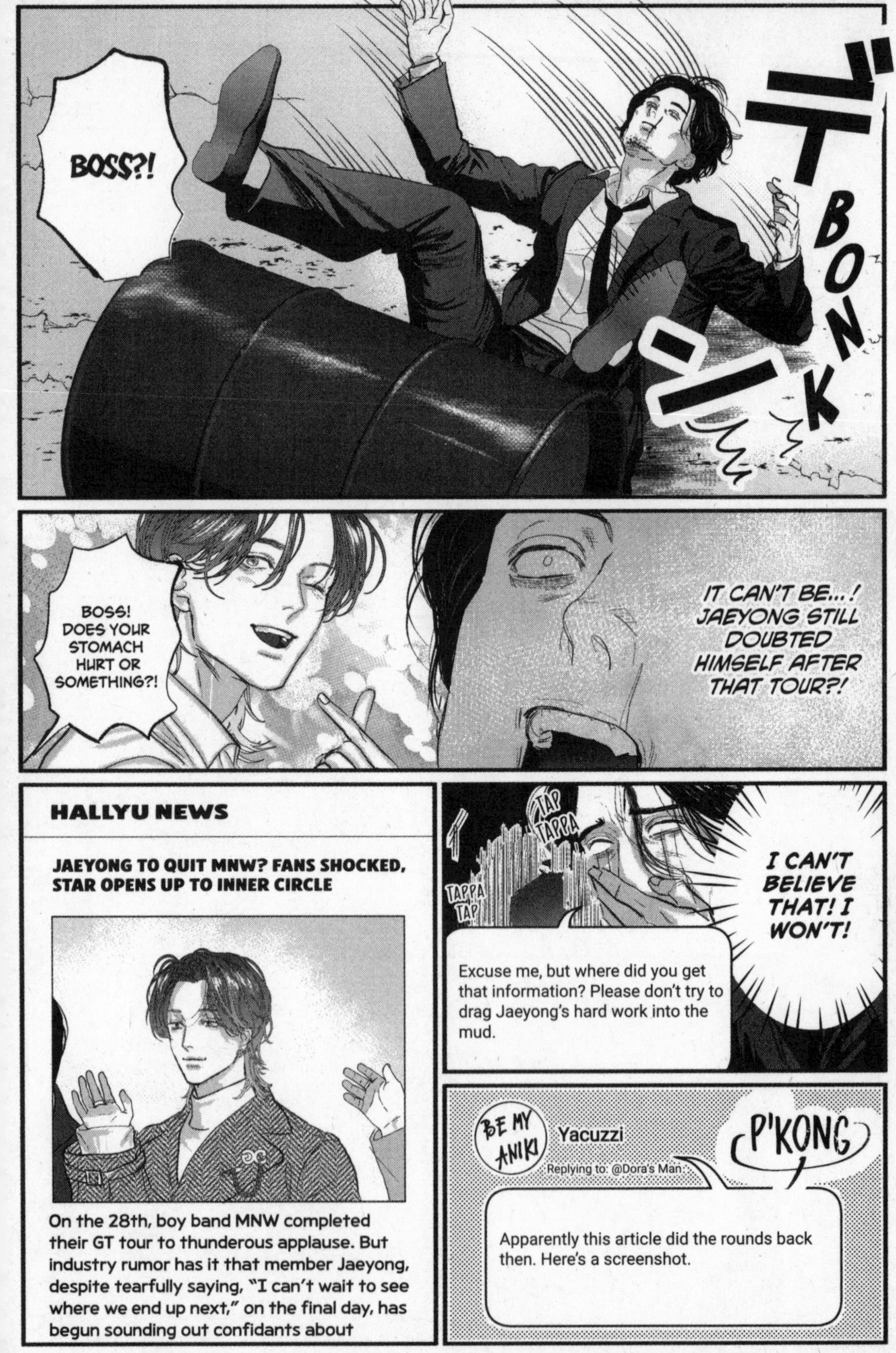
BOSS?!
BONK
IT CAN'T BE...! JAEYONG STILL DOUBTED HIMSELF AFTER THAT TOUR?!
BOSS! DOES YOUR STOMACH HURT OR SOMETHING?!
I CAN'T BELIEVE THAT! I WON'T!
TAP TAPPA
TAPPA TAP
Excuse me, but where did you get that information? Please don't try to drag Jaeyong's hard work into the mud.
P'KONG
BE MY ANIKI
Yacuzzi
Replying to: @Dora's Man
Apparently this article did the rounds back then. Here's a screenshot.
HALLYU NEWS
JAEYONG TO QUIT MNW? FANS SHOCKED, STAR OPENS UP TO INNER CIRCLE
On the 28th, boy band MNW completed their GT tour to thunderous applause. But industry rumor has it that member Jaeyong, despite tearfully saying, "I can't wait to see where we end up next," on the final day, has begun sounding out confidants about

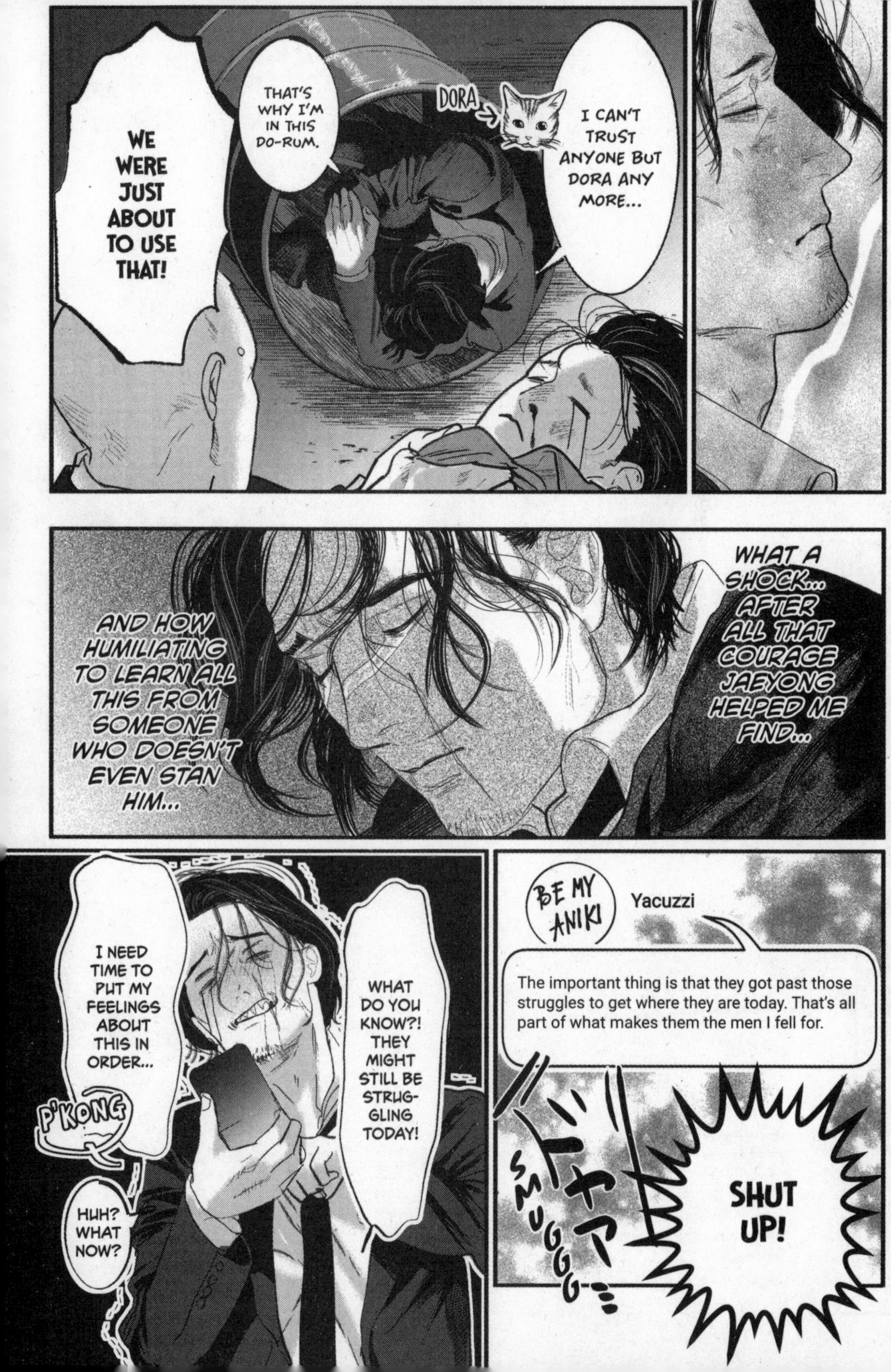
I CAN'T TRUST ANYONE BUT DORA ANY MORE...
DORA
THAT'S WHY I'M IN THIS DO-RUM.
WE WERE JUST ABOUT TO USE THAT!
WHAT A SHOCK... AFTER ALL THAT COURAGE JAEYONG HELPED ME FIND...
AND HOW HUMILIATING TO LEARN ALL THIS FROM SOMEONE WHO DOESN'T EVEN STAN HIM...
BE MY ANIKI
Yacuzzi
The important thing is that they got past those struggles to get where they are today. That's all part of what makes them the men I fell for.
SHUT UP!
SMUGGG...
WHAT DO YOU KNOW?! THEY MIGHT STILL BE STRUG-GLING TODAY!
I NEED TIME TO PUT MY FEELINGS ABOUT THIS IN ORDER...
P'KONG
HUH? WHAT NOW?

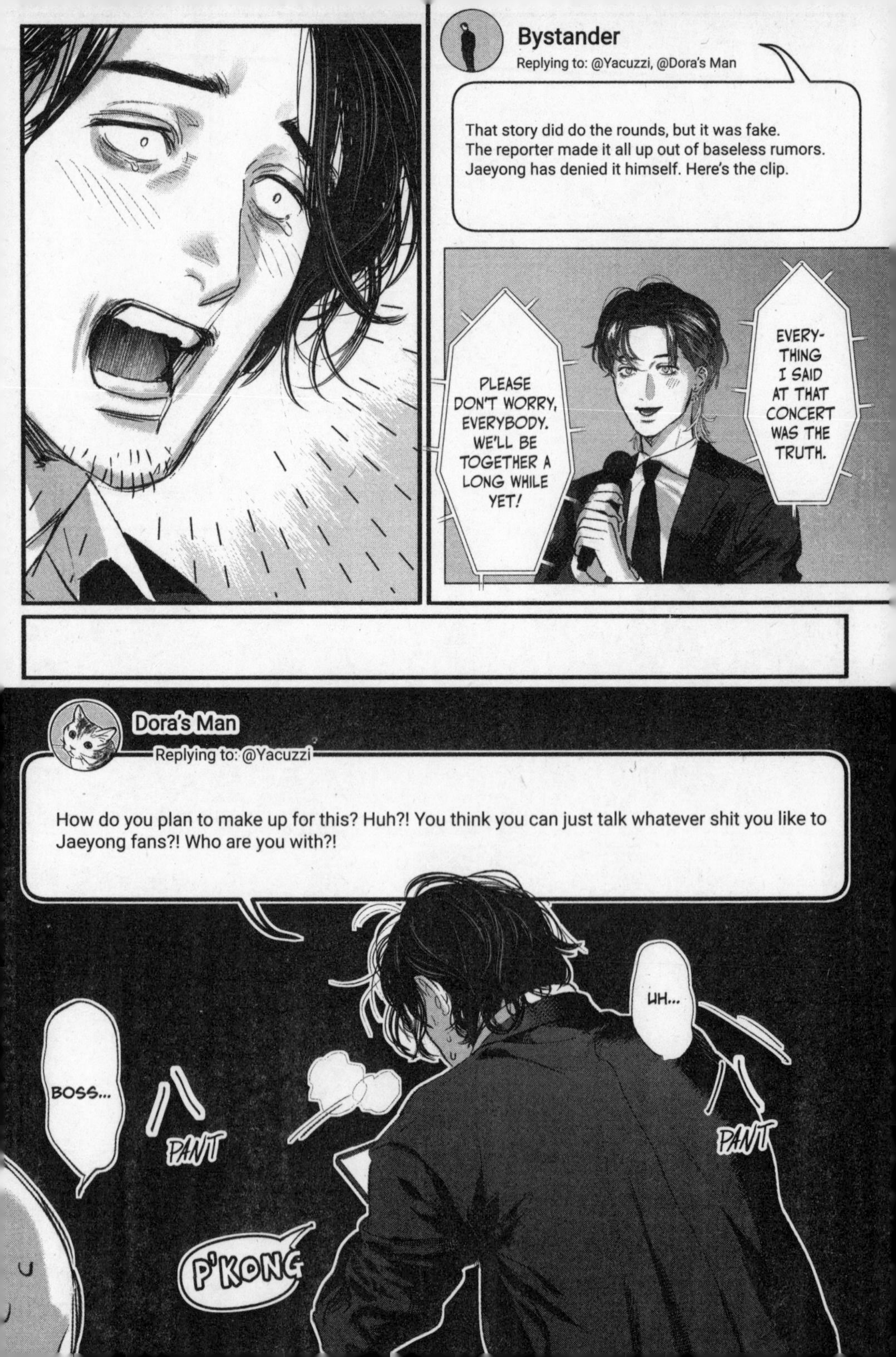
Bystander
Replying to: @Yacuzzi, @Dora's Man
That story did do the rounds, but it was fake. The reporter made it all up out of baseless rumors. Jaeyong has denied it himself. Here's the clip.
EVERY-THING I SAID AT THAT CONCERT WAS THE TRUTH.
PLEASE DON'T WORRY, EVERYBODY. WE'LL BE TOGETHER A LONG WHILE YET!
Dora's Man
Replying to: @Yacuzzi
How do you plan to make up for this? Huh?! You think you can just talk whatever shit you like to Jaeyong fans?! Who are you with?!
UH...
PANT
BOSS...
PANT
P'KONG

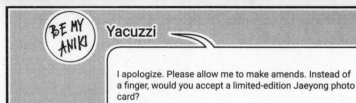

Yacuzzi

I apologize. Please allow me to make amends. Instead of a finger, would you accept a limited-edition Jaeyong photo card?

Dora's Man

It's all good. I'm sorry I flew off the handle. But I do want that card. Can you DM me?

⌐ HEH

I apologize for losing my cool in your replies. I would like that photo card, if you're still offering.

No, I'm the one who should apologize for not checking my sources. Are you free to meet sometime this weekend?

WHAT THE HELL?! HE'S A GOOD GUY AFTER ALL!

Yes, I am! How about 4:00 on Saturday, outside the Elta building? I'm looking foward to it!

Got it. See you then.

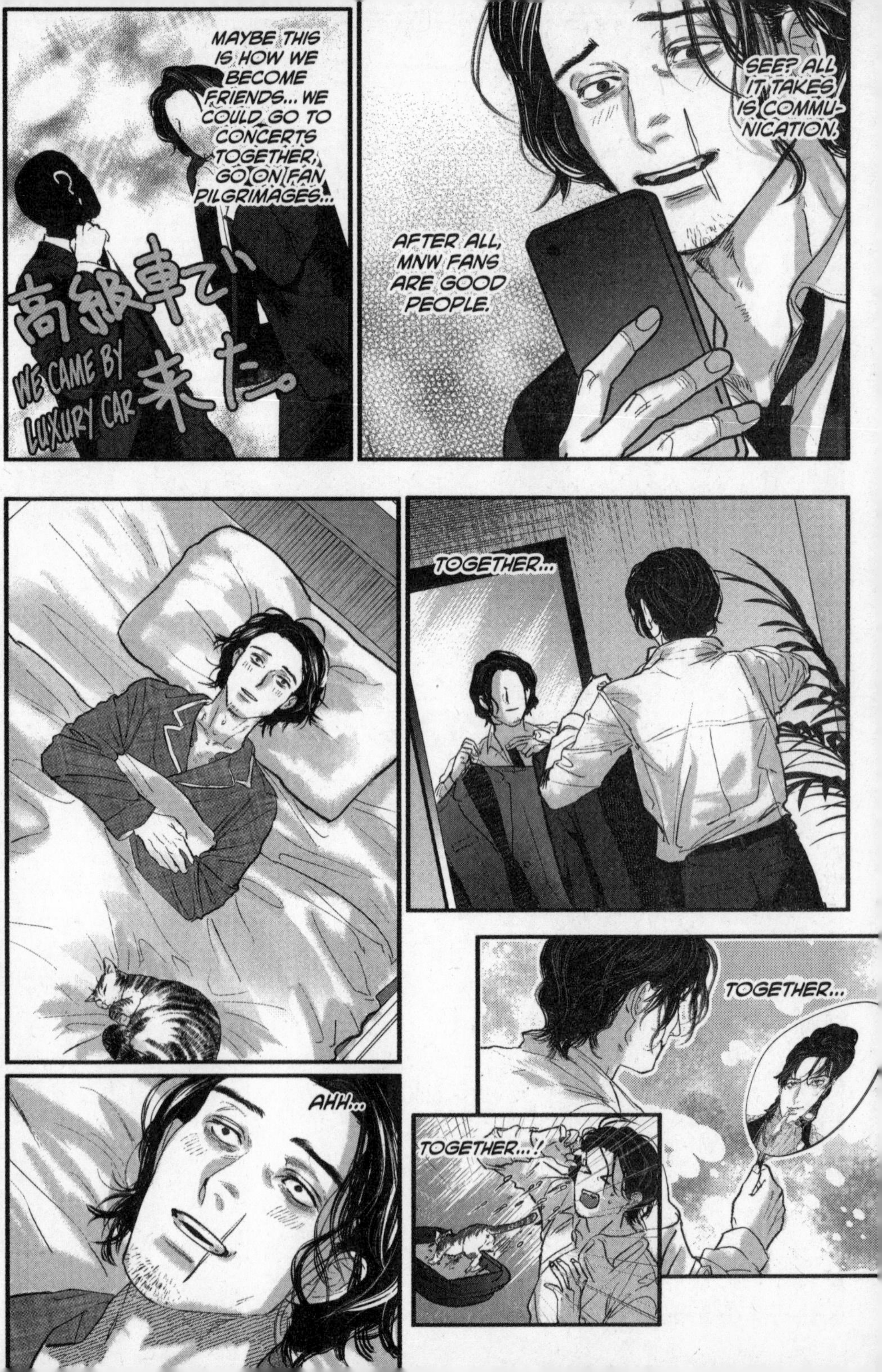
SEE? ALL IT TAKES IS COMMUNICATION.
AFTER ALL, MNW FANS ARE GOOD PEOPLE.
MAYBE THIS IS HOW WE BECOME FRIENDS... WE COULD GO TO CONCERTS TOGETHER, GO ON FAN PILGRIMAGES...
?
高級車で来た。
WE CAME BY LUXURY CAR
TOGETHER...
TOGETHER...
TOGETHER...!
AHH...

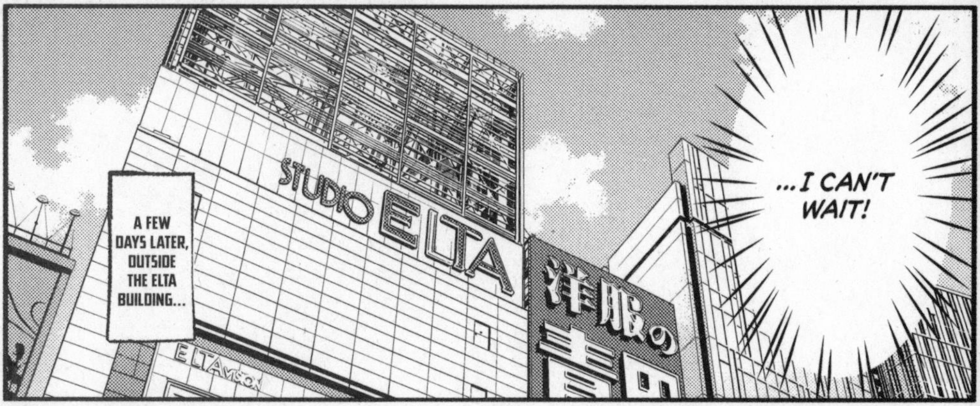
...I CAN'T WAIT!
A FEW DAYS LATER, OUTSIDE THE ELTA BUILDING...
STUDIO ELTA
洋服の

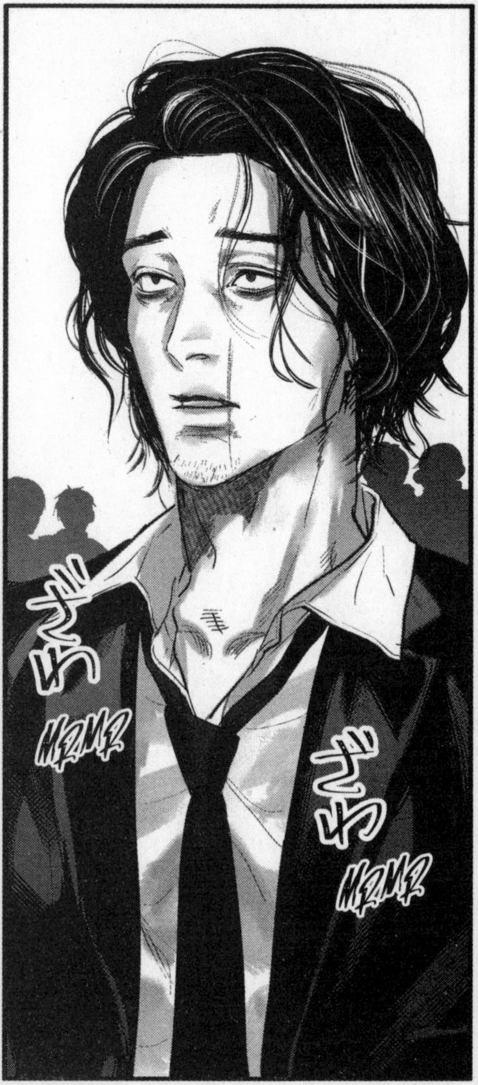
ざわ
MURMUR
ざわ
MURMUR

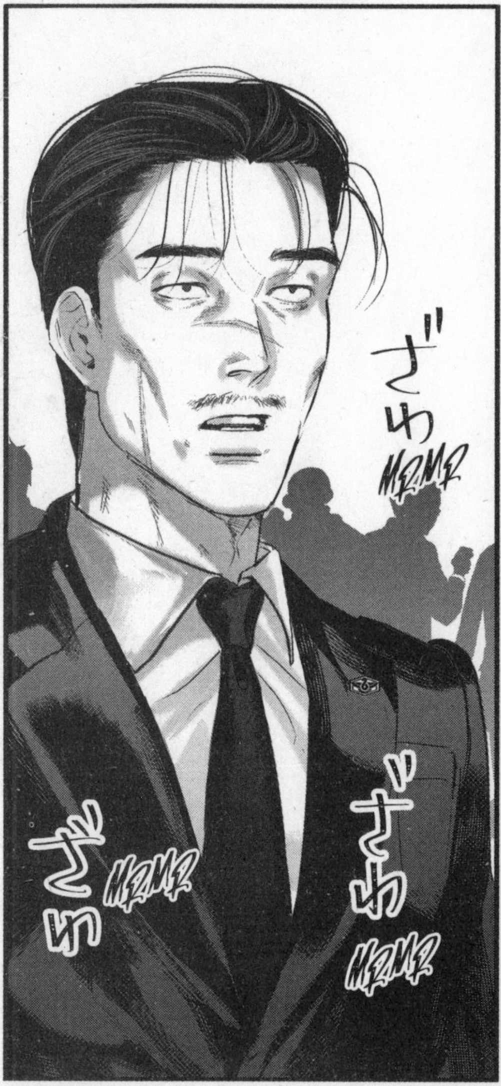
ざわ
MURMUR
ざわ
MURMUR
ざわ
MURMUR

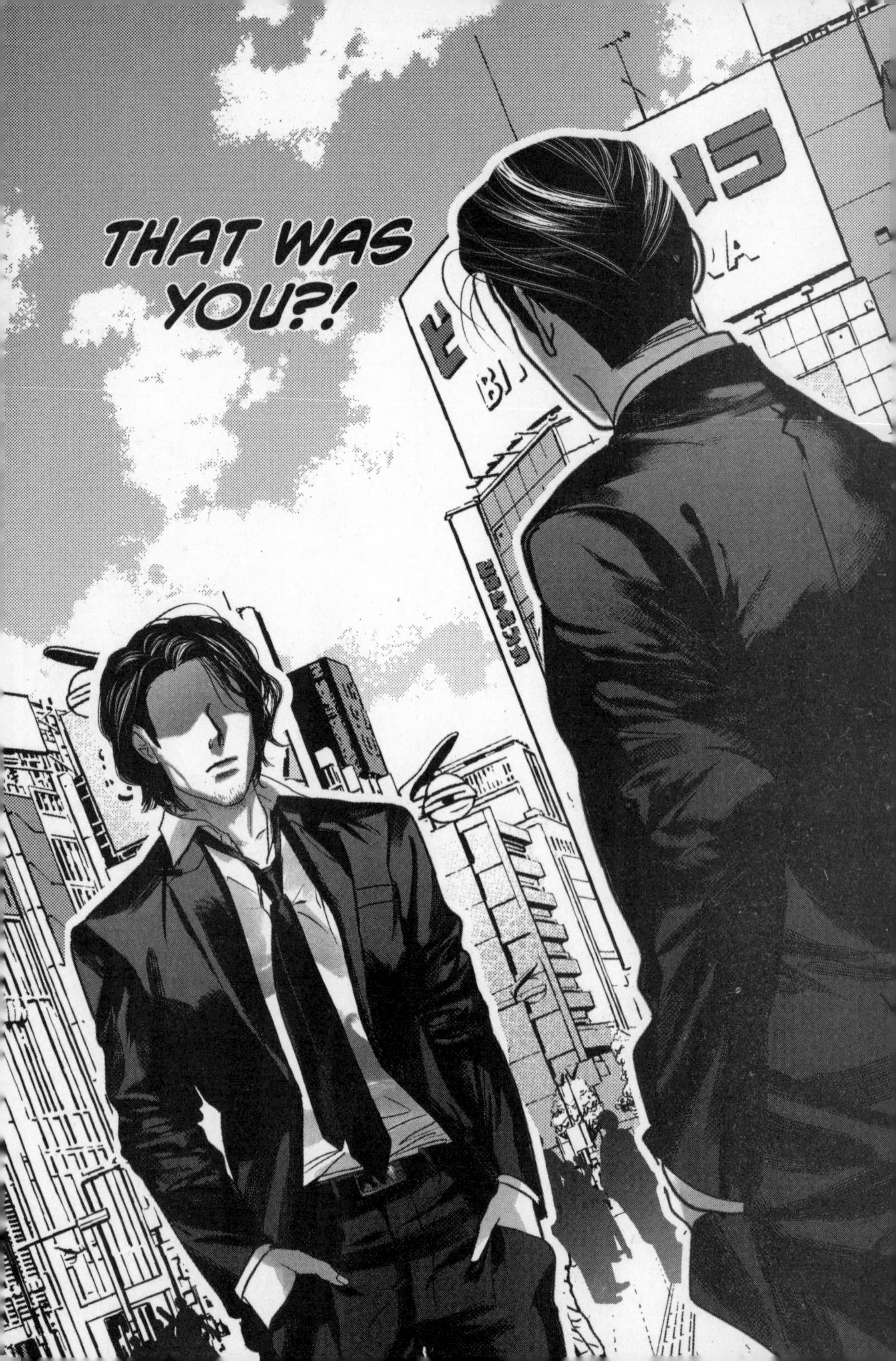
THAT WAS YOU?!

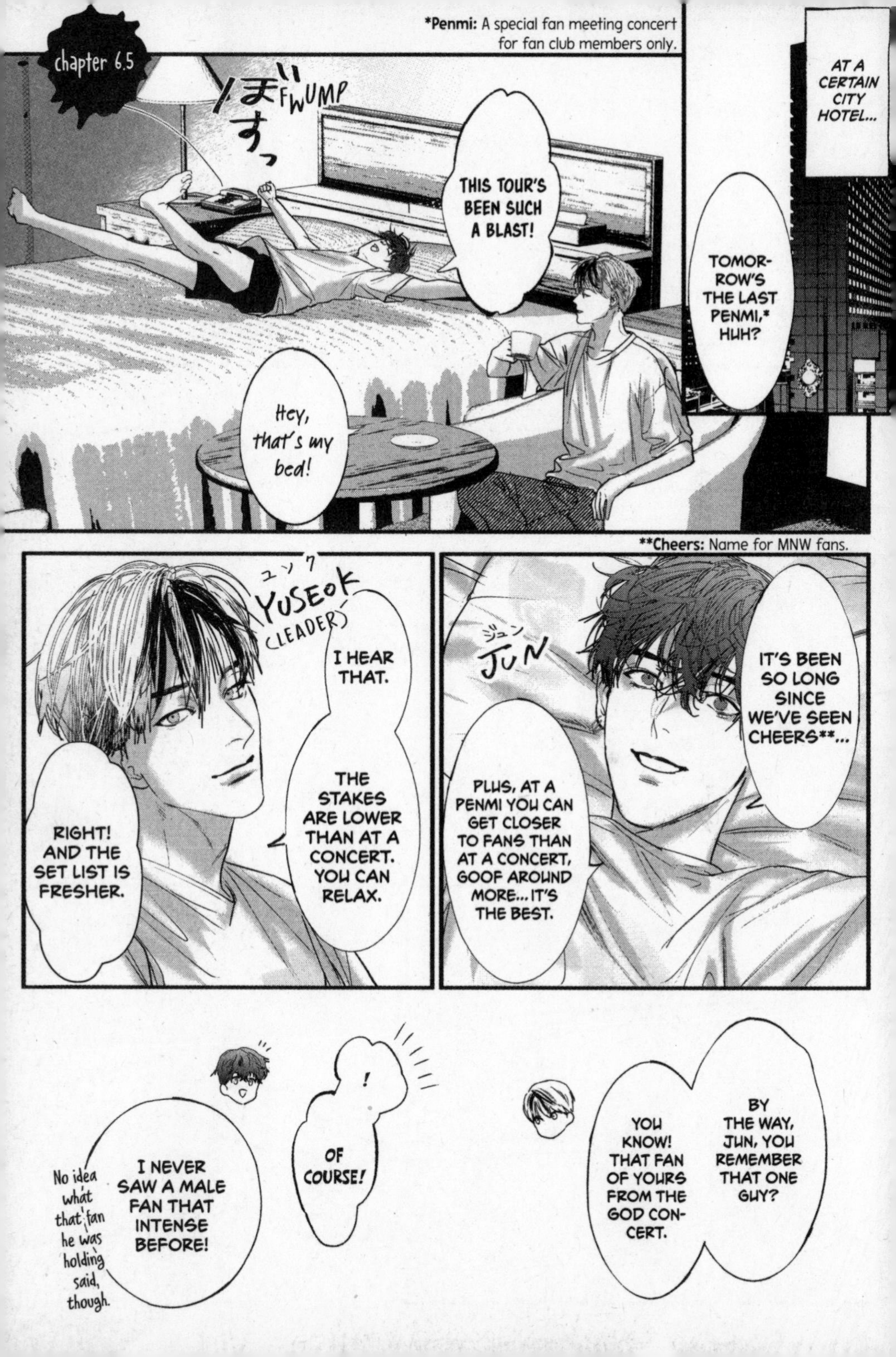
chapter 6.5
AT A CERTAIN CITY HOTEL...
TOMORROW'S THE LAST PENMI,* HUH?
THIS TOUR'S BEEN SUCH A BLAST!
FWUMP
Hey, that's my bed!
JUN
IT'S BEEN SO LONG SINCE WE'VE SEEN CHEERS**...
PLUS, AT A PENMI YOU CAN GET CLOSER TO FANS THAN AT A CONCERT, GOOF AROUND MORE... IT'S THE BEST.
YUSEOK (LEADER)
I HEAR THAT.
THE STAKES ARE LOWER THAN AT A CONCERT. YOU CAN RELAX.
RIGHT! AND THE SET LIST IS FRESHER.
BY THE WAY, JUN, YOU REMEMBER THAT ONE GUY?
YOU KNOW! THAT FAN OF YOURS FROM THE GOD CONCERT.
!
OF COURSE!
I NEVER SAW A MALE FAN THAT INTENSE BEFORE!
No idea what that fan he was holding said, though.

*Penmi: A special fan meeting concert for fan club members only.

**Cheers: Name for MNW fans.

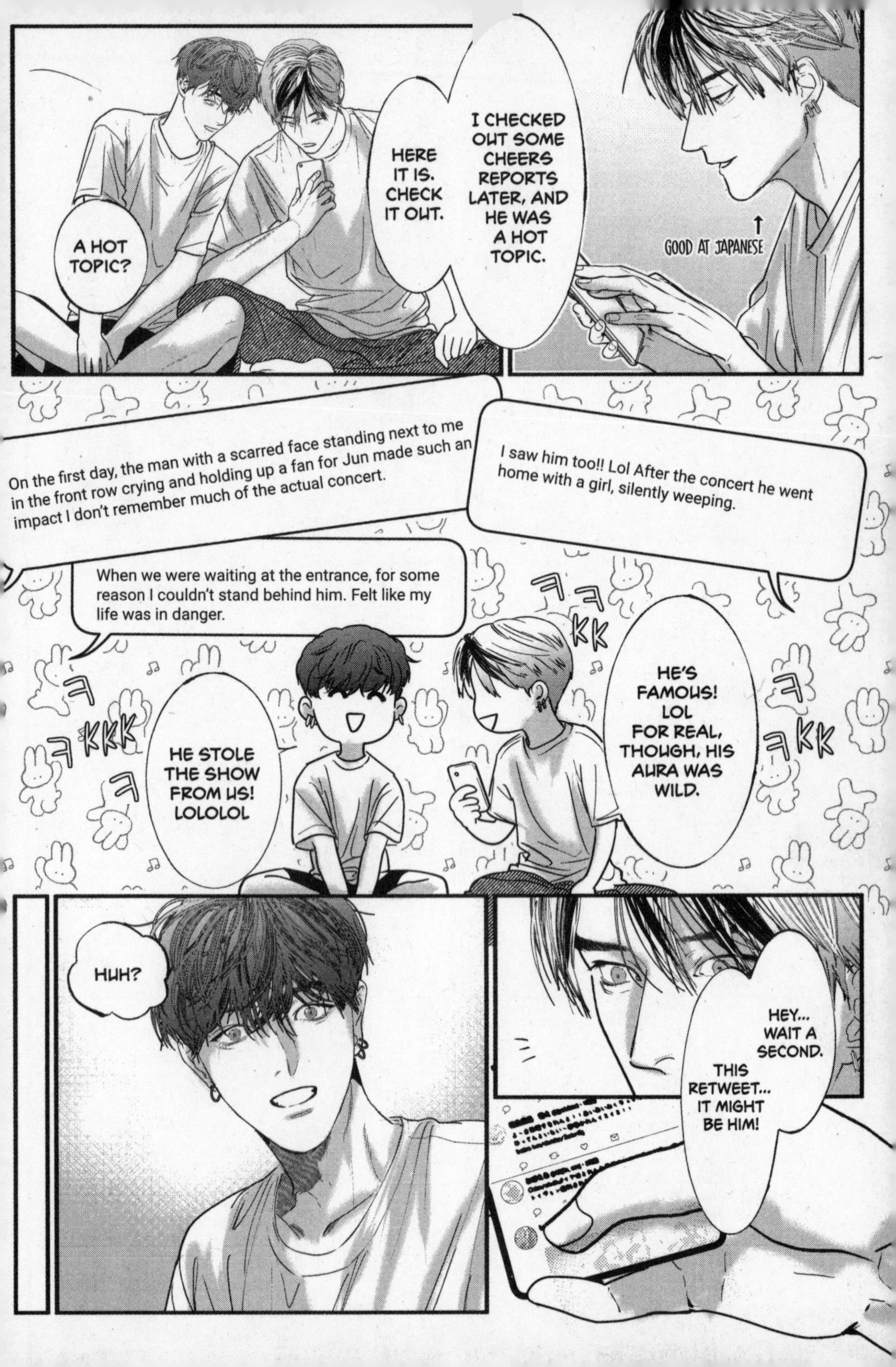
I CHECKED OUT SOME CHEERS REPORTS LATER, AND HE WAS A HOT TOPIC.
GOOD AT JAPANESE
HERE IT IS. CHECK IT OUT.
A HOT TOPIC?
On the first day, the man with a scarred face standing next to me in the front row crying and holding up a fan for Jun made such an impact I don't remember much of the actual concert.
I saw him too!! Lol After the concert he went home with a girl, silently weeping.
When we were waiting at the entrance, for some reason I couldn't stand behind him. Felt like my life was in danger.
ㅋㅋ KK
HE'S FAMOUS! LOL FOR REAL, THOUGH, HIS AURA WAS WILD.
ㅋ KK
ㅋ KKK ㅋ
HE STOLE THE SHOW FROM US! LOLOLOL
HEY... WAIT A SECOND.
THIS RETWEET... IT MIGHT BE HIM!
HUH?

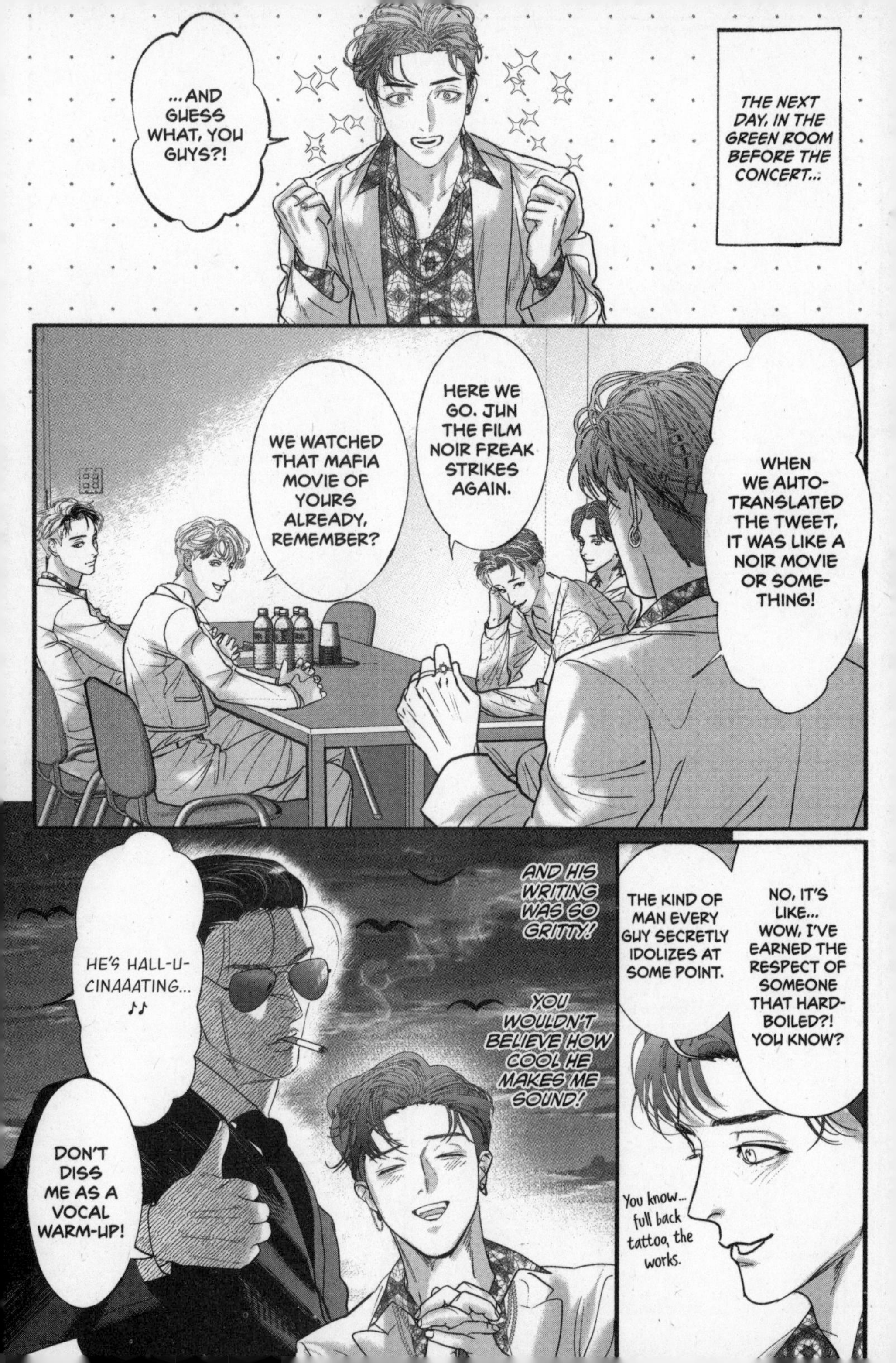
THE NEXT DAY, IN THE GREEN ROOM BEFORE THE CONCERT...
...AND GUESS WHAT, YOU GUYS?!
WHEN WE AUTO-TRANSLATED THE TWEET, IT WAS LIKE A NOIR MOVIE OR SOMETHING!
HERE WE GO. JUN THE FILM NOIR FREAK STRIKES AGAIN.
WE WATCHED THAT MAFIA MOVIE OF YOURS ALREADY, REMEMBER?
NO, IT'S LIKE... WOW, I'VE EARNED THE RESPECT OF SOMEONE THAT HARD-BOILED?! YOU KNOW?
THE KIND OF MAN EVERY GUY SECRETLY IDOLIZES AT SOME POINT.
You know... full back tattoo, the works.
AND HIS WRITING WAS SO GRITTY!
YOU WOULDN'T BELIEVE HOW COOL HE MAKES ME SOUND!
HE'S HALL-U-CINAAATING... ♪♪
DON'T DISS ME AS A VOCAL WARM-UP!

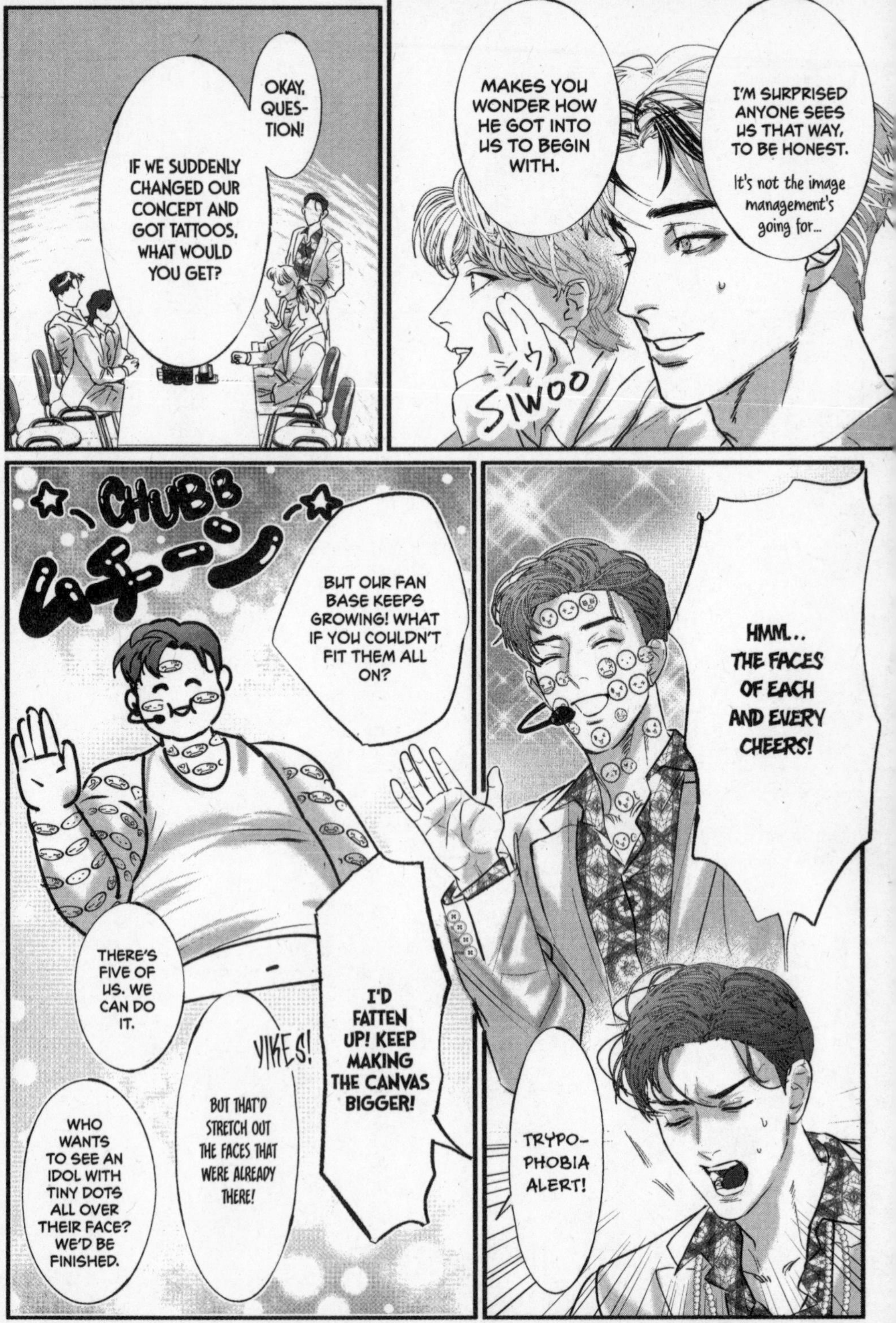
I'M SURPRISED ANYONE SEES US THAT WAY, TO BE HONEST.
It's not the image management's going for...
MAKES YOU WONDER HOW HE GOT INTO US TO BEGIN WITH.
SIWOO
OKAY, QUES-TION!
IF WE SUDDENLY CHANGED OUR CONCEPT AND GOT TATTOOS, WHAT WOULD YOU GET?
HMM.. THE FACES OF EACH AND EVERY CHEERS!
TRYPO-PHOBIA ALERT!
CHUBB
BUT OUR FAN BASE KEEPS GROWING! WHAT IF YOU COULDN'T FIT THEM ALL ON?
I'D FATTEN UP! KEEP MAKING THE CANVAS BIGGER!
THERE'S FIVE OF US. WE CAN DO IT.
YIKES!
BUT THAT'D STRETCH OUT THE FACES THAT WERE ALREADY THERE!
WHO WANTS TO SEE AN IDOL WITH TINY DOTS ALL OVER THEIR FACE? WE'D BE FINISHED.

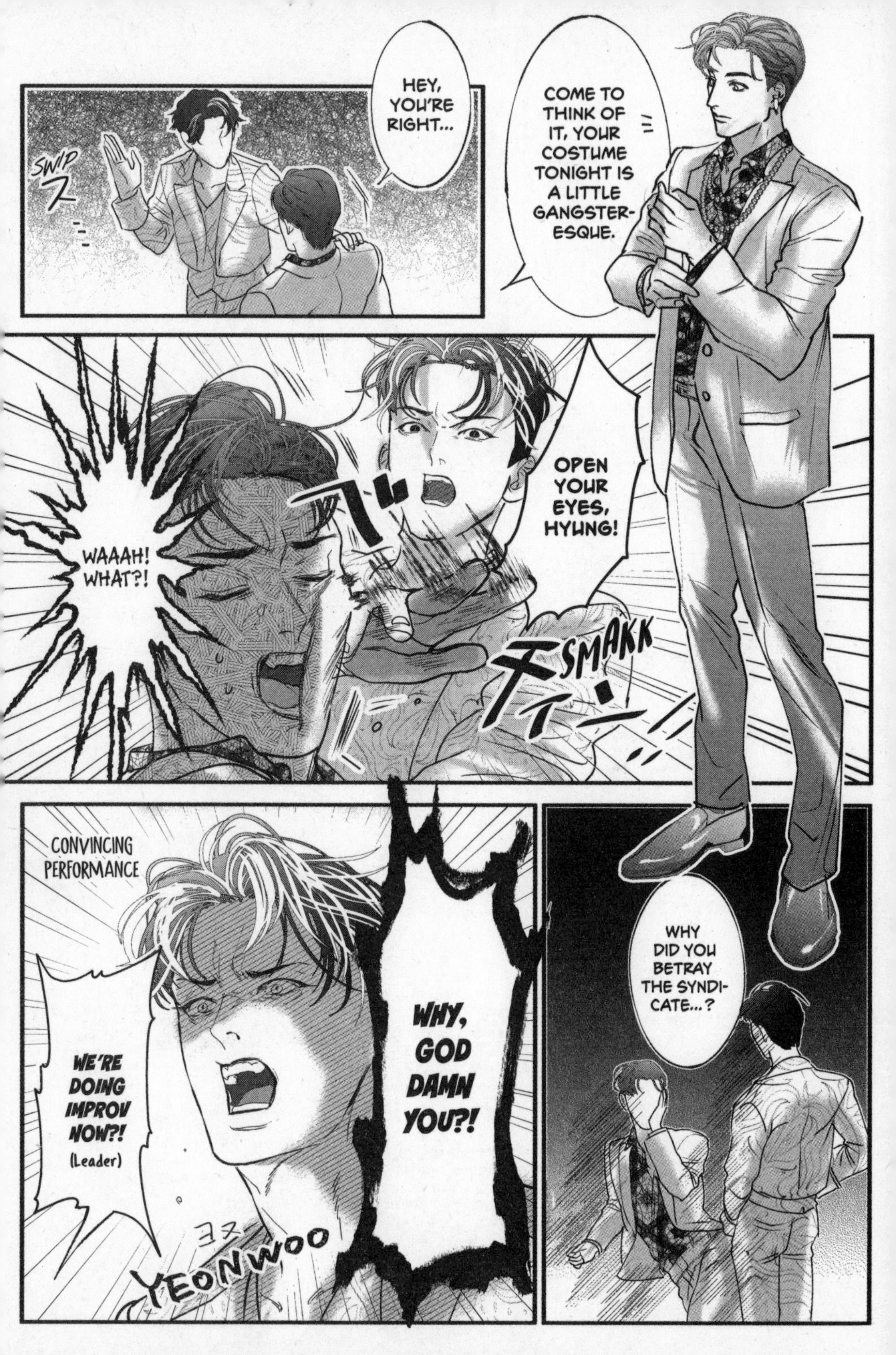
COME TO THINK OF IT, YOUR COSTUME TONIGHT IS A LITTLE GANGSTER-ESQUE.
HEY, YOU'RE RIGHT...
SWIP
OPEN YOUR EYES, HYUNG!
SMAKK
WAAAH! WHAT?!
WHY DID YOU BETRAY THE SYNDICATE...?
WHY, GOD DAMN YOU?!
WE'RE DOING IMPROV NOW?!
(Leader)
CONVINCING PERFORMANCE
YEONWOO

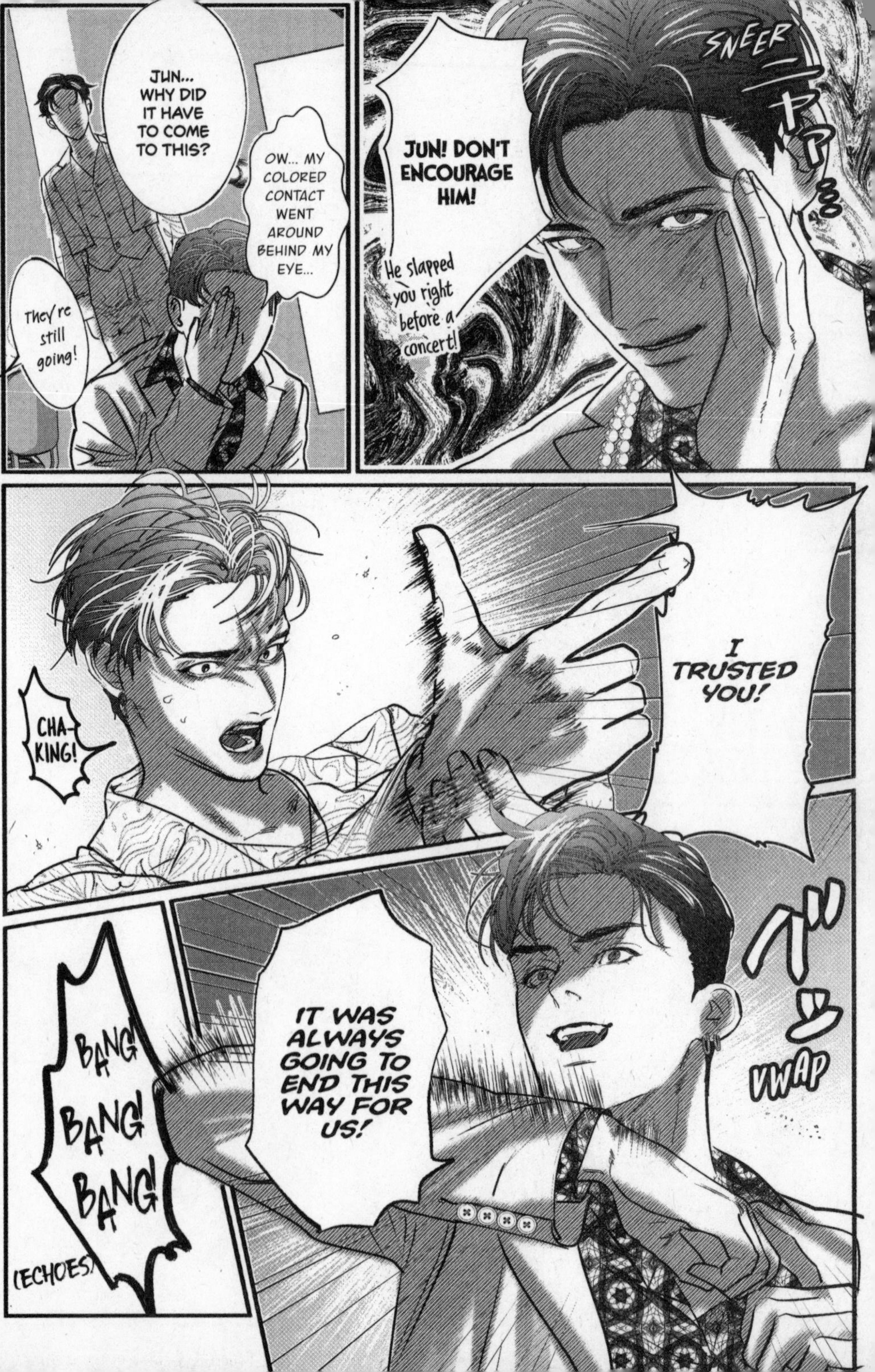
SNEER
JUN! DON'T ENCOURAGE HIM!
He slapped you right before a concert!
JUN... WHY DID IT HAVE TO COME TO THIS?
OW... MY COLORED CONTACT WENT AROUND BEHIND MY EYE...
They're still going!
I TRUSTED YOU!
CHA-KING!
VWAP
IT WAS ALWAYS GOING TO END THIS WAY FOR US!
BANG BANG! BANG!
(ECHOES)

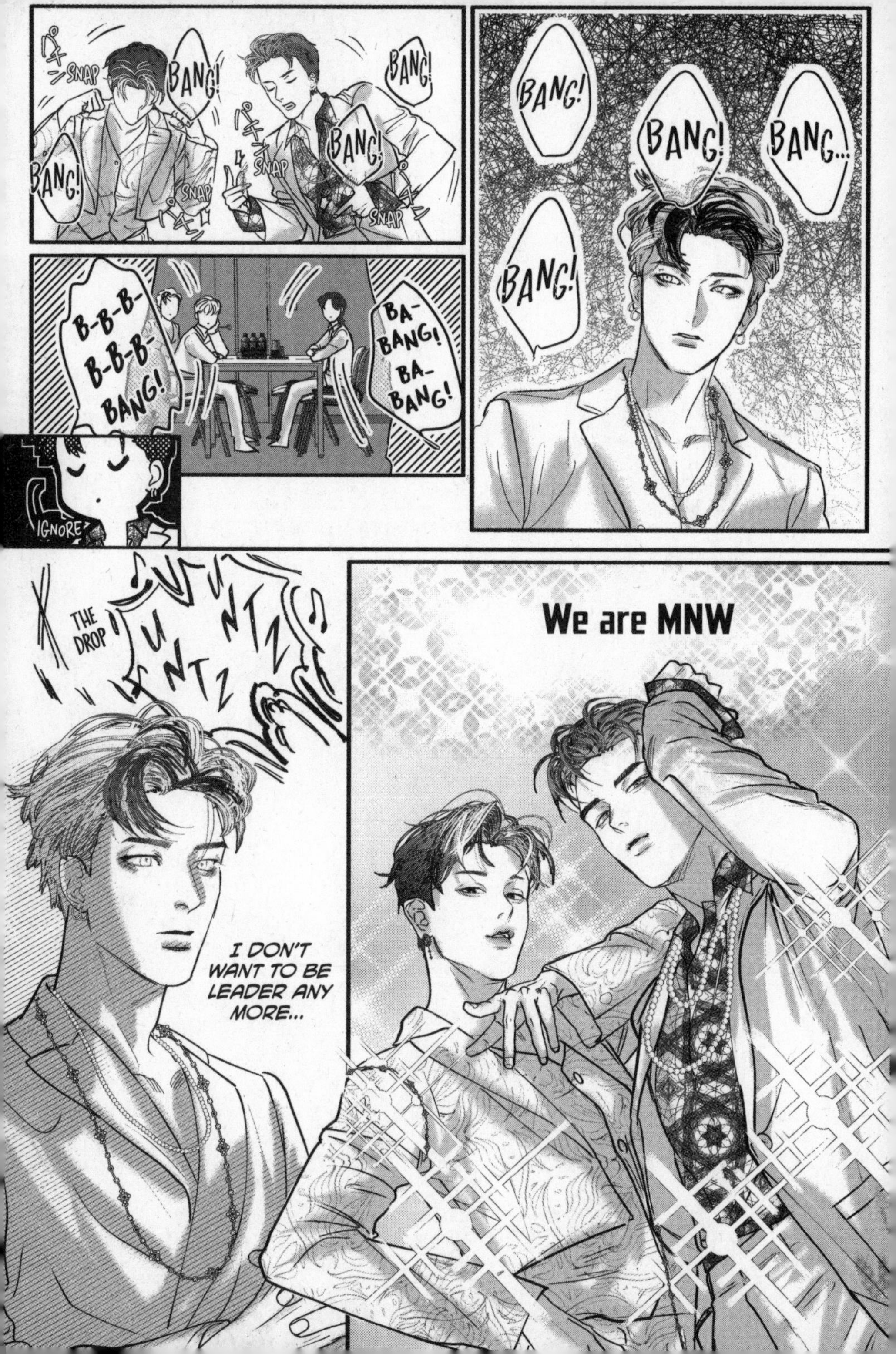

BANG...
BANG!
BANG!
BANG!
BANG!
SNAP
BANG!
SNAP
BANG!
SNAP
BANG!
SNAP
BA-BANG! BA-BANG!
B-B-B-B-B-B-BANG!
IGNORE
We are MNW
THE DROP
UNTZ UNTZ
I DON'T WANT TO BE LEADER ANY MORE...

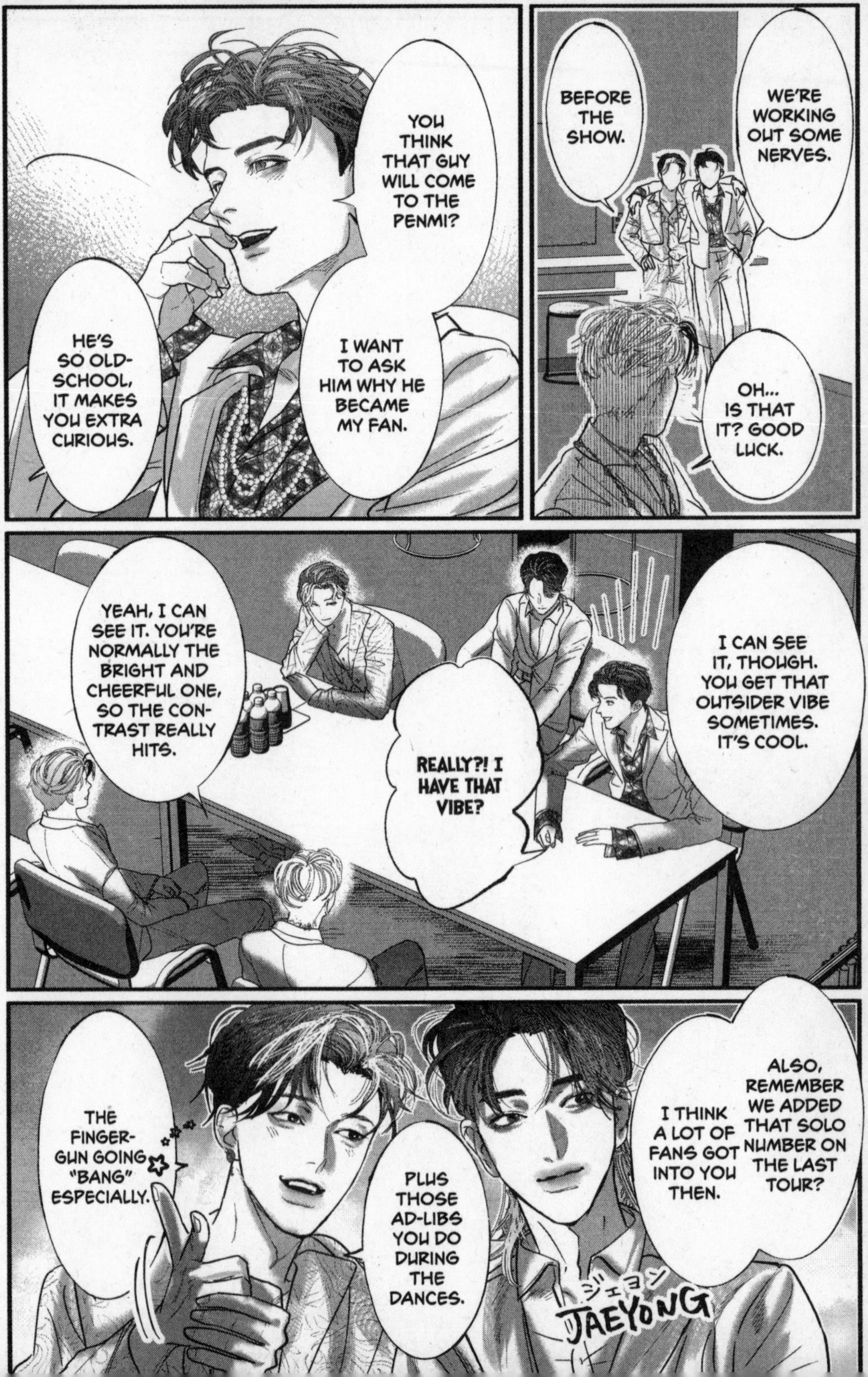
WE'RE WORKING OUT SOME NERVES.
BEFORE THE SHOW.
OH... IS THAT IT? GOOD LUCK.
YOU THINK THAT GUY WILL COME TO THE PENMI?
I WANT TO ASK HIM WHY HE BECAME MY FAN.
HE'S SO OLD-SCHOOL, IT MAKES YOU EXTRA CURIOUS.
I CAN SEE IT, THOUGH. YOU GET THAT OUTSIDER VIBE SOMETIMES. IT'S COOL.
REALLY?! I HAVE THAT VIBE?
YEAH, I CAN SEE IT. YOU'RE NORMALLY THE BRIGHT AND CHEERFUL ONE, SO THE CONTRAST REALLY HITS.
ALSO, REMEMBER WE ADDED THAT SOLO NUMBER ON THE LAST TOUR?
I THINK A LOT OF FANS GOT INTO YOU THEN.
PLUS THOSE AD-LIBS YOU DO DURING THE DANCES.
THE FINGER-GUN GOING "BANG" ESPECIALLY.
ジェヨン
JAEYONG

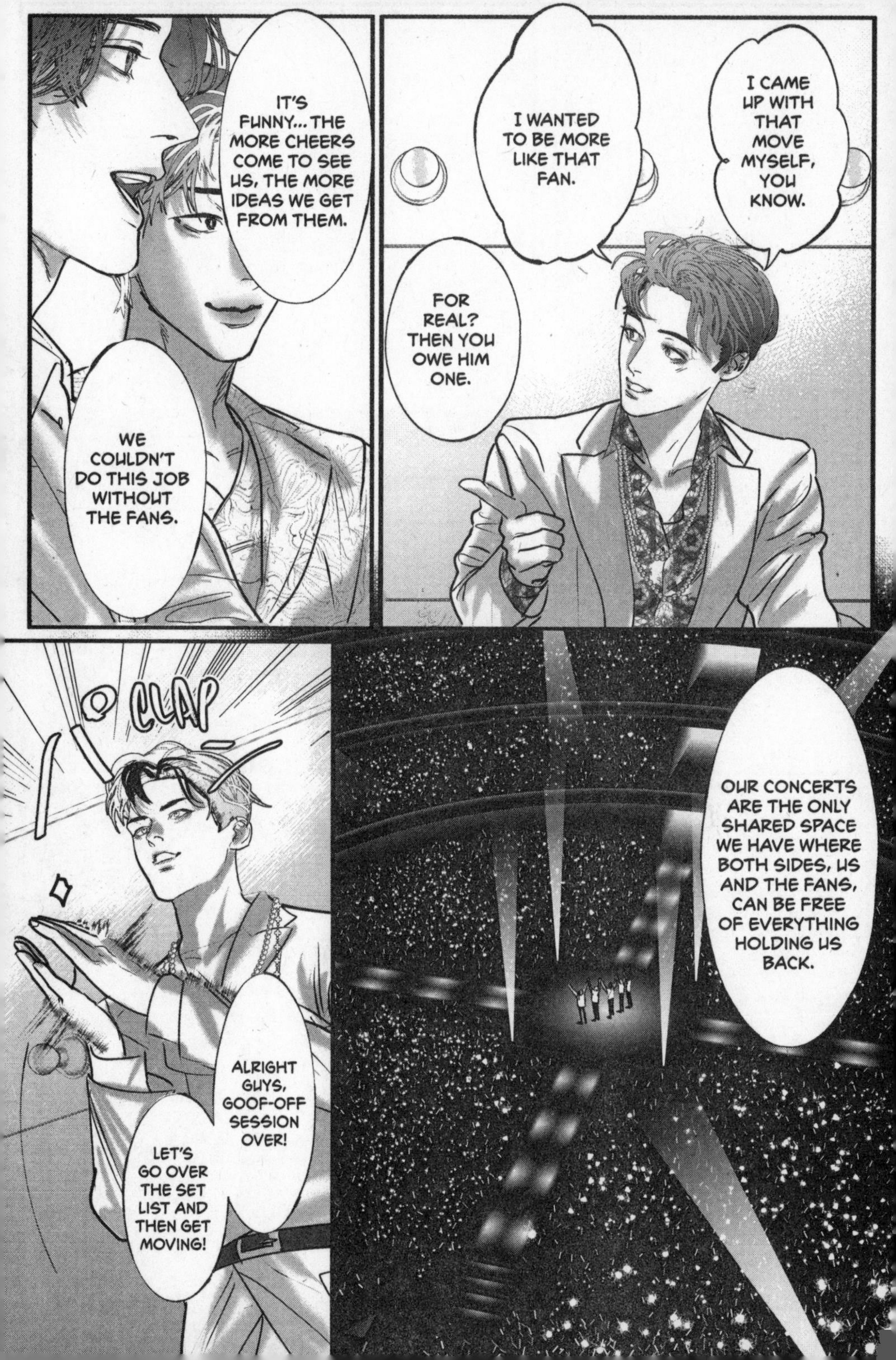
I CAME UP WITH THAT MOVE MYSELF, YOU KNOW.
I WANTED TO BE MORE LIKE THAT FAN.
FOR REAL? THEN YOU OWE HIM ONE.
IT'S FUNNY... THE MORE CHEERS COME TO SEE US, THE MORE IDEAS WE GET FROM THEM.
WE COULDN'T DO THIS JOB WITHOUT THE FANS.
OUR CONCERTS ARE THE ONLY SHARED SPACE WE HAVE WHERE BOTH SIDES, US AND THE FANS, CAN BE FREE OF EVERYTHING HOLDING US BACK.
CLAP
ALRIGHT GUYS, GOOF-OFF SESSION OVER!
LET'S GO OVER THE SET LIST AND THEN GET MOVING!

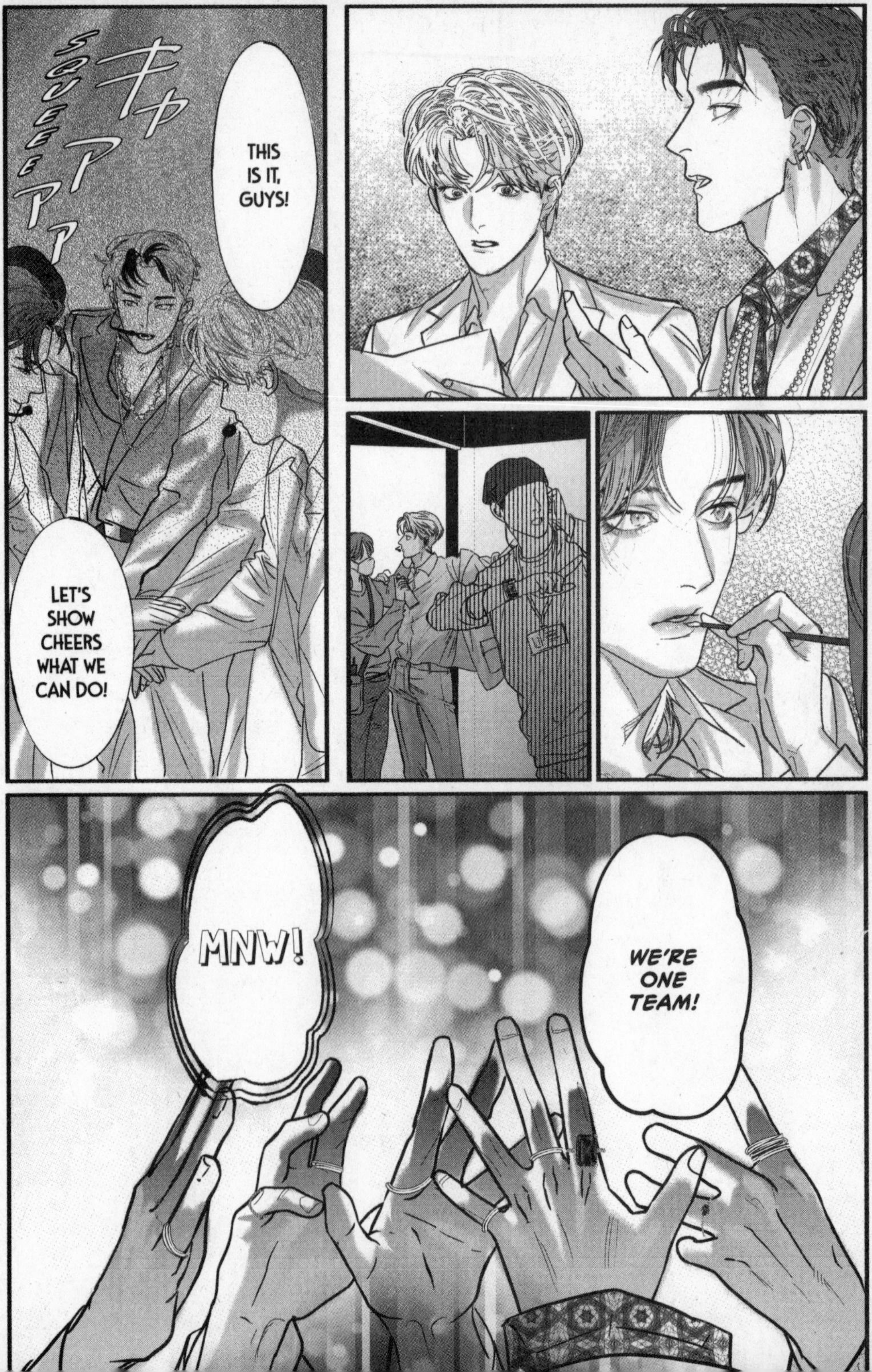
THIS IS IT, GUYS!
キャアア
SQUEEEE
LET'S SHOW CHEERS WHAT WE CAN DO!
WE'RE ONE TEAM!
MNW!

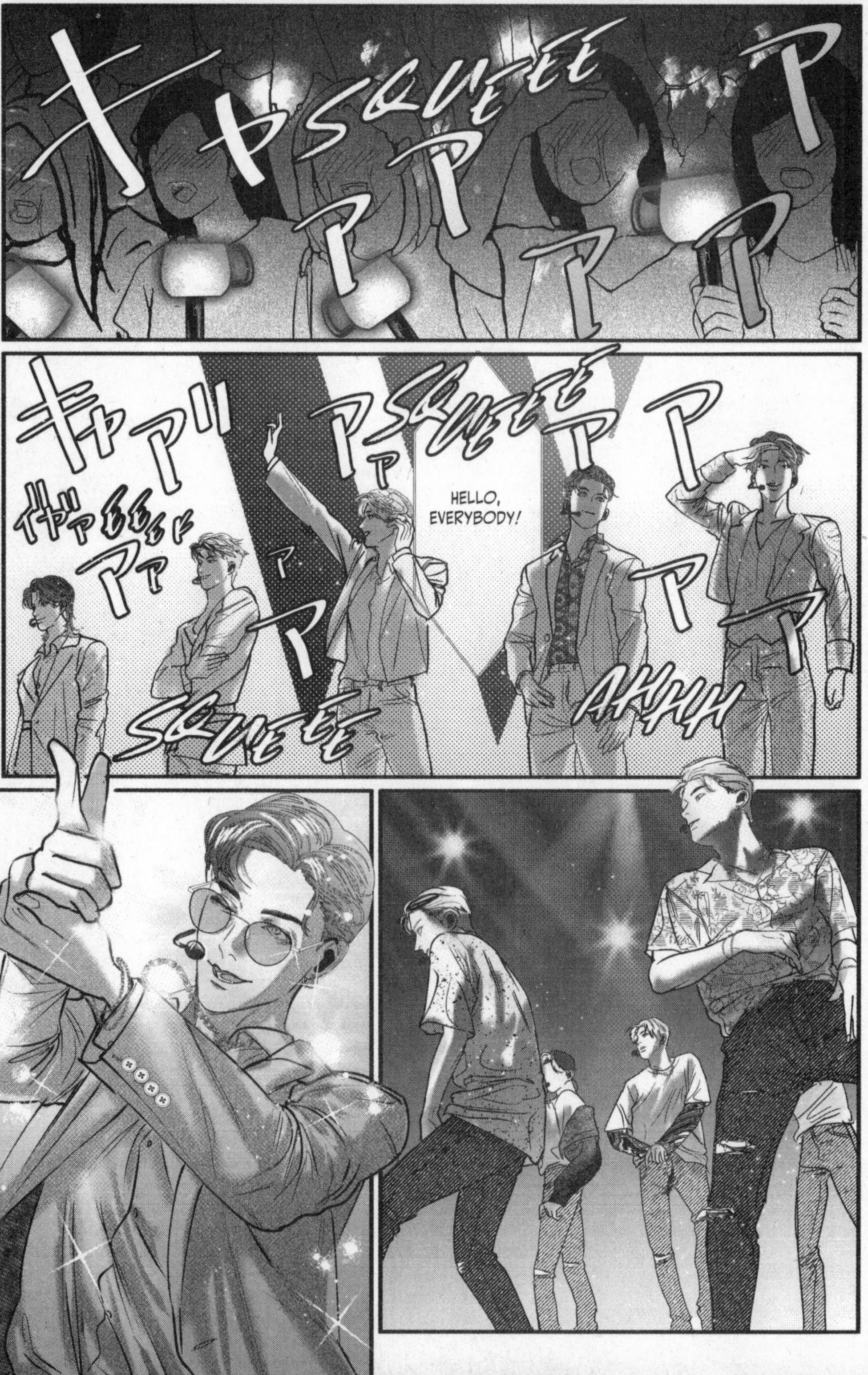
SQUEEE
SQUEEE
HELLO, EVERYBODY!
AHHH
SQUEEE

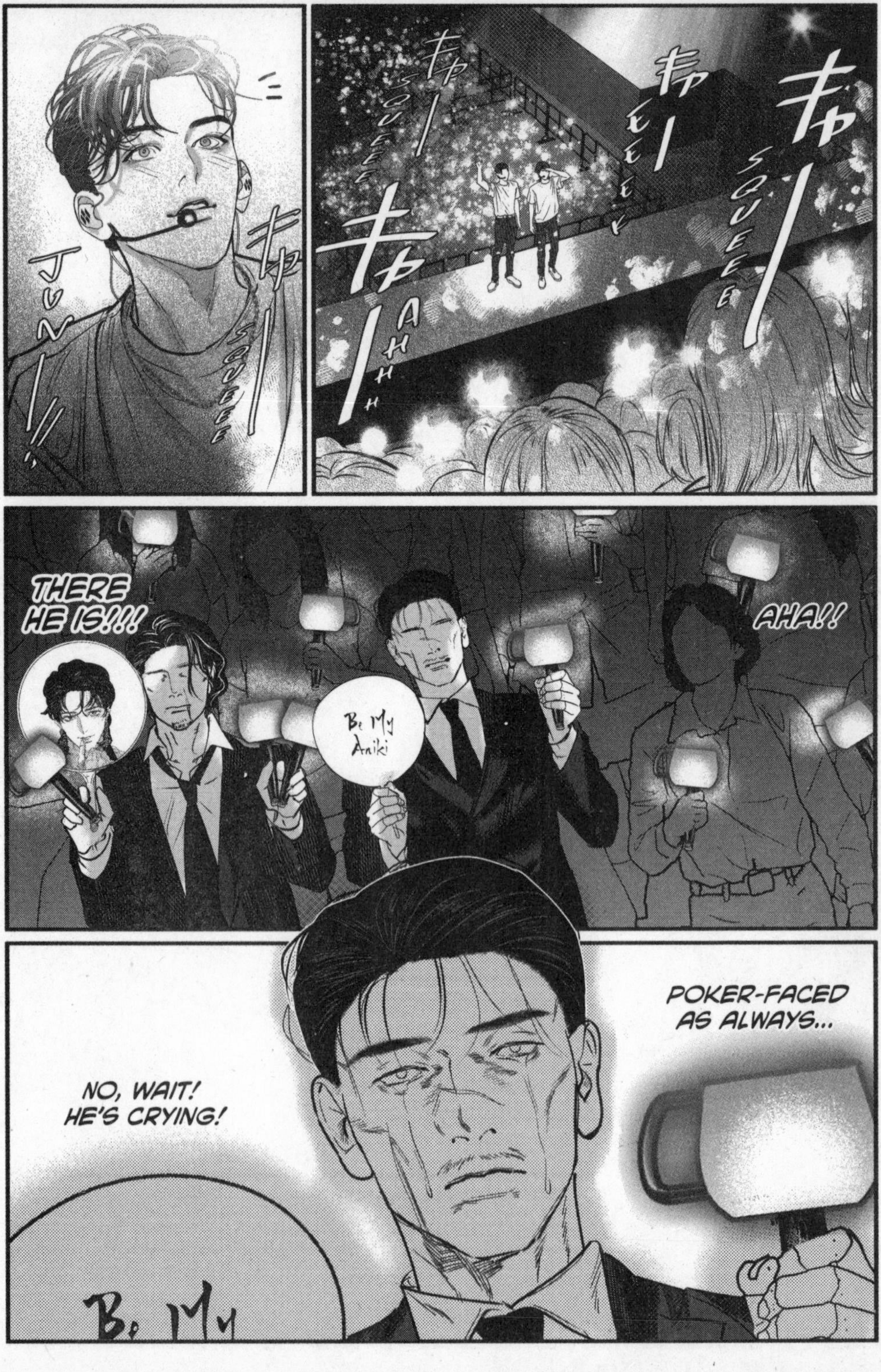
キャー
SQUEEEE
キャー
SQUEEEE
キャー
SQUEEEE
キャー
AHHHH
キャー
SQUEEEE
JUN—!!
AHA!!
Be My Aniki
THERE HE IS!!!
POKER-FACED AS ALWAYS...
NO, WAIT! HE'S CRYING!
Be My

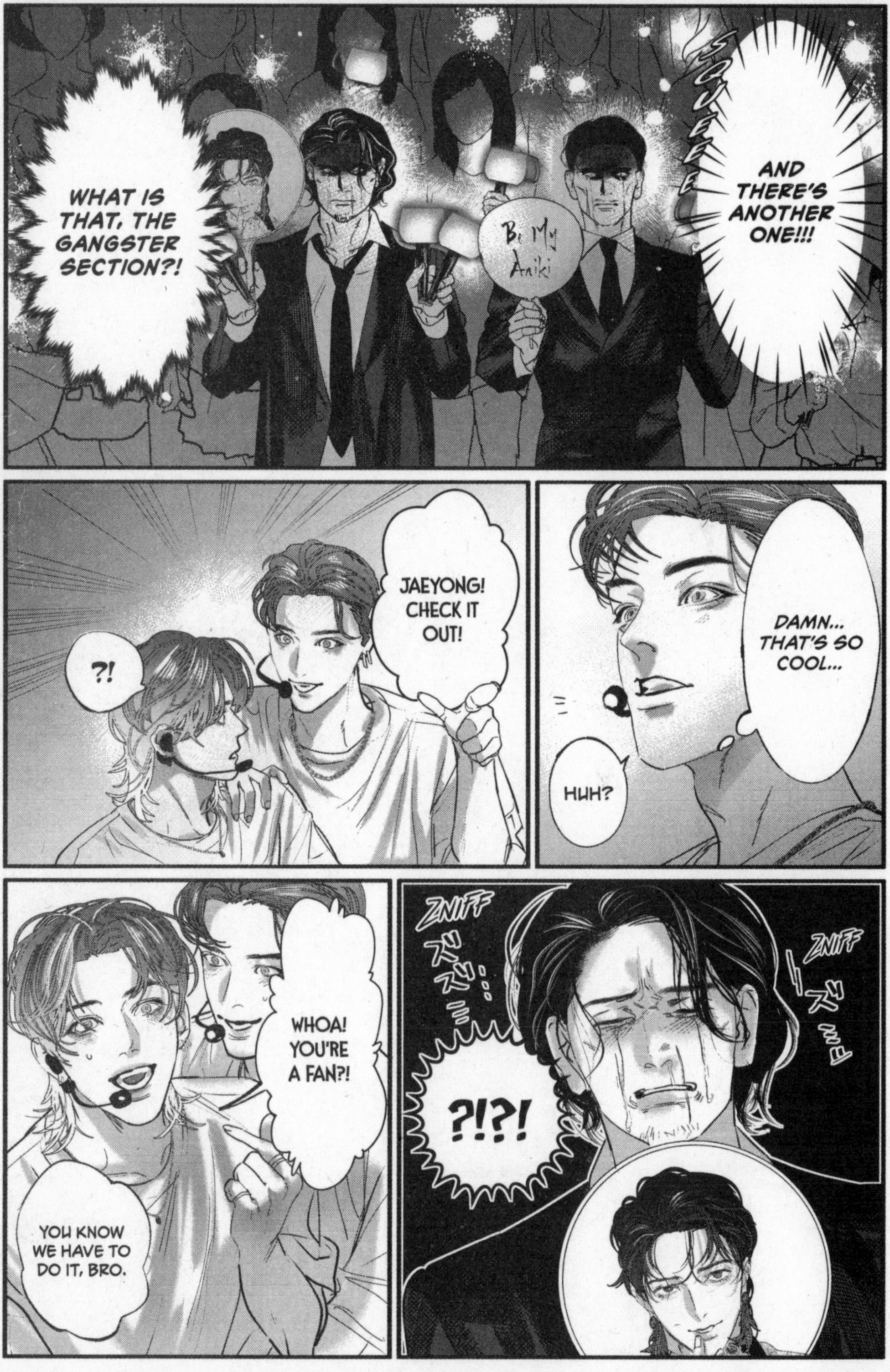
SQUEEE
AND THERE'S ANOTHER ONE!!!
Be My Aniki
WHAT IS THAT, THE GANGSTER SECTION?!
DAMN... THAT'S SO COOL...
HUH?
JAEYONG! CHECK IT OUT!
?!
ZNIFF
ZNIFF
?!?!
WHOA! YOU'RE A FAN?!
YOU KNOW WE HAVE TO DO IT, BRO.

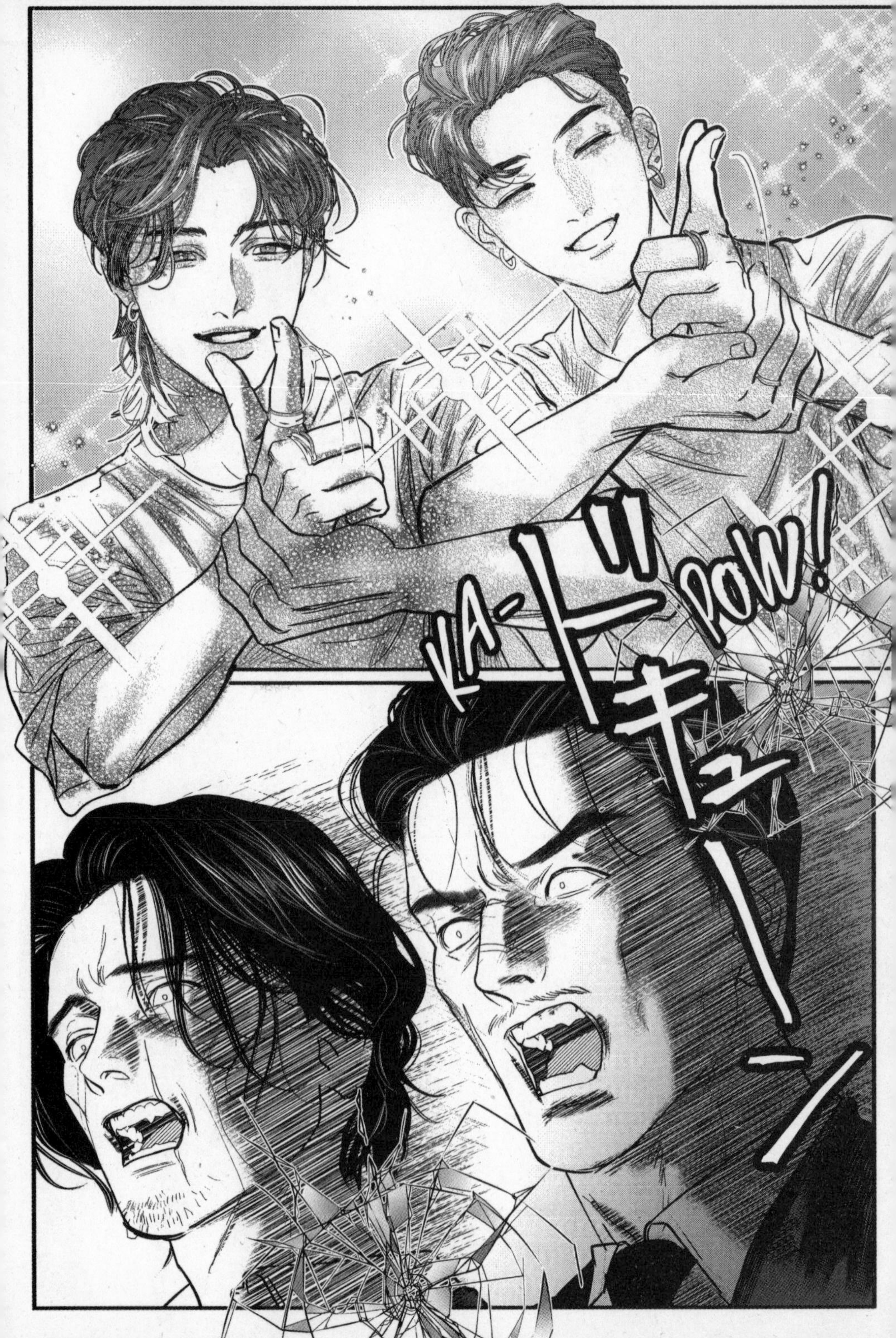

KA-POW!
ドキューン

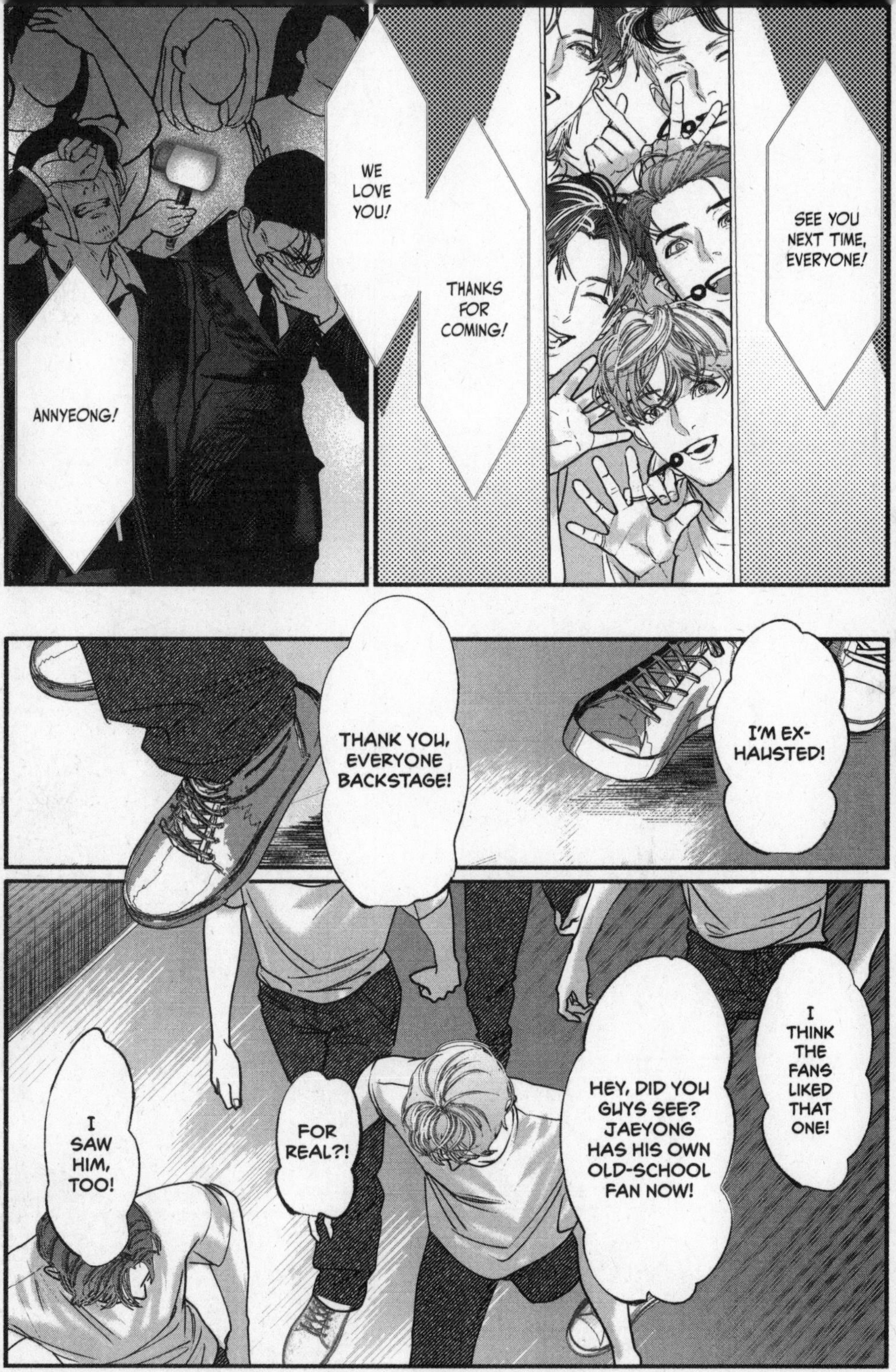
SEE YOU NEXT TIME, EVERYONE!
THANKS FOR COMING!
WE LOVE YOU!
ANNYEONG!
I'M EX-HAUSTED!
THANK YOU, EVERYONE BACKSTAGE!
I THINK THE FANS LIKED THAT ONE!
HEY, DID YOU GUYS SEE? JAEYONG HAS HIS OWN OLD-SCHOOL FAN NOW!
FOR REAL?!
I SAW HIM, TOO!

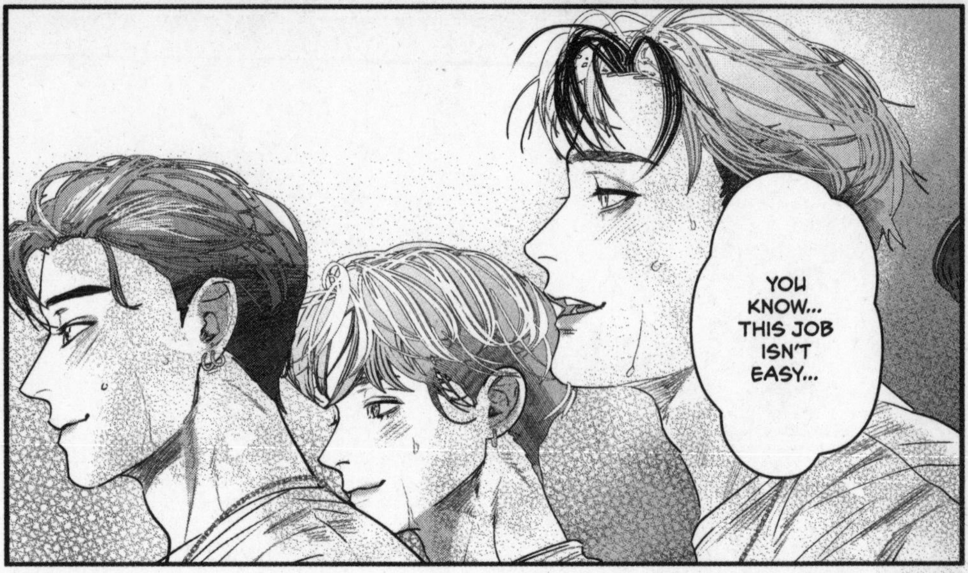
YOU KNOW... THIS JOB ISN'T EASY...
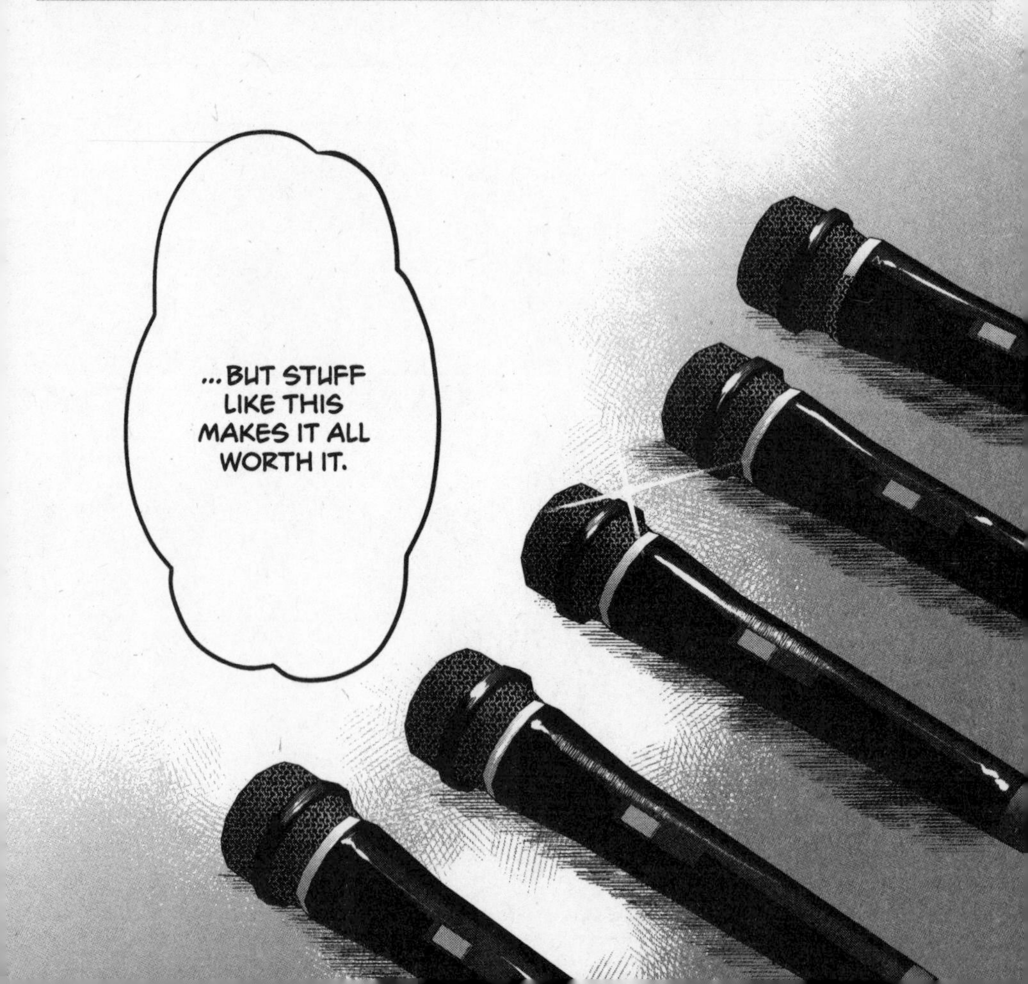
...BUT STUFF LIKE THIS MAKES IT ALL WORTH IT.

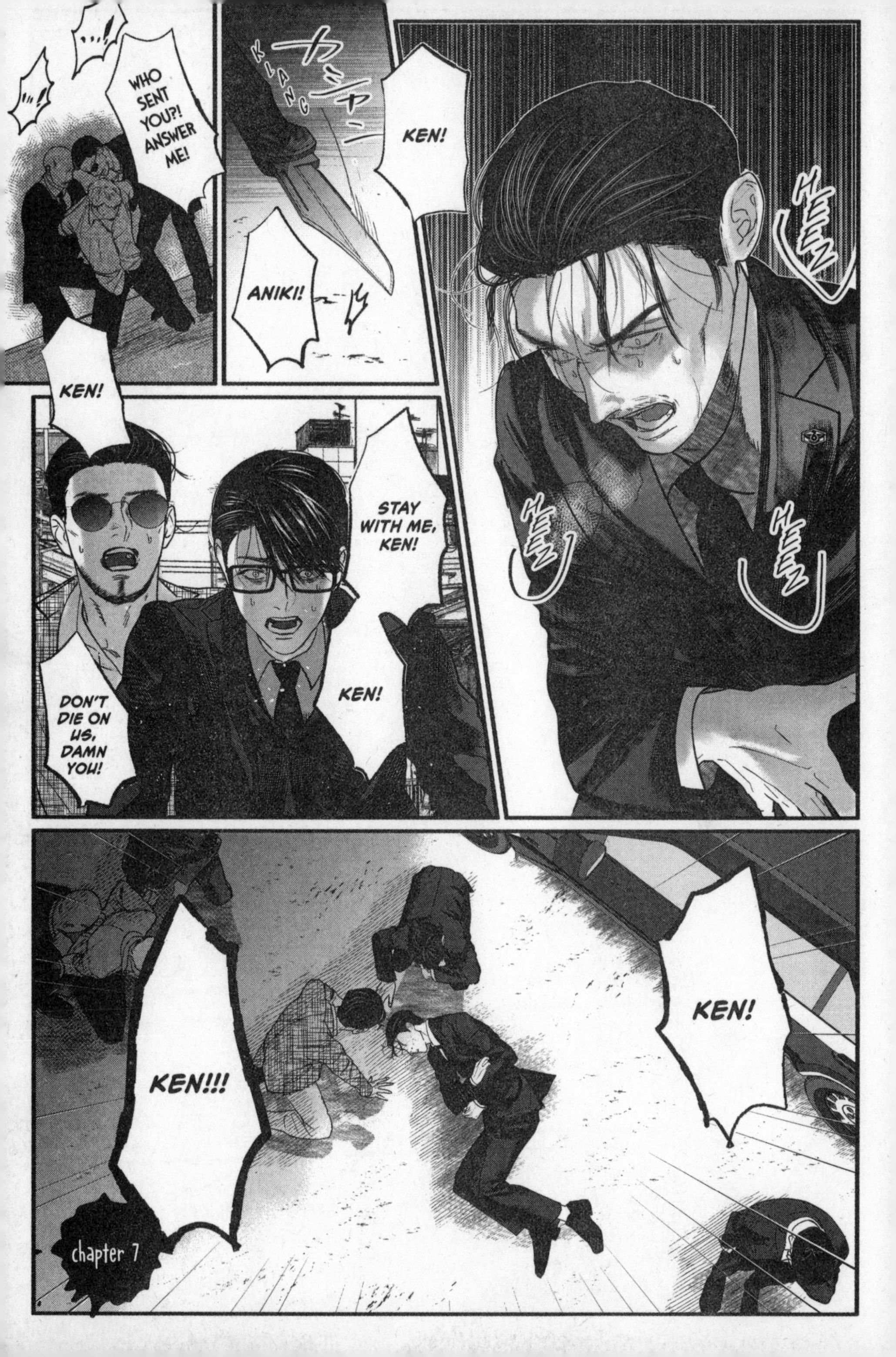

KEN!
KLANG
ANIKI!
!!...
...!!
WHO SENT YOU?! ANSWER ME!
KEN!
STAY WITH ME, KEN!
KEN!
DON'T DIE ON US, DAMN YOU!
KEN!
KEN!!!
chapter 7

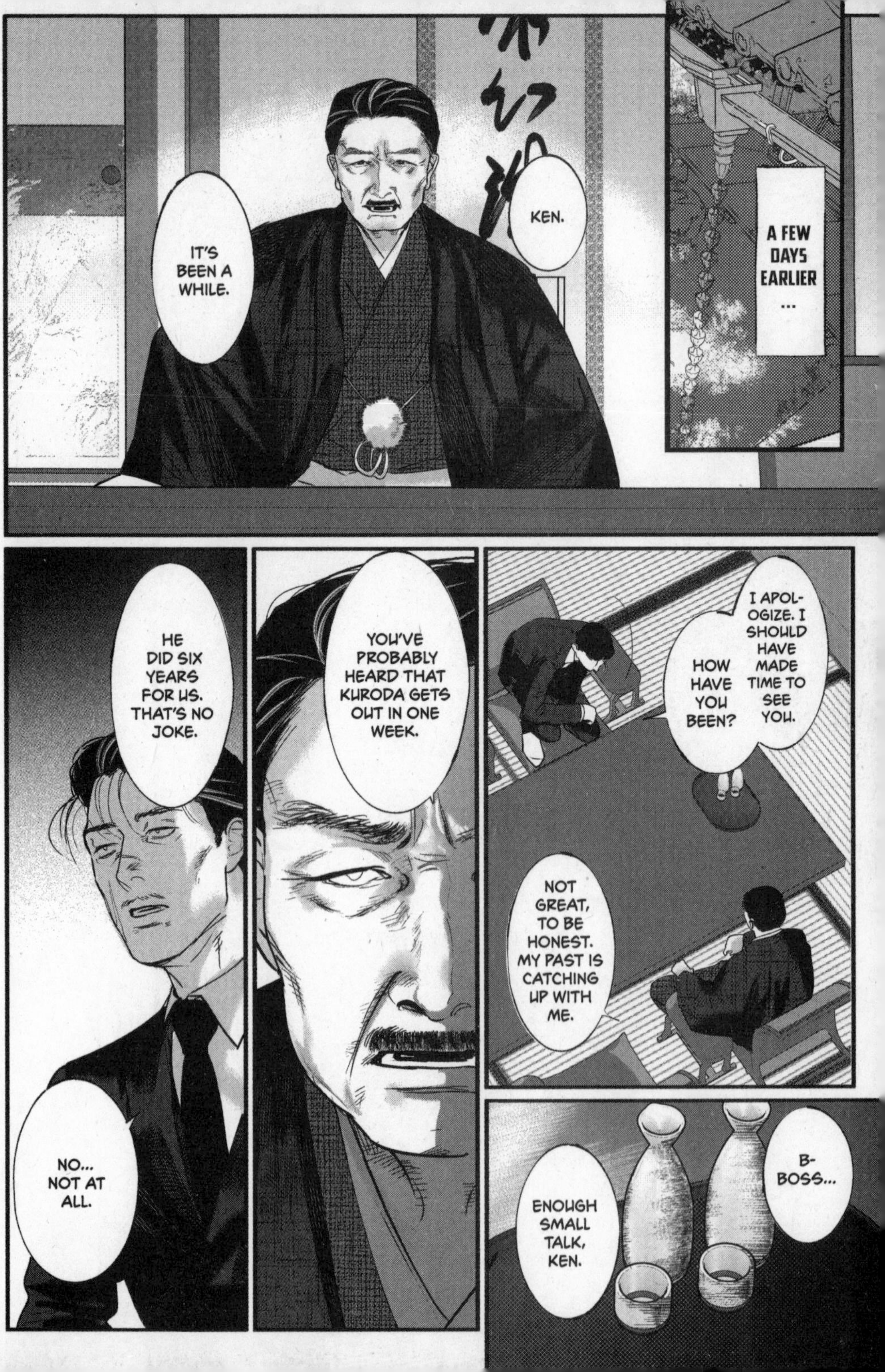
A FEW DAYS EARLIER ...
KEN.
IT'S BEEN A WHILE.
I APOLOGIZE. I SHOULD HAVE MADE TIME TO SEE YOU.
HOW HAVE YOU BEEN?
NOT GREAT, TO BE HONEST. MY PAST IS CATCHING UP WITH ME.
B-BOSS...
ENOUGH SMALL TALK, KEN.
YOU'VE PROBABLY HEARD THAT KURODA GETS OUT IN ONE WEEK.
HE DID SIX YEARS FOR US. THAT'S NO JOKE.
NO... NOT AT ALL.

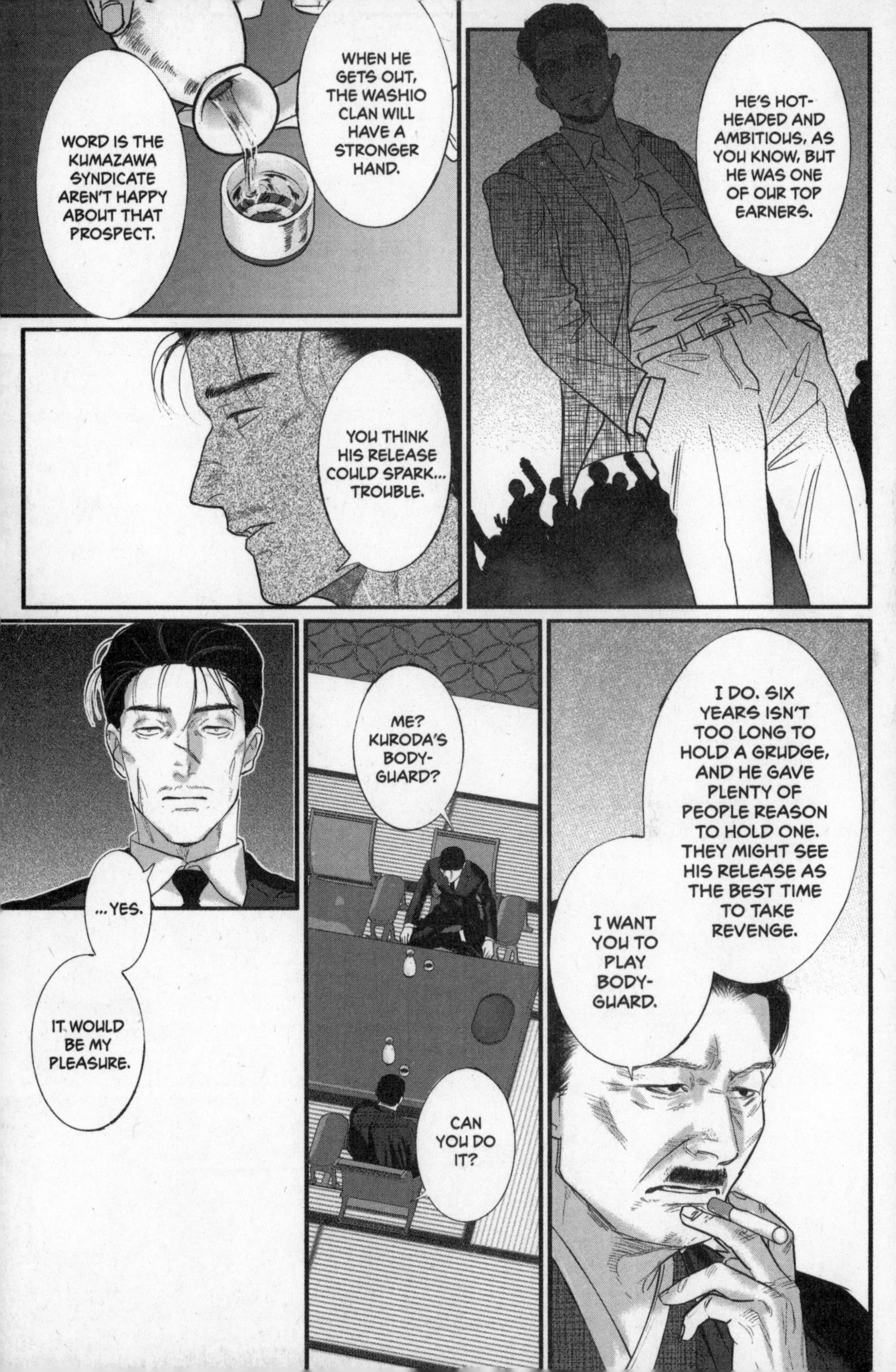

HE'S HOT-HEADED AND AMBITIOUS, AS YOU KNOW, BUT HE WAS ONE OF OUR TOP EARNERS.
WHEN HE GETS OUT, THE WASHIO CLAN WILL HAVE A STRONGER HAND.
WORD IS THE KUMAZAWA SYNDICATE AREN'T HAPPY ABOUT THAT PROSPECT.
YOU THINK HIS RELEASE COULD SPARK... TROUBLE.
I DO. SIX YEARS ISN'T TOO LONG TO HOLD A GRUDGE, AND HE GAVE PLENTY OF PEOPLE REASON TO HOLD ONE. THEY MIGHT SEE HIS RELEASE AS THE BEST TIME TO TAKE REVENGE.
I WANT YOU TO PLAY BODY-GUARD.
ME? KURODA'S BODY-GUARD?
CAN YOU DO IT?
...YES.
IT WOULD BE MY PLEASURE.

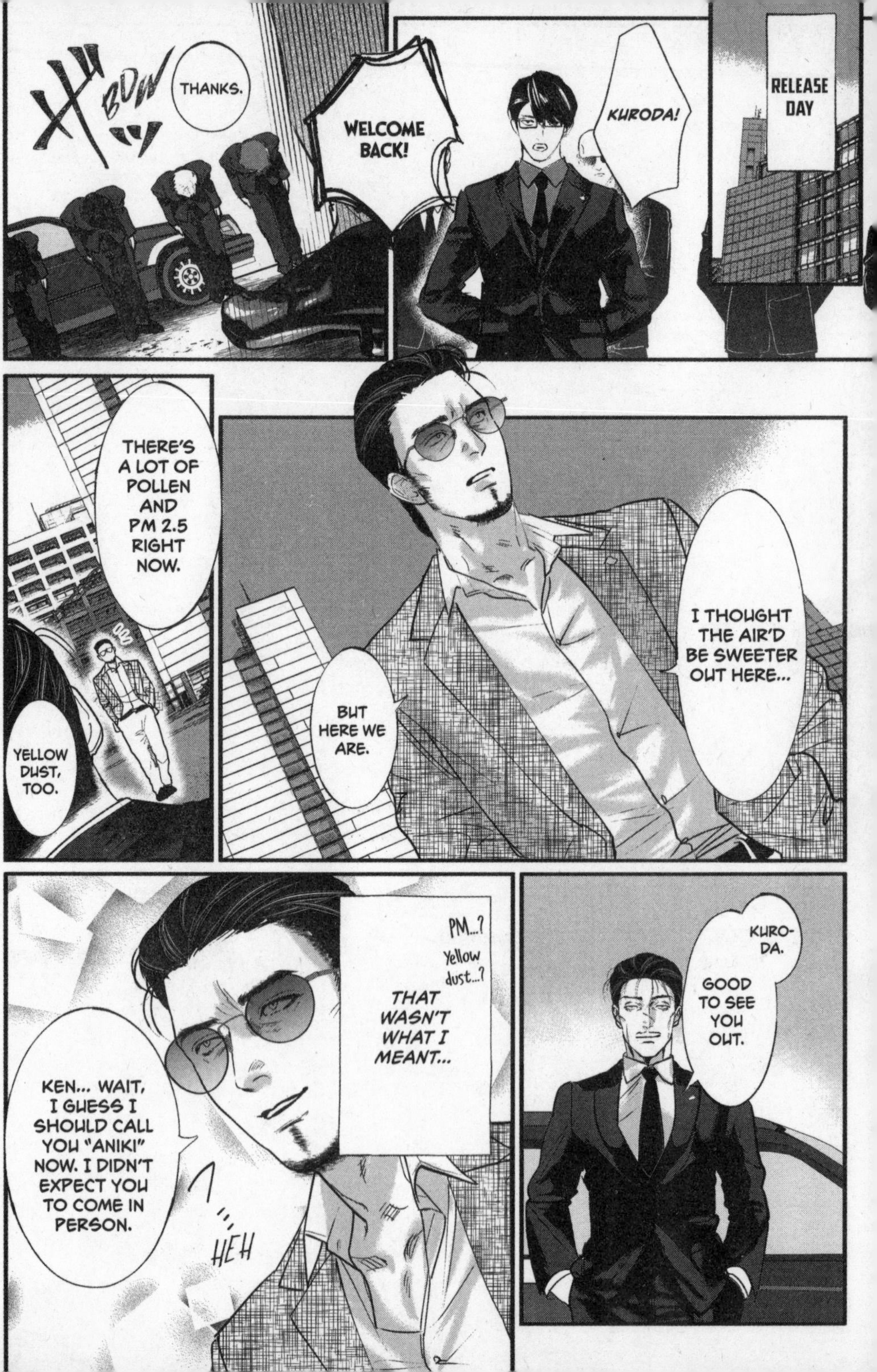
RELEASE DAY
KURODA!
WELCOME BACK!
THANKS.
BOW
I THOUGHT THE AIR'D BE SWEETER OUT HERE...
BUT HERE WE ARE.
THERE'S A LOT OF POLLEN AND PM 2.5 RIGHT NOW.
YELLOW DUST, TOO.
KURO-DA.
GOOD TO SEE YOU OUT.
PM...? Yellow dust...?
THAT WASN'T WHAT I MEANT...
KEN... WAIT, I GUESS I SHOULD CALL YOU "ANIKI" NOW. I DIDN'T EXPECT YOU TO COME IN PERSON.
HEH

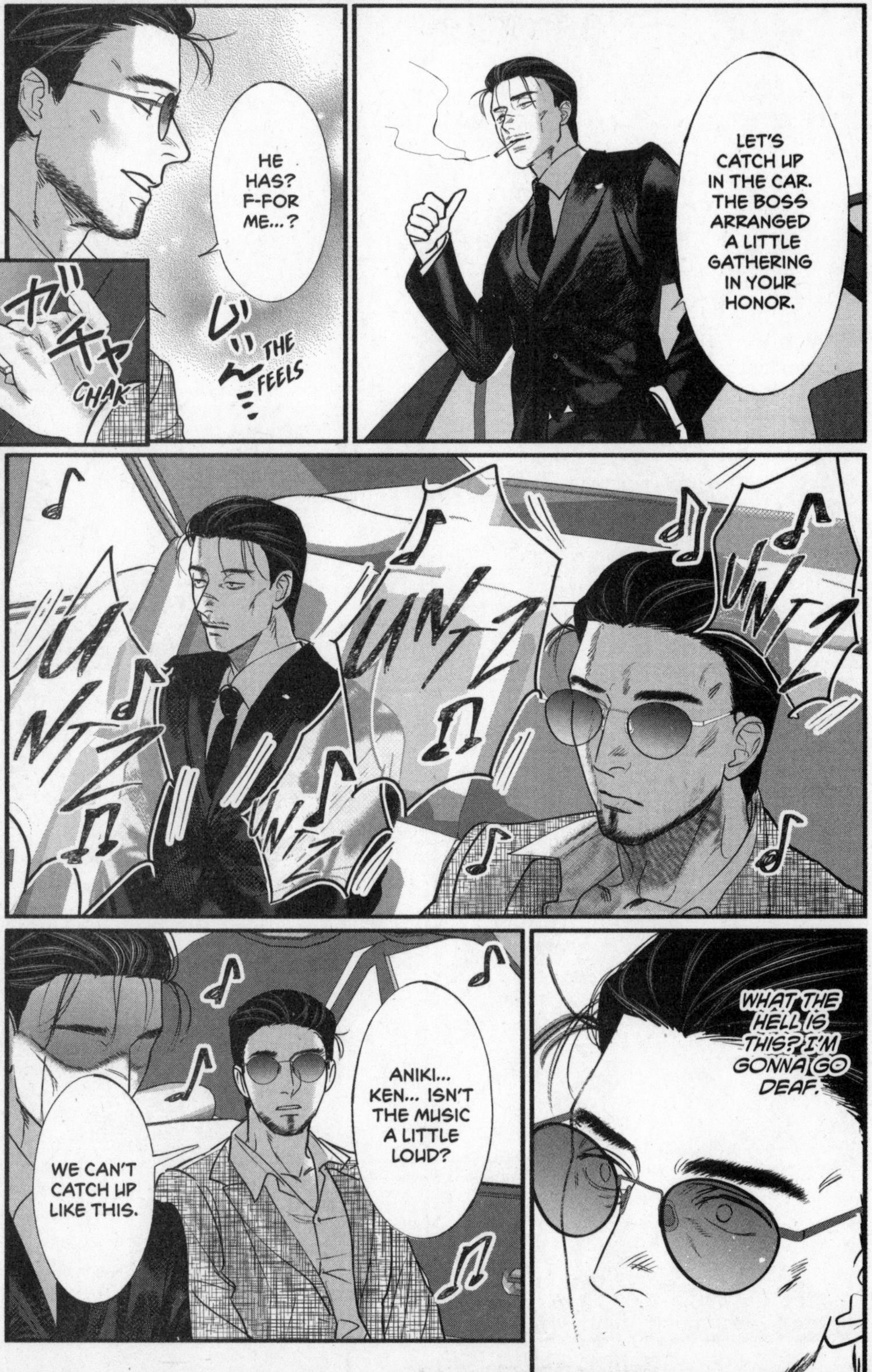
LET'S CATCH UP IN THE CAR. THE BOSS ARRANGED A LITTLE GATHERING IN YOUR HONOR.
HE HAS? F-FOR ME...?
THE FEELS
CHAK
UNTZ
UNTZ
UNTZ
UNTZ
WHAT THE HELL IS THIS? I'M GONNA GO DEAF.
ANIKI... KEN... ISN'T THE MUSIC A LITTLE LOUD?
WE CAN'T CATCH UP LIKE THIS.

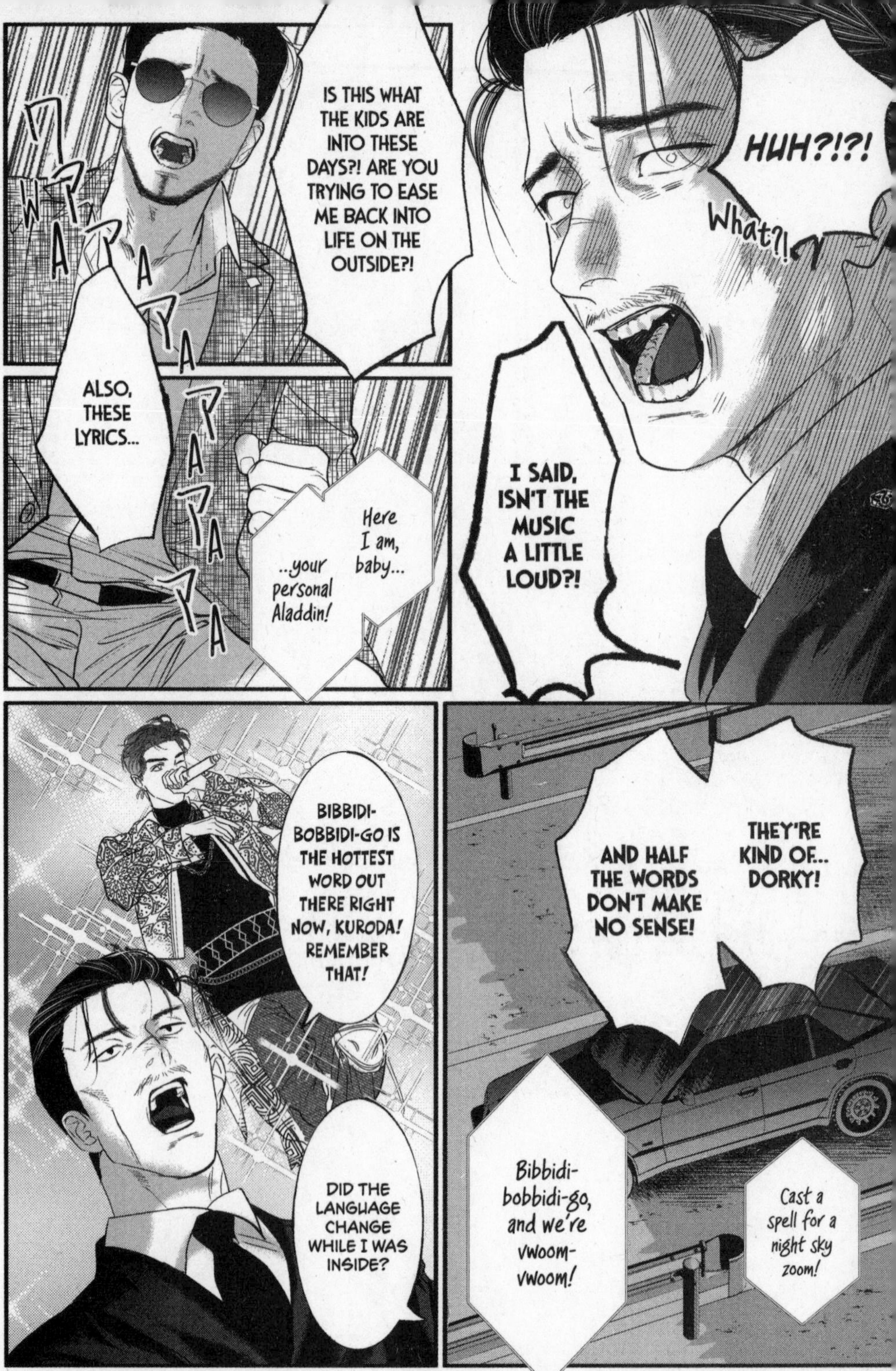
HUH?!?!
What?!
I SAID, ISN'T THE MUSIC A LITTLE LOUD?!
IS THIS WHAT THE KIDS ARE INTO THESE DAYS?! ARE YOU TRYING TO EASE ME BACK INTO LIFE ON THE OUTSIDE?!
ALSO, THESE LYRICS...
Here I am, baby...
...your personal Aladdin!
THEY'RE KIND OF... DORKY!
AND HALF THE WORDS DON'T MAKE NO SENSE!
Cast a spell for a night sky zoom!
Bibbidi-bobbidi-go, and we're vwoom-vwoom!
BIBBIDI-BOBBIDI-GO IS THE HOTTEST WORD OUT THERE RIGHT NOW, KURODA! REMEMBER THAT!
DID THE LANGUAGE CHANGE WHILE I WAS INSIDE?

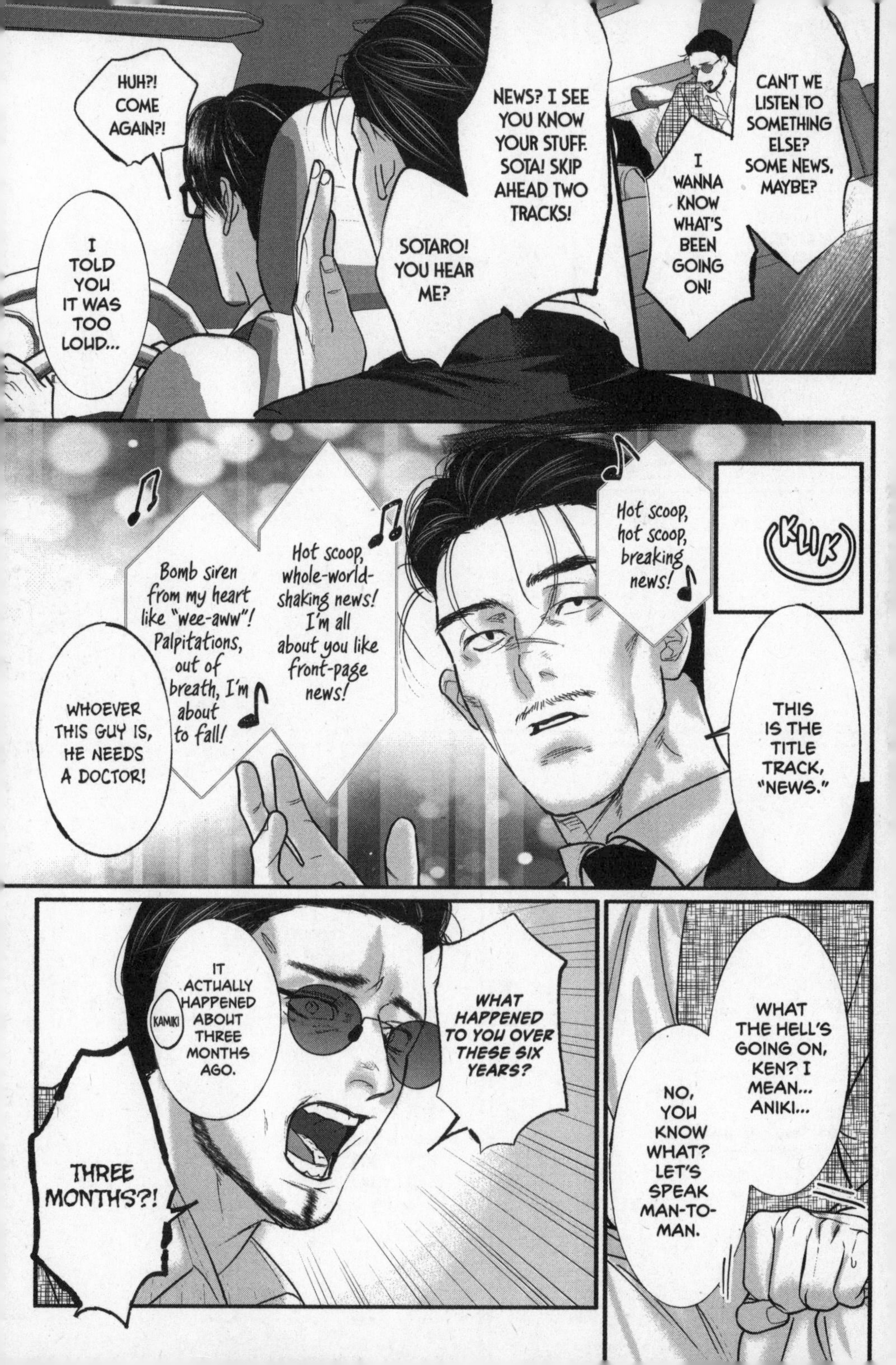
CAN'T WE LISTEN TO SOMETHING ELSE? SOME NEWS, MAYBE?
I WANNA KNOW WHAT'S BEEN GOING ON!
NEWS? I SEE YOU KNOW YOUR STUFF. SOTA! SKIP AHEAD TWO TRACKS!
SOTARO! YOU HEAR ME?
HUH?! COME AGAIN?!
I TOLD YOU IT WAS TOO LOUD...
KLIK
THIS IS THE TITLE TRACK, "NEWS."
Hot scoop, hot scoop, breaking news!
Hot scoop, whole-world-shaking news! I'm all about you like front-page news!
Bomb siren from my heart like "wee-aww"! Palpitations, out of breath, I'm about to fall!
WHOEVER THIS GUY IS, HE NEEDS A DOCTOR!
WHAT THE HELL'S GOING ON, KEN? I MEAN... ANIKI...
NO, YOU KNOW WHAT? LET'S SPEAK MAN-TO-MAN.
WHAT HAPPENED TO YOU OVER THESE SIX YEARS?
KAMIKI
IT ACTUALLY HAPPENED ABOUT THREE MONTHS AGO.
THREE MONTHS?!

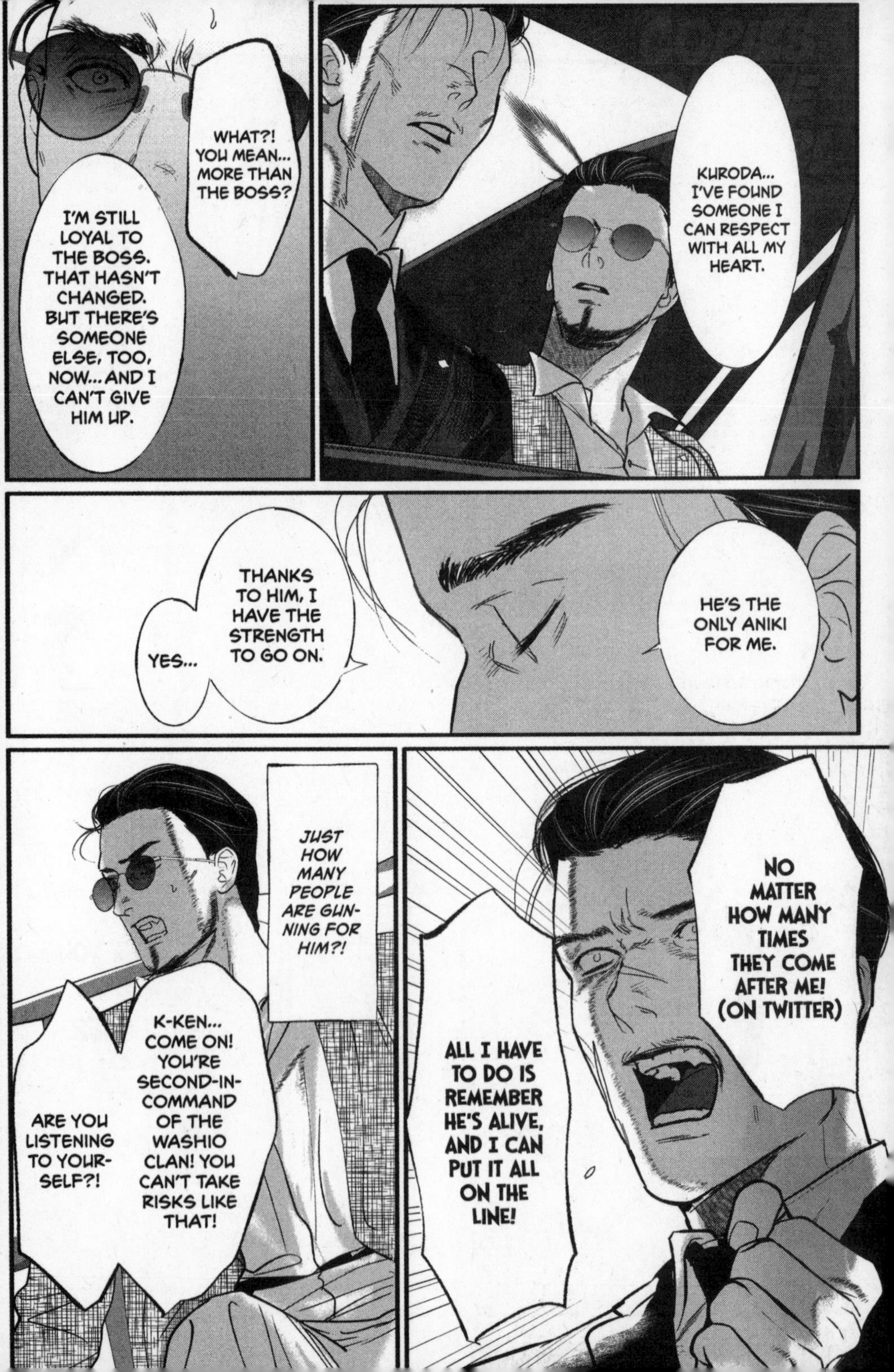
KURODA... I'VE FOUND SOMEONE I CAN RESPECT WITH ALL MY HEART.
WHAT?! YOU MEAN... MORE THAN THE BOSS?
I'M STILL LOYAL TO THE BOSS. THAT HASN'T CHANGED. BUT THERE'S SOMEONE ELSE, TOO, NOW... AND I CAN'T GIVE HIM UP.
HE'S THE ONLY ANIKI FOR ME.
YES... THANKS TO HIM, I HAVE THE STRENGTH TO GO ON.
NO MATTER HOW MANY TIMES THEY COME AFTER ME! (ON TWITTER)
ALL I HAVE TO DO IS REMEMBER HE'S ALIVE, AND I CAN PUT IT ALL ON THE LINE!
JUST HOW MANY PEOPLE ARE GUNNING FOR HIM?!
K-KEN... COME ON! YOU'RE SECOND-IN-COMMAND OF THE WASHIO CLAN! YOU CAN'T TAKE RISKS LIKE THAT!
ARE YOU LISTENING TO YOURSELF?!

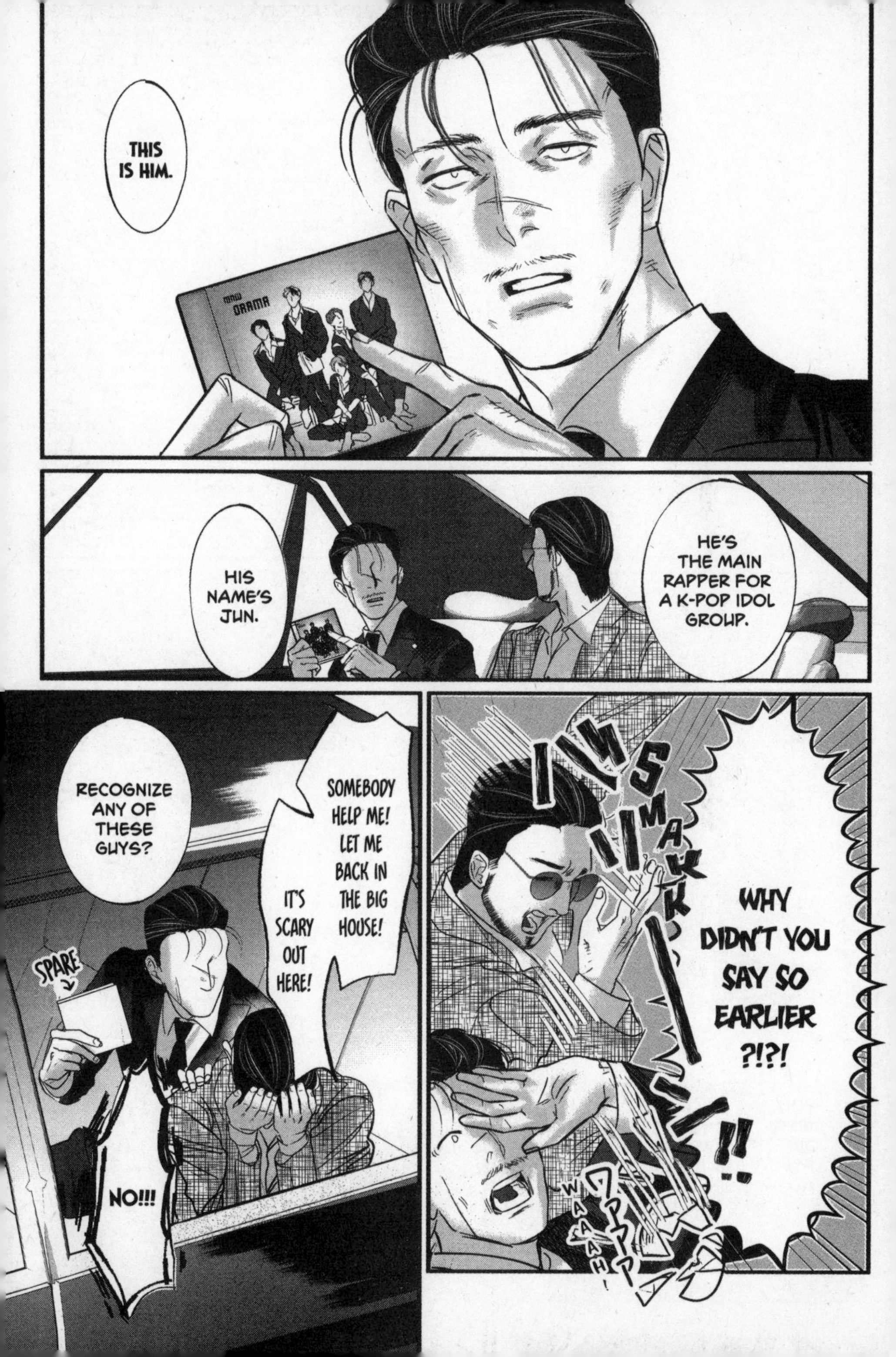
THIS IS HIM.
DRAMA
HE'S THE MAIN RAPPER FOR A K-POP IDOL GROUP.
HIS NAME'S JUN.
SMAKK
WHY DIDN'T YOU SAY SO EARLIER ?!?!
!!
WAAAAH!
SOMEBODY HELP ME! LET ME BACK IN THE BIG HOUSE!
IT'S SCARY OUT HERE!
RECOGNIZE ANY OF THESE GUYS?
SPARE
NO!!!

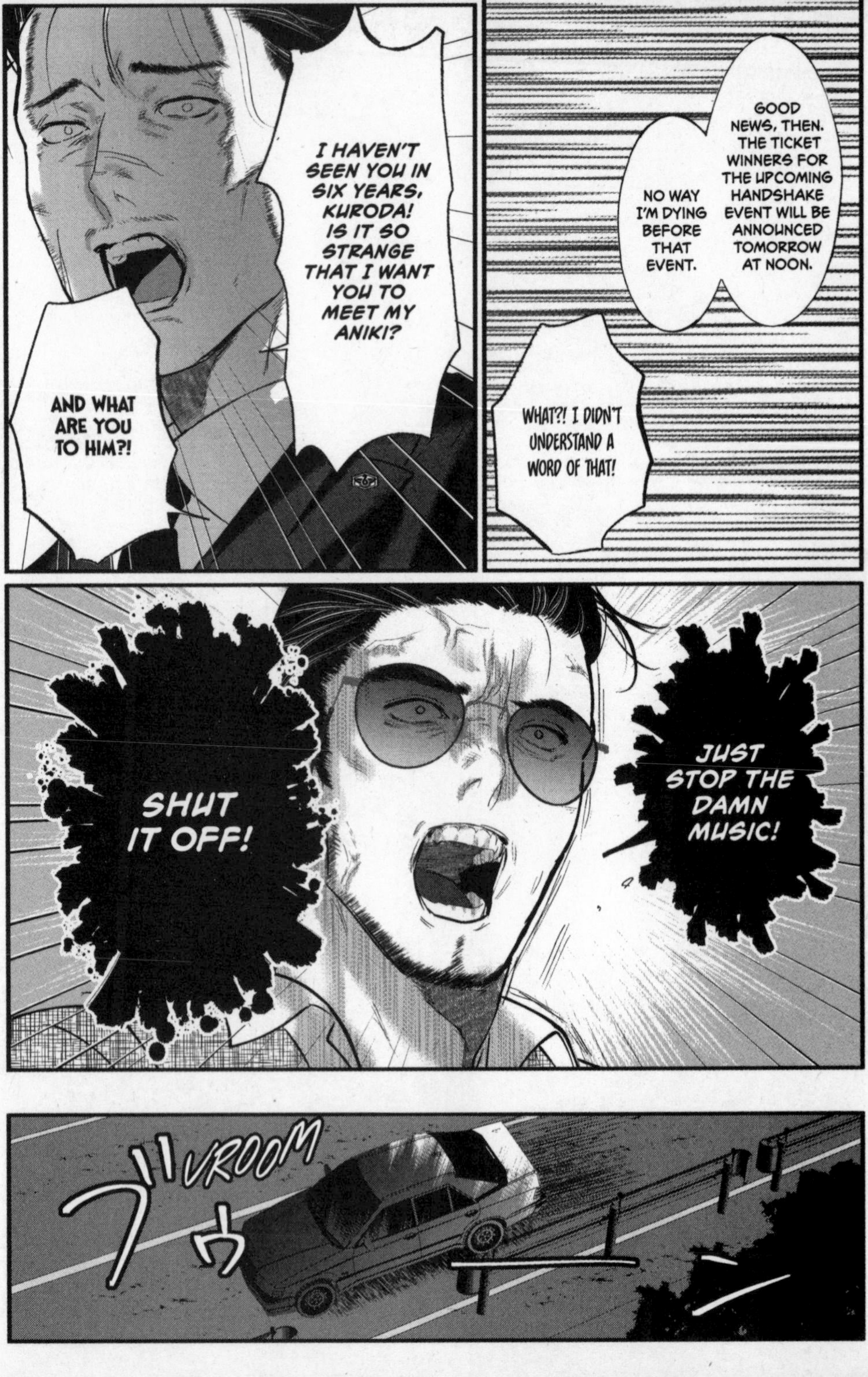
GOOD NEWS, THEN. THE TICKET WINNERS FOR THE UPCOMING HANDSHAKE EVENT WILL BE ANNOUNCED TOMORROW AT NOON.
NO WAY I'M DYING BEFORE THAT EVENT.
WHAT?! I DIDN'T UNDERSTAND A WORD OF THAT!
I HAVEN'T SEEN YOU IN SIX YEARS, KURODA! IS IT SO STRANGE THAT I WANT YOU TO MEET MY ANIKI?
AND WHAT ARE YOU TO HIM?!
JUST STOP THE DAMN MUSIC!
SHUT IT OFF!
ヴゥ
VROOM

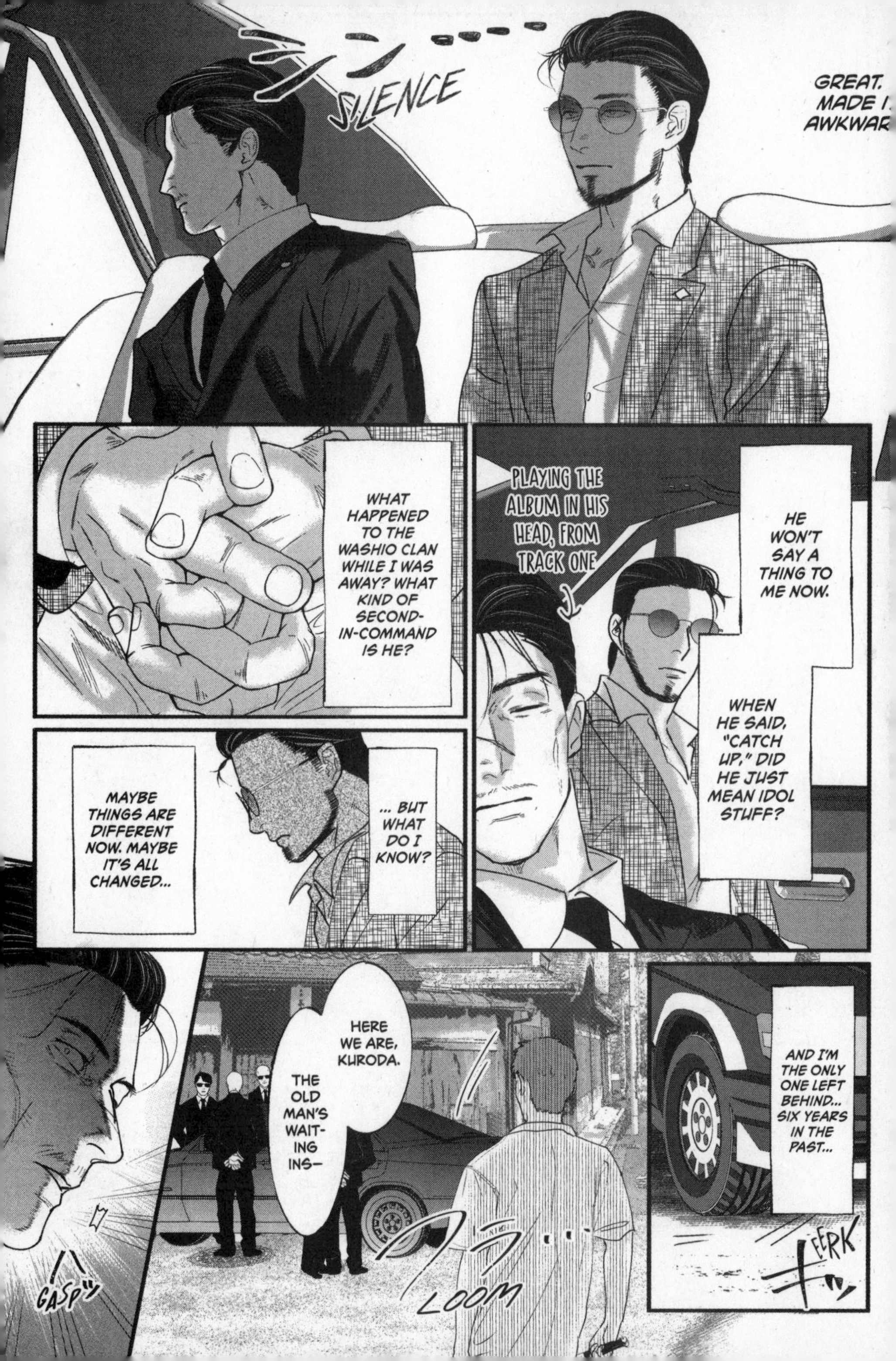
SILENCE
GREAT. MADE I AWKWAR
PLAYING THE ALBUM IN HIS HEAD, FROM TRACK ONE
HE WON'T SAY A THING TO ME NOW.
WHEN HE SAID, "CATCH UP," DID HE JUST MEAN IDOL STUFF?
WHAT HAPPENED TO THE WASHIO CLAN WHILE I WAS AWAY? WHAT KIND OF SECOND-IN-COMMAND IS HE?
... BUT WHAT DO I KNOW?
MAYBE THINGS ARE DIFFERENT NOW. MAYBE IT'S ALL CHANGED...
AND I'M THE ONLY ONE LEFT BEHIND... SIX YEARS IN THE PAST...
EERK
HERE WE ARE, KURODA.
THE OLD MAN'S WAIT-ING INS—
LOOM
GASP

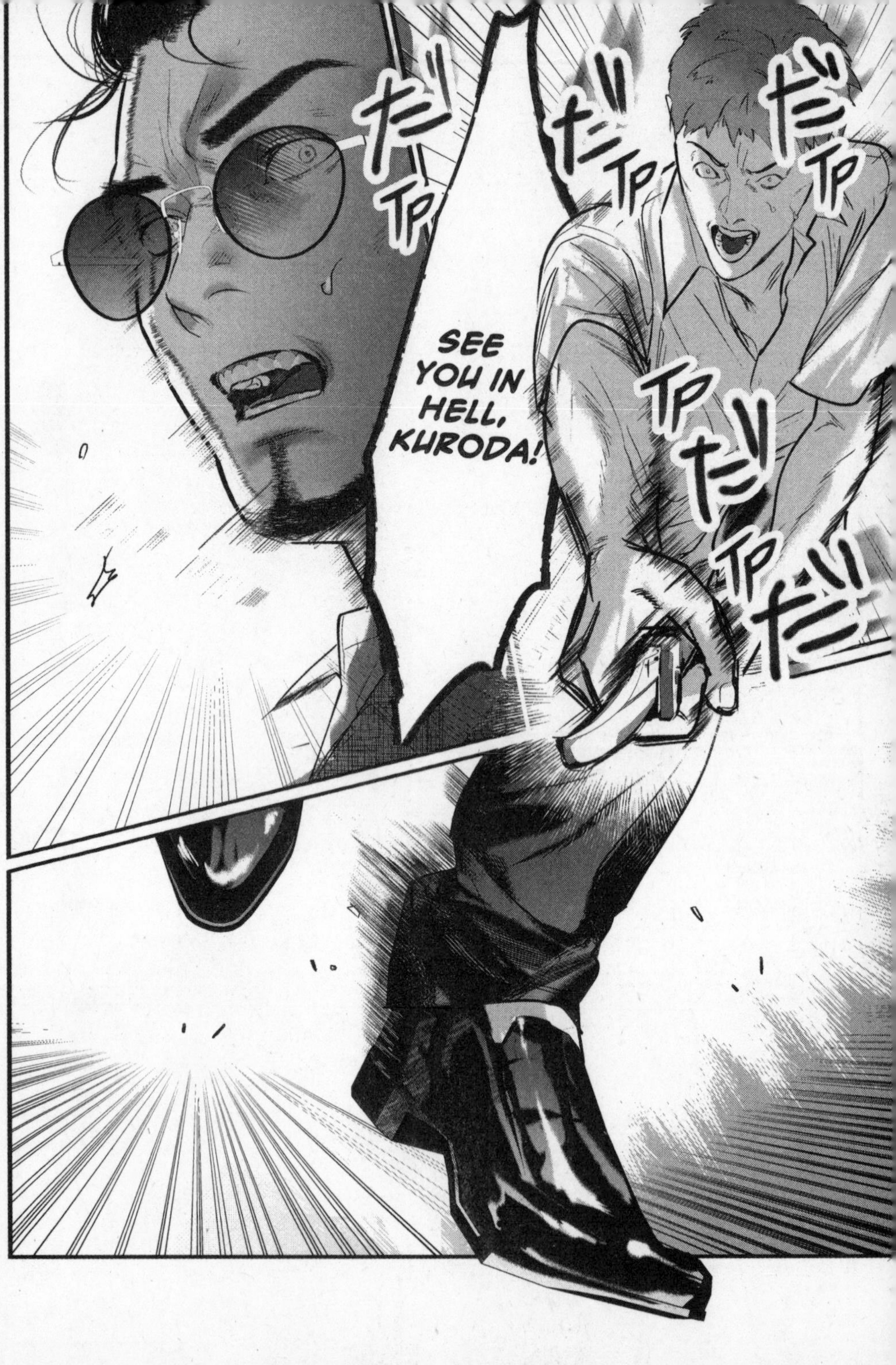
だ TP
だ TP
だ TP
SEE YOU IN HELL, KURODA!
TP だ
TP だ

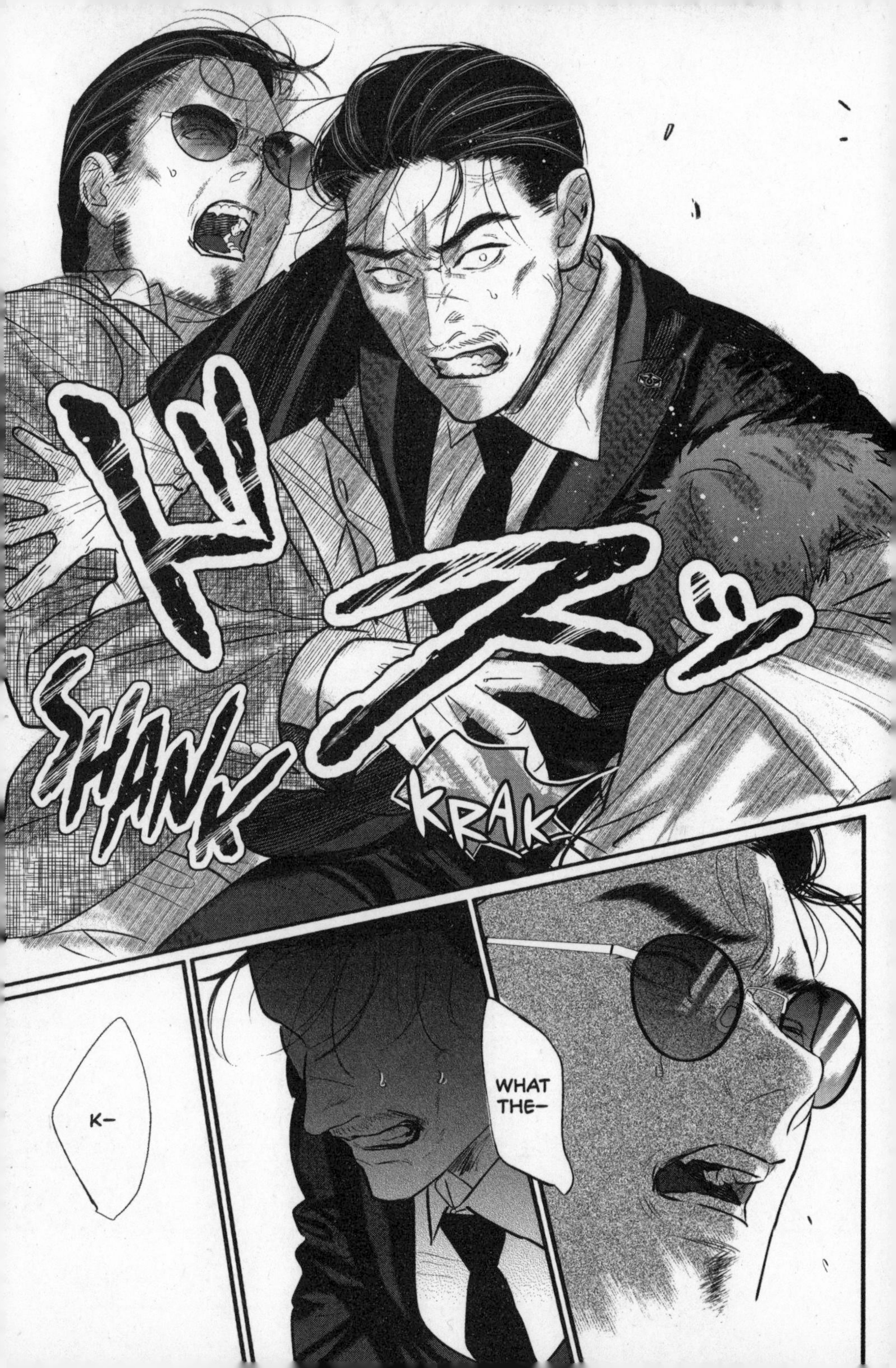
SHANK
KRAK
WHAT THE–
K–

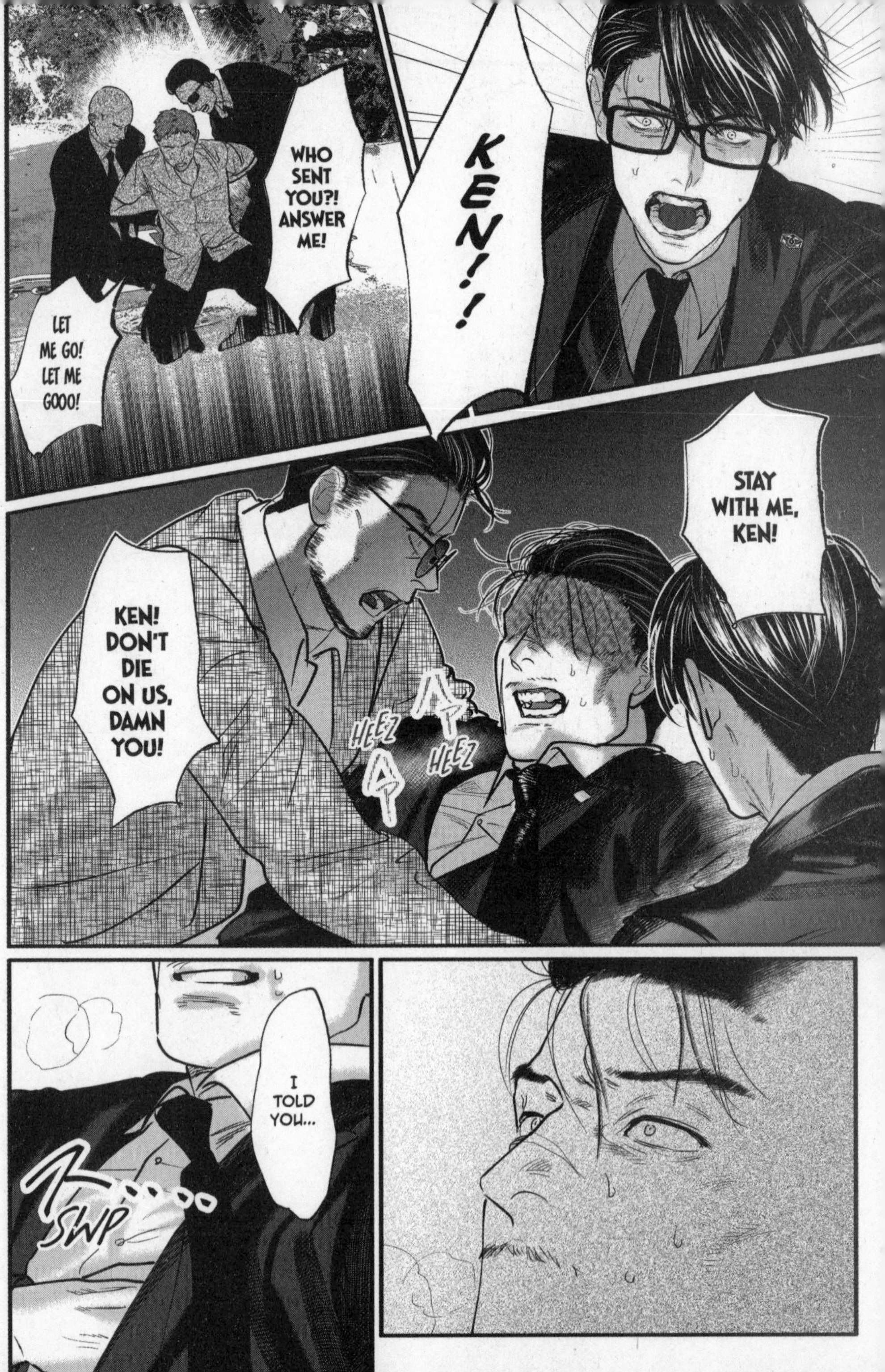
KEN!!
WHO SENT YOU?! ANSWER ME!
LET ME GO! LET ME GOOO!
STAY WITH ME, KEN!
KEN! DON'T DIE ON US, DAMN YOU!
HEEZ
HEEZ
I TOLD YOU...
SWP

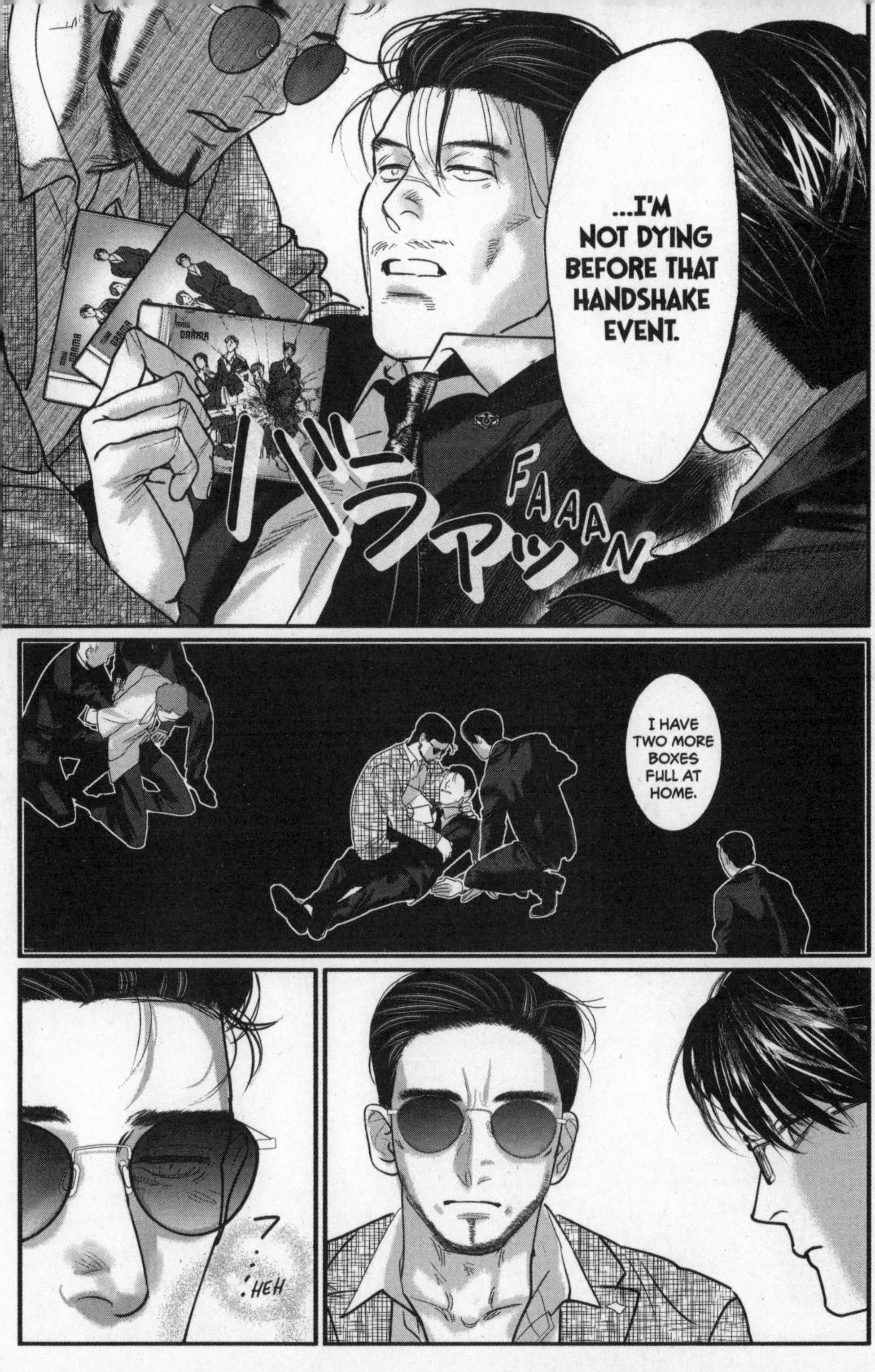
...I'M NOT DYING BEFORE THAT HANDSHAKE EVENT.
ドファッ
FAAAN
I HAVE TWO MORE BOXES FULL AT HOME.
...HEH

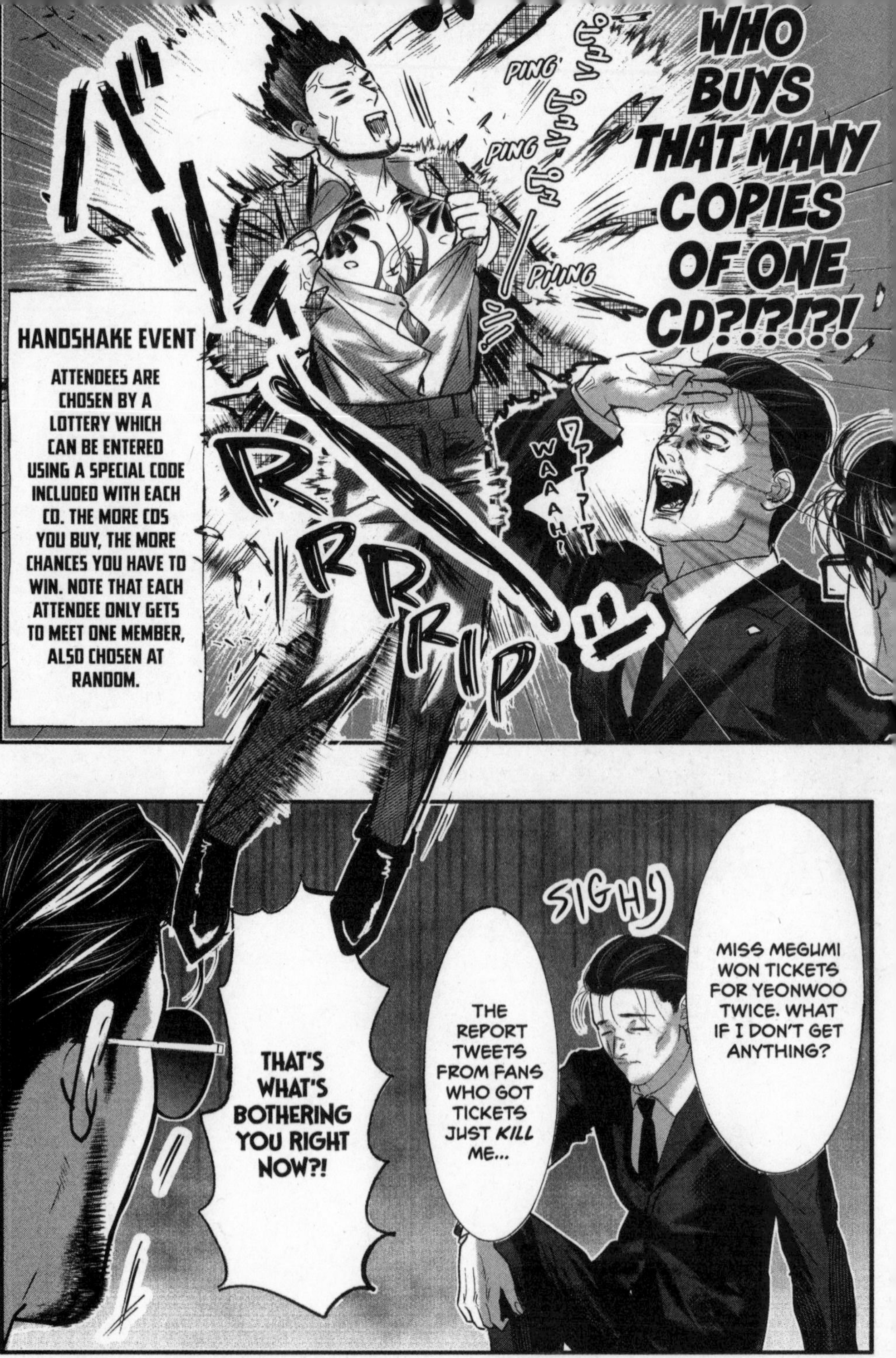
WHO BUYS THAT MANY COPIES OF ONE CD?!?!?!
PING
PING
PIIING
WAAAAH!
RRRRIP
HANDSHAKE EVENT
ATTENDEES ARE CHOSEN BY A LOTTERY WHICH CAN BE ENTERED USING A SPECIAL CODE INCLUDED WITH EACH CD. THE MORE CDS YOU BUY, THE MORE CHANCES YOU HAVE TO WIN. NOTE THAT EACH ATTENDEE ONLY GETS TO MEET ONE MEMBER, ALSO CHOSEN AT RANDOM.
MISS MEGUMI WON TICKETS FOR YEONWOO TWICE. WHAT IF I DON'T GET ANYTHING?
SIGH
THE REPORT TWEETS FROM FANS WHO GOT TICKETS JUST *KILL* ME...
THAT'S WHAT'S BOTHERING YOU RIGHT NOW?!

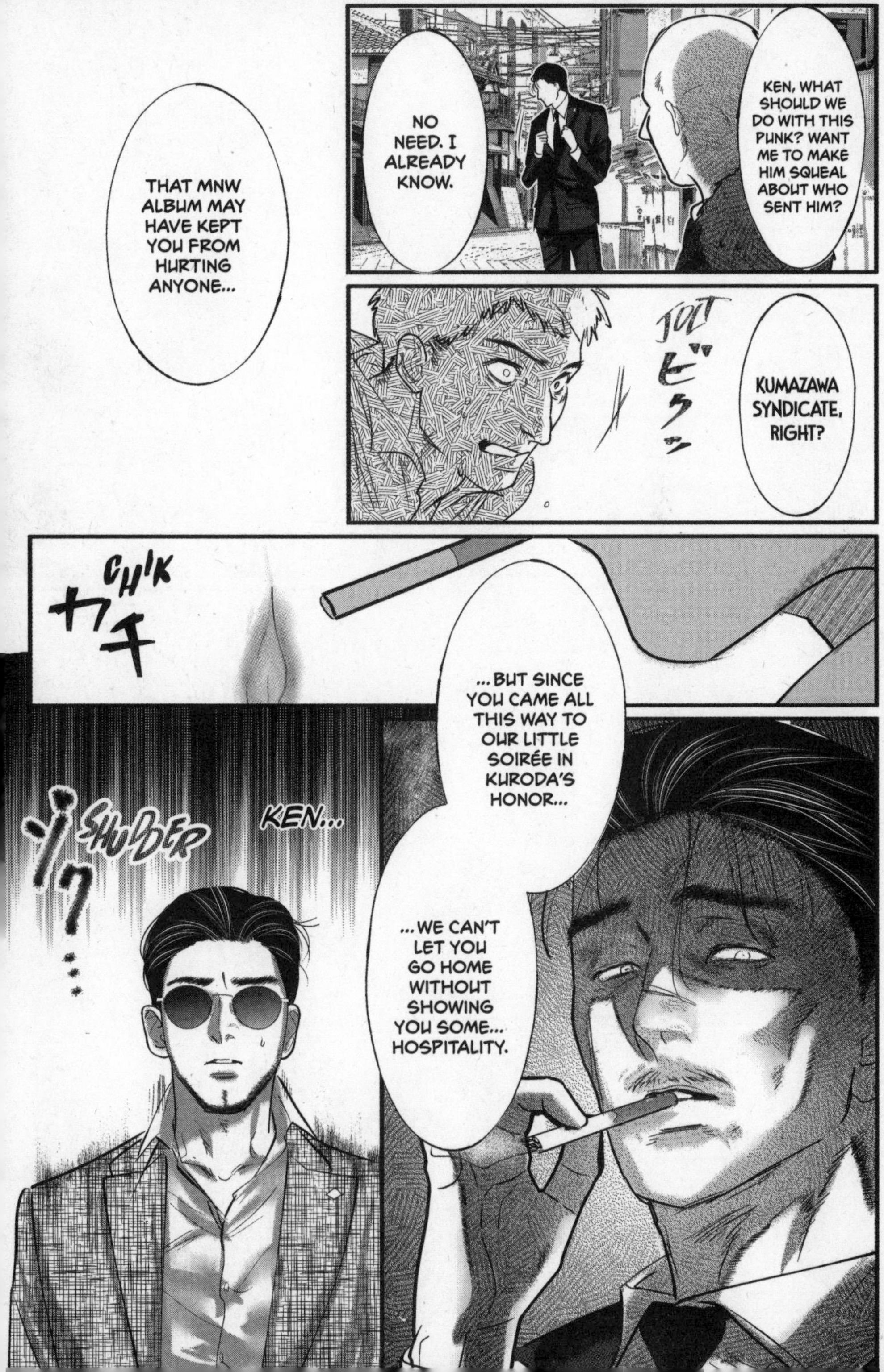
KEN, WHAT SHOULD WE DO WITH THIS PUNK? WANT ME TO MAKE HIM SQUEAL ABOUT WHO SENT HIM?
NO NEED. I ALREADY KNOW.
KUMAZAWA SYNDICATE, RIGHT?
JOLT
ビクッ
THAT MNW ALBUM MAY HAVE KEPT YOU FROM HURTING ANYONE...
CHIK
カチ
...BUT SINCE YOU CAME ALL THIS WAY TO OUR LITTLE SOIRÉE IN KURODA'S HONOR...
...WE CAN'T LET YOU GO HOME WITHOUT SHOWING YOU SOME... HOSPITALITY.
KEN...
SHUDDER
ゾク...

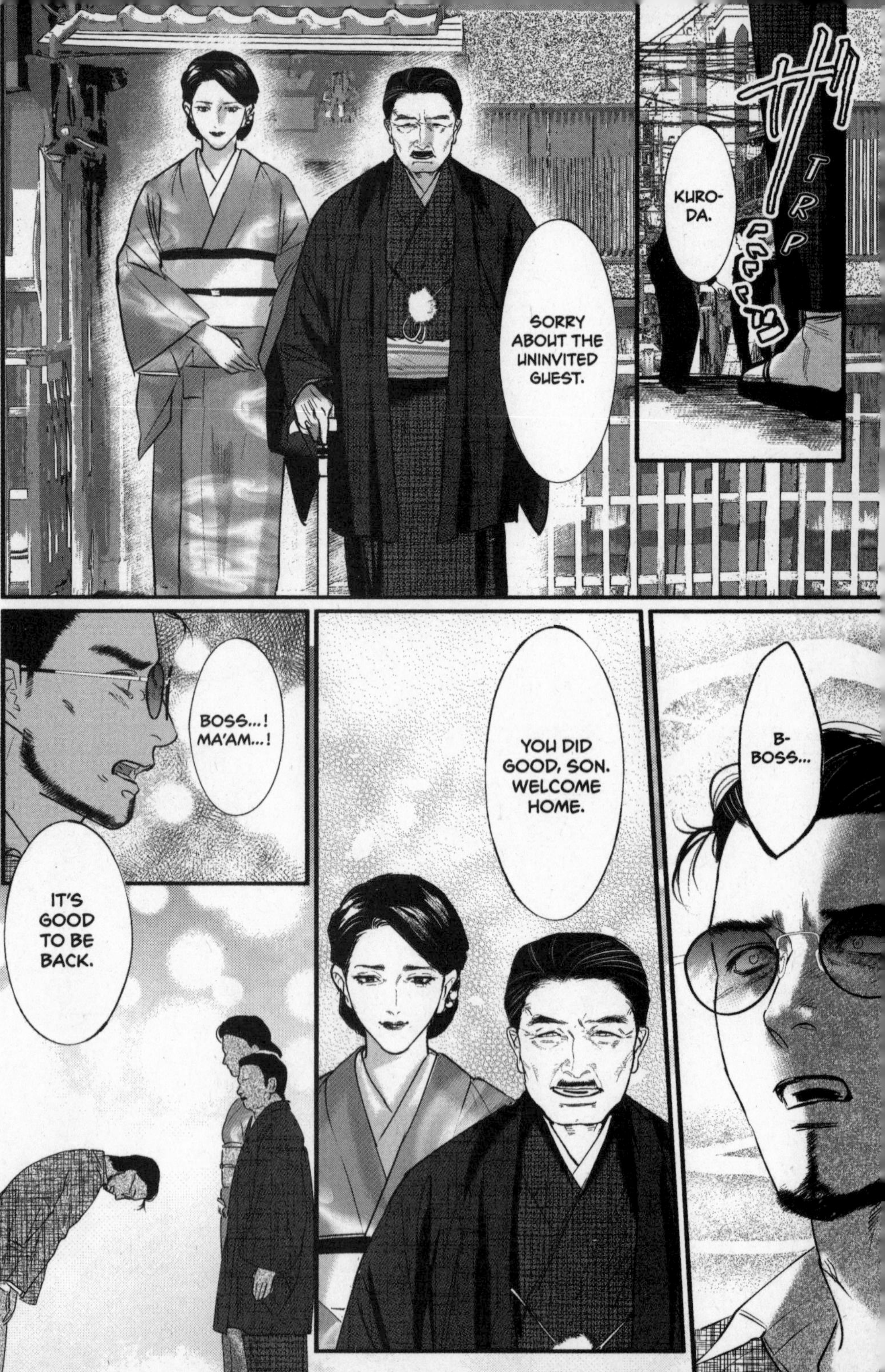
TRP
KURO-DA.
SORRY ABOUT THE UNINVITED GUEST.
B-BOSS...
YOU DID GOOD, SON. WELCOME HOME.
BOSS...! MA'AM...!
IT'S GOOD TO BE BACK.

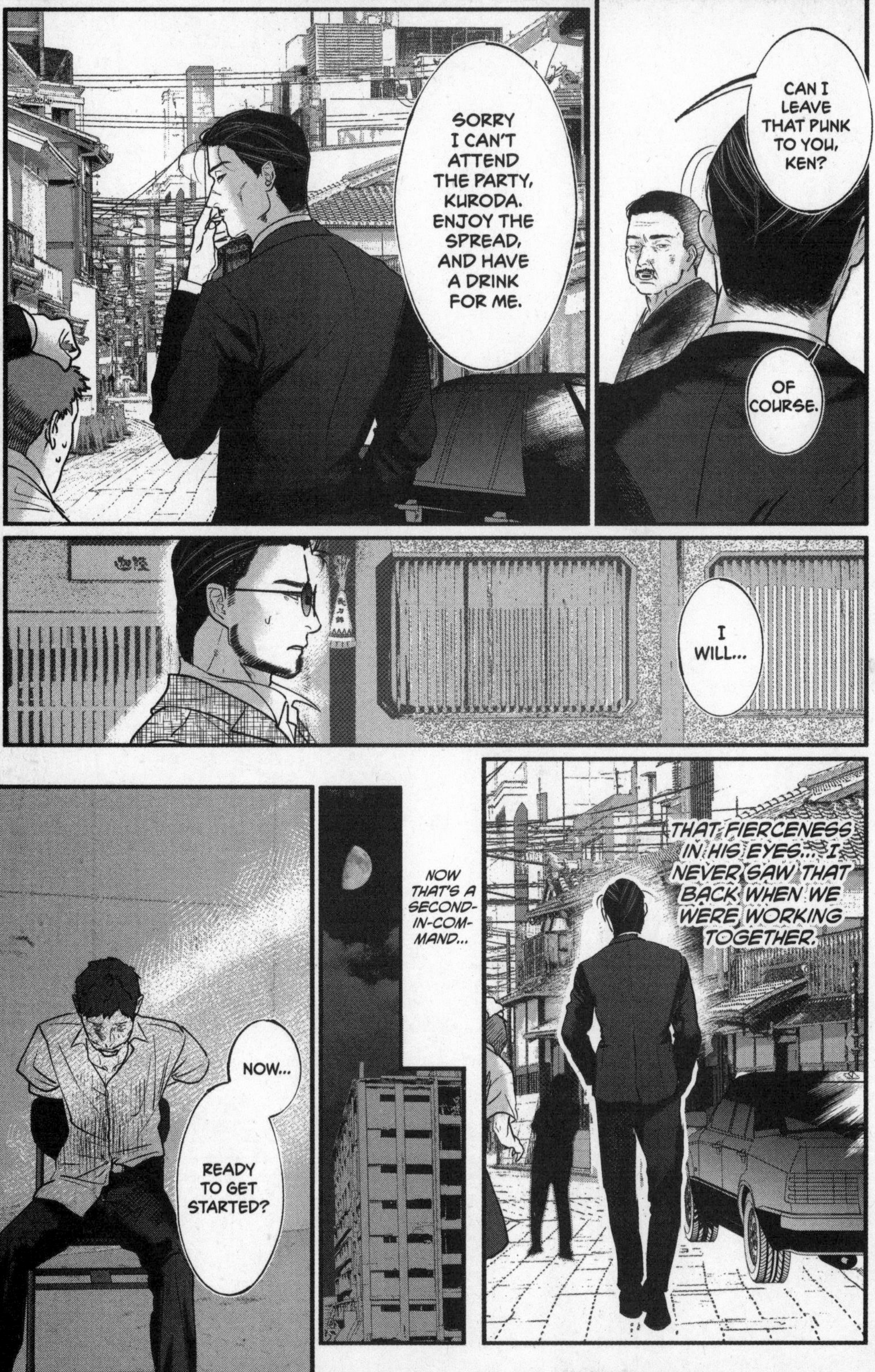
CAN I LEAVE THAT PUNK TO YOU, KEN?
OF COURSE.
SORRY I CAN'T ATTEND THE PARTY, KURODA. ENJOY THE SPREAD, AND HAVE A DRINK FOR ME.
I WILL...
THAT FIERCENESS IN HIS EYES... I NEVER SAW THAT BACK WHEN WE WERE WORKING TOGETHER.
NOW THAT'S A SECOND-IN-COMMAND...
NOW...
READY TO GET STARTED?

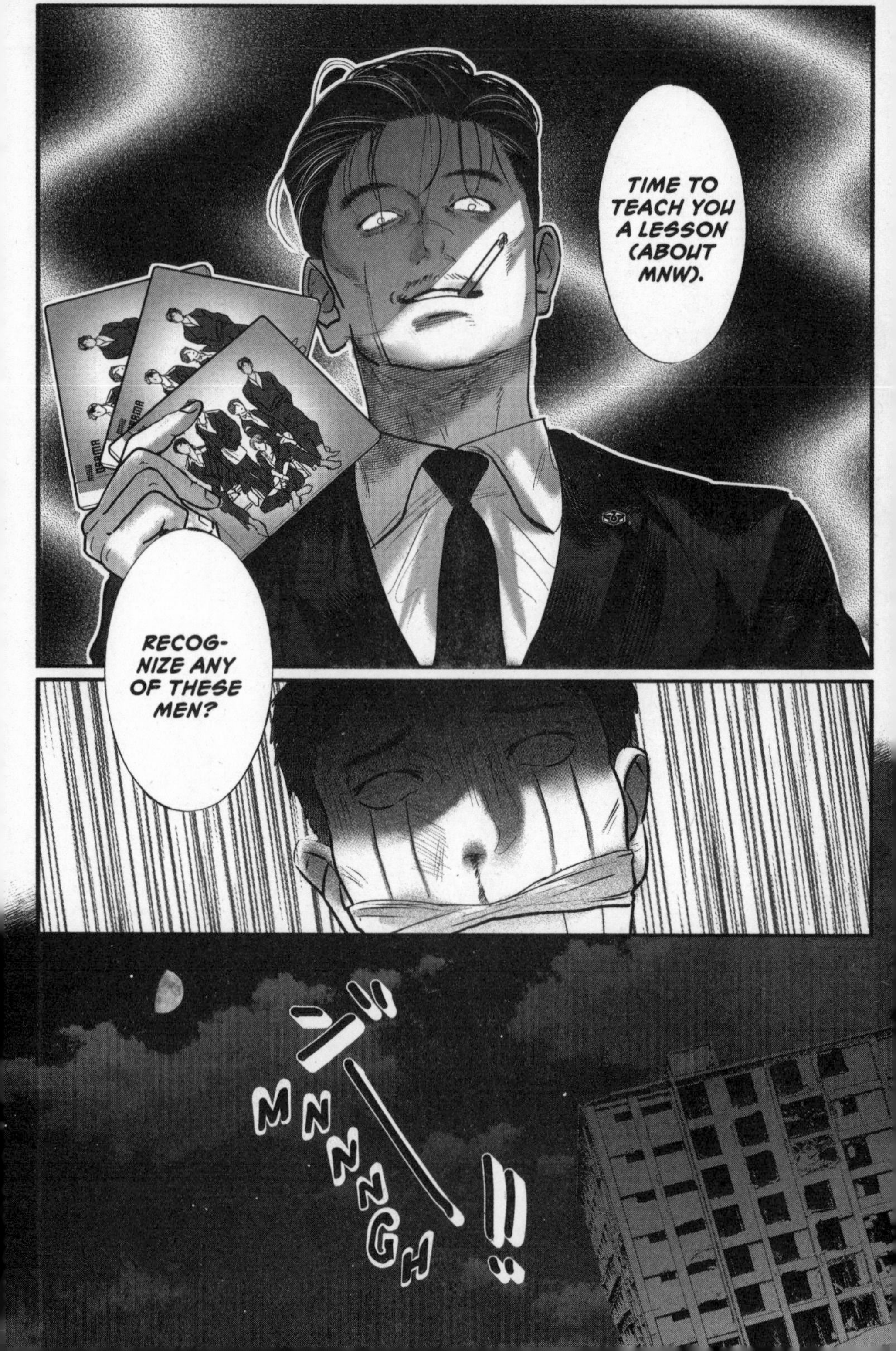
TIME TO TEACH YOU A LESSON (ABOUT MNW).
RECOG-NIZE ANY OF THESE MEN?
MNNNGH!!

Afterword

First-time readers, it's nice to meet you.

I never imagined I'd do a gag manga, but it was a lot of fun to draw, and I enjoyed entrusting Ken and his pals with my own stanning activities.

My sincere gratitude to Suzuki-san, the editor who gave me this opportunity; my friends, who gave me ideas; everyone who supported me; my family; and, of course, everyone who read this.

Thank you all very much.

Teki Yatsuda

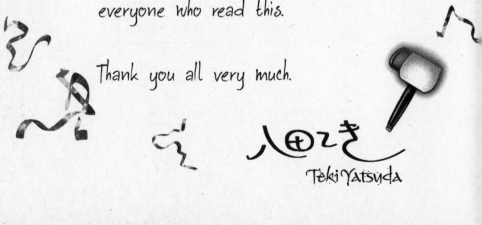

Translation Notes

Be my aniki, page 16

Aniki literally meaning "big brother," has a special meaning in underworld groups (and legit groups organized along similar lines). Your *aniki* is someone you love, respect, and obey; in exchange, they take you under their wing and become both teacher and protector.

Be My Aniki
OKAY! LITTLE HEAVY!

He only ever used to listen to manly, old ballads, page 25

The "manly, old ballads" refererred to are *enka* and *kayokyoku*, which are two old-fashioned genres of pop music strongly associated with the traditional, conservative underworld.

HE ONLY EVER USED TO LISTEN TO MANLY, OLD BALLADS, BUT NOW ALL HE PLAYS IN THE CAR IS THAT WEIRD FANCY POP MUSIC.
UNTZ
(THE DROP)
UNTZ

Odawara Castle, page 43

Odawara Castle, located in Kanagawa Prefecture, was known for its very strong defense throughout the Warring States Period (1467-1600), remaining for five generations under the control of the Odawara Hojo clan, who invested in improving its fortification. However, during the Battle of Odawara in 1590, Toyotomi Hideyoshi, one of the three "Great Unifiers" of Japan, forced the surrender of the Odawara Hojo clan without storming the castle through a combination of a three-month siege and bluff. This reference could be interpreted in many ways, as Megumi alludes to the resilience of hardcore fans in a tense battle.

Fans are always ready for battle!
ALLOW ME TO EXPLAIN!
FANS LOVE TO DRAG REGULAR FOLKS INTO THEIR ARGUMENTS! THE MORE PEOPLE AROUND WHEN THEY'RE PROMOTING THEIR BIASES, THE BETTER!
THE IMPREG-NABLE ODAWARA CASTLE

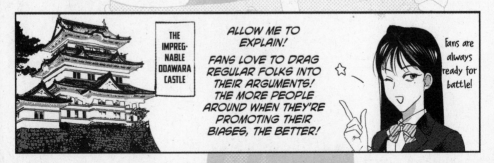

Translation Notes

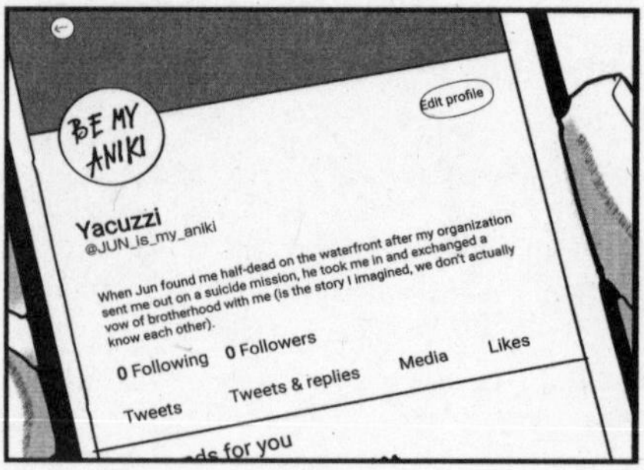
BE MY ANIKI
Edit profile
Yacuzzi
@JUN_is_my_aniki
When Jun found me half-dead on the waterfront after my organization sent me out on a suicide mission, he took me in and exchanged a vow of brotherhood with me (is the story I imagined, we don't actually know each other).
0 Following 0 Followers
Tweets
Tweets & replies
Media
Likes

Yacuzzi, page 54

Ken's Twitter handle, chosen by Megumi, in the original Japanese is *gokudu,* which is a kind of cute version of *gokudo* (alternative word for yakuza). This is a style of *gyaru-moji,* which is a type of Japanese writing popular amongst urban Japanese youth. Yacuzzi was created to continue with a similarly goofy, but yakuza-related, name.

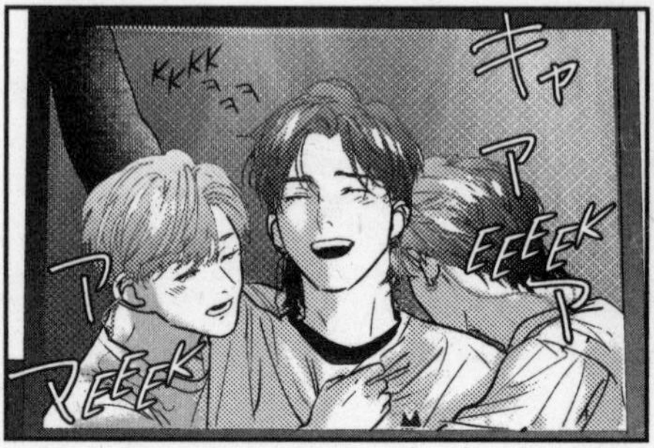
キャア
EEEEK
KKKK
ㅋㅋㅋ
EEEEK

KKKK, page 72

KKKK, sometimes romanized *kekekeke,* is the Korean online equivalent of "hahaha" or "lol." The number of Ks can vary!

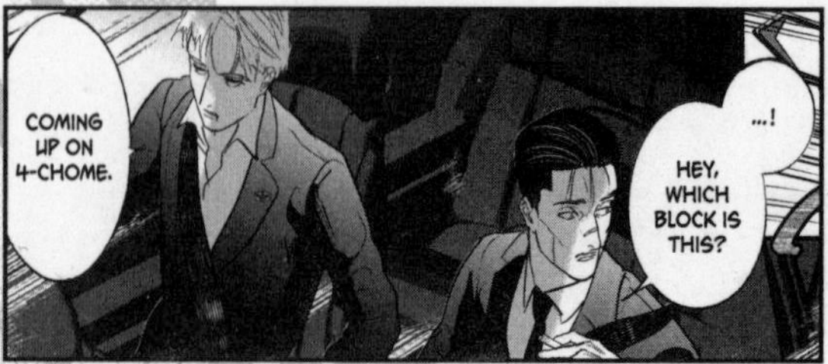
...!
HEY, WHICH BLOCK IS THIS?
COMING UP ON 4-CHOME.

Coming up on 4-chome, page 75

In Japanese cities, addresses are given by block number. In this case, 4-chome literally means "4th block."

Translation Notes

Kabukicho Ichibangai, page 89

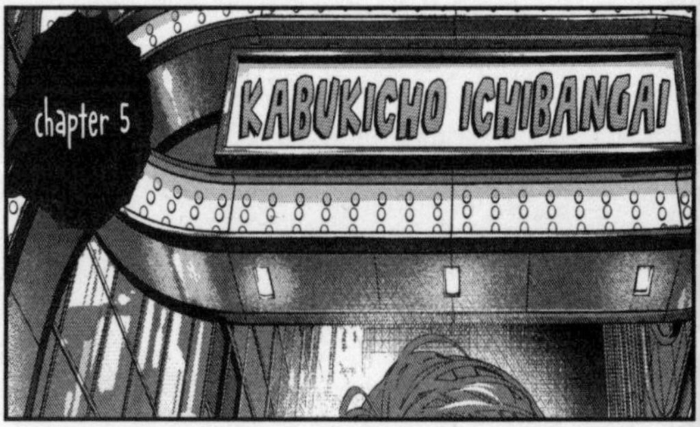
chapter 5
KABUKICHO ICHIBANGAI

Kabukicho is Shinjuku's huge entertainment district, a "town that never sleeps" with everything from movie theaters, restaurants, and bars (including the famous Golden Gai area) to hostess clubs and love hotels. Historically, many of these enterprises have been associated with organized crime . Ichibangai roughly means "Main Street" or "First Avenue," and the big Ichibangai gate (pictured here) is the unofficial "front door" of Kabukicho.

She got him to order a bottle?!, page 95

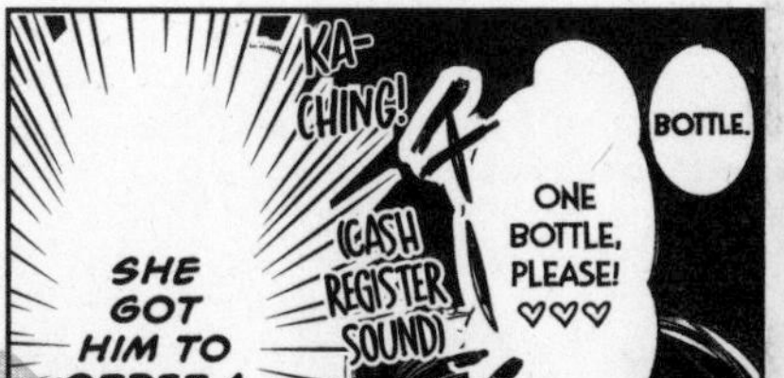
BOTTLE.
ONE BOTTLE, PLEASE! ♡♡♡
KA-CHING!
(CASH REGISTER SOUND)
SHE GOT HIM TO ORDER A BOTTLE?!
ヒェ
YEEEE!

Hostesses usually earn commissions based on how many drinks (and snacks, and so on) they can get patrons to order. Ordering a bottle is more expensive than ordering a glass, so it is often viewed as a "gift" to a favored hostess, even if they don't plan to drink it all. Ordering a bottle of something especially expensive is a correspondingly bigger gift.

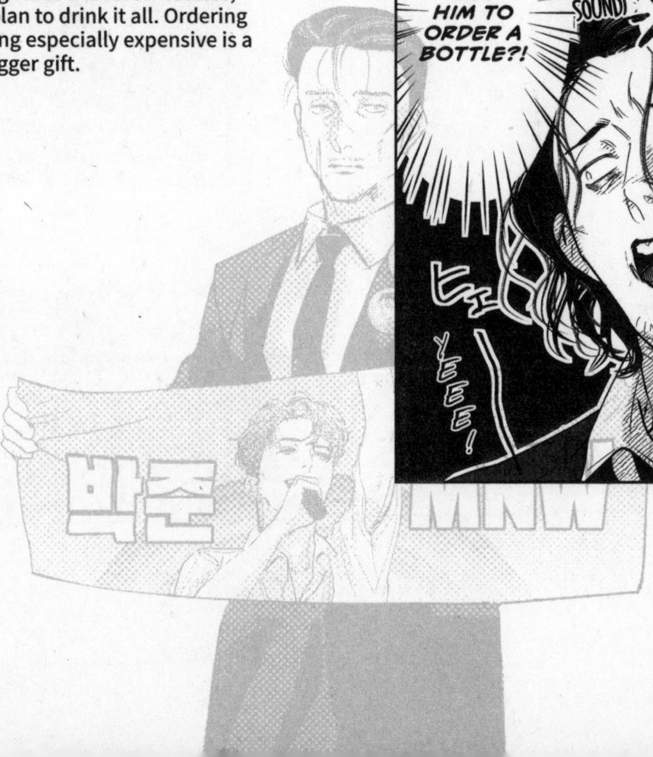
박준
MNW

Translation Notes

nstead of a finger, would you accept a limited-edition Jaeyong photo card?, page 107

Cutting off one of your fingers is a way of showing remorse or accepting responsibility for a bad outcome in yakuza society.

BE MY ANIKI
Yacuzzi
I apologize. Please allow me to make amends. Instead of a finger, would you accept a limited-edition Jaeyong photo card?

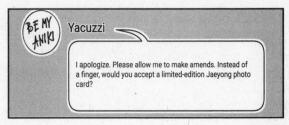

We came by luxury car, page 108

This is a reference to the Japanese meme "We came by bicycle" *(chari de kita),* showing four kids doing tough-guy poses and bragging about their wheels.

MAYBE THIS IS HOW WE BECOME FRIENDS... WE COULD GO TO CONCERTS TOGETHER, GO ON FAN PILGRIMAGES...
高級車で来た。
WE CAME BY LUXURY CAR

Open your eyes, hyung!, page 115

Hyung is a Korean word for "older brother" and can be used both among friends (of different ages) and, as here, in dramatic gangster scenes (not entirely unlike aniki).

OPEN YOUR EYES, HYUNG!
SMAKK
WAAAH! WHAT?!

THE YAKUZA'S Bias

Young characters and steampunk setting, like *Howl's Moving Castle* and *Battle Angel Alita*

Beyond the Clouds © 2018 Nicke / Ki-oon

A boy with a talent for machines and a mysterious girl whose wings he's fixed will take you beyond the clouds! In the tradition of the high-flying, resonant adventure stories of Studio Ghibli comes a gorgeous tale about the longing of young hearts for adventure and friendship!

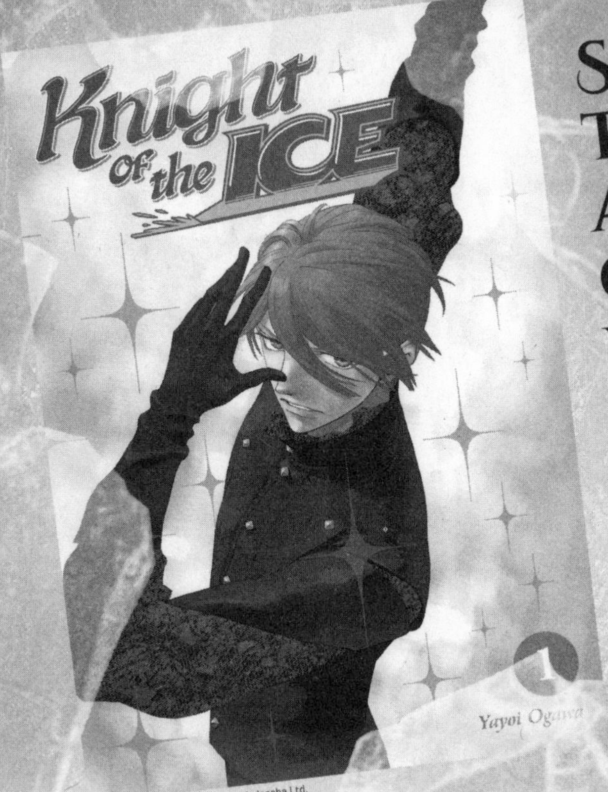
Knight of the ICE
1
Yayoi Ogawa
Knight of the Ice ©Yayoi Ogawa/Kodansha Ltd.

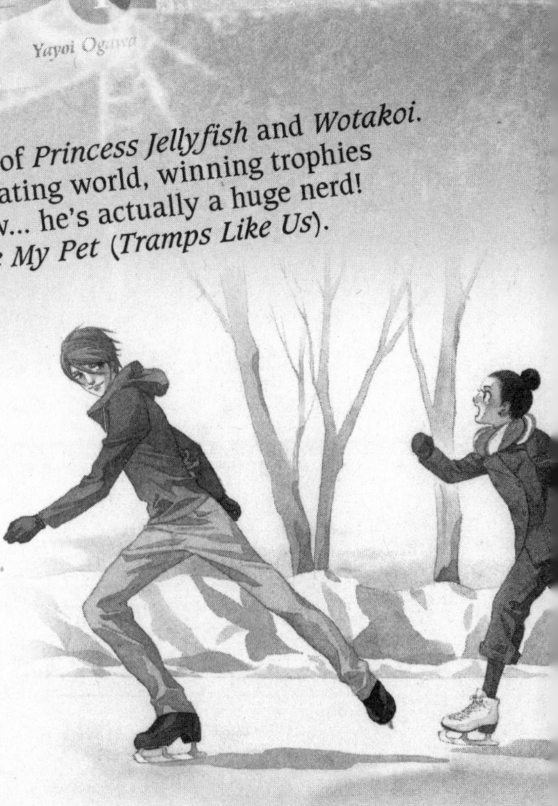

A SMART, NEW ROMANTIC COMEDY FOR FANS OF *SHORTCAKE CAKE* AND *TERRACE HOUSE*!

LIVING ROOM

Keiko Iwashita

MATSUNAGA-SAN

KC
KODANSHA
COMICS

A romance manga starring high school girl Meeko, who learns to live on her own in a boarding house whose living room is home to the odd (but handsome) Matsunaga-san. She begins to adjust to her new life away from her parents, but Meeko soon learns that no matter how far away from home she is, she's still a young girl at heart — especially when she finds herself falling for Matsunaga-san.

PERFECT WORLD

Rie Aruga

A TOUCHING
NEW SERIES
ABOUT LOVE AND
COPING WITH
DISABILITY

An office party reunites Tsugumi with her high school crush Itsuki. He's realized his dream of becoming an architect, but along the way, he experienced a spinal injury that put him in a wheelchair. Now Tsugumi's rekindled feelings will butt up against prejudices she never considered — and Itsuki will have to decide if he's ready to let someone into his heart...

"Depicts with great delicacy and courage the difficulties some with disabilities experience getting involved in romantic relationships... Rie Aruga refuses to romanticize, pushing her heroine to face the reality of disability. She invites her readers to the same tasks of empathy, knowledge and recognition."
—Slate.fr

"An important entry [in manga romance]... The emotional core of both plot and characters indicates thoughtfulness... [Aruga's] research is readily apparent in the text and artwork, making this feel like a real story."
—Anime News Network

KC
KODANSHA
COMICS

Something's Wrong With Us

NATSUMI ANDO

The dark, psychological, sexy shojo series readers have been waiting for!

A spine-chilling and steamy romance between a Japanese sweets maker and the man who framed her mother for murder!

Following in her mother's footsteps, Nao became a traditional Japanese sweets maker, and with unparalleled artistry and a bright attitude, she gets an offer to work at a world-class confectionary company. But when she meets the young, handsome owner, she recognizes his cold stare...

The adorable new odd-couple cat comedy manga from the creator of the beloved *Chi's Sweet Home*, in full color!

Sue & Tai-chan

Konami Kanata

Sue is an aging housecat who's looking forward to living out her life in peace... but her plans change when the mischievous black tomcat Tai-chan enters the picture! Hey! Sue never signed up to be a catsitter! *Sue & Tai-chan* is the latest from the reigning meow-narch of cute kitty comics, Konami Kanata.

KC KODANSHA COMICS

THE SWEET SCENT OF LOVE IS IN THE AIR! FOR FANS OF OFFBEAT ROMANCES LIKE *WOTAKOI*

Sweat and Soap © Kintetsu Yamada / Kodansha Ltd.

In an office romance, there's a fine line between sexy and awkward... and that line is where Asako — a woman who sweats copiously — meets Koutarou — a perfume developer who can't get enough of Asako's, er, scent. Don't miss a romcom manga like no other!

SAINT ☆ YOUNG MEN

A LONG AWAITED ARRIVAL IN PREMIUM 2-IN-1 HARDCOVER

After centuries of hard work, Jesus and Buddha take a break from their heavenly duties to relax among the people of Japan, and their adventures in this lighthearted buddy comedy are sure to bring mirth and merriment to all!

"Brilliant...the physical comedy and facial expressions will make you literally LOL."
—Sam Humphries
(host of *DC Daily*; writer, *Green Lanterns*, *Legendary Star-Lord*)

◄ KAMOME ►
SHIRAHAMA

Witch Hat Atelier

A magical manga
adventure for
fans of Disney
and Studio
Ghibli!

The magical adventure that took Japan by storm is finally here, from acclaimed DC and Marvel cover artist Kamome Shirahama!

In a world where everyone takes wonders like magic spells and dragons for granted, Coco is a girl with a simple dream: She wants to be a witch. But everybody knows magicians are born, not made, and Coco was not born with a gift for magic. Resigned to her un-magical life, Coco is about to give up on her dream to become a witch...until the day she meets Qifrey, a mysterious, traveling magician. After secretly seeing Qifrey perform magic in a way she's never seen before, Coco soon learns what everybody "knows" might not be the truth, and discovers that her magical dream may not be as far away as it may seem...

KC
KODANSHA
COMICS

The beloved characters from *Cardcaptor Sakura* return in a brand new, reimagined fantasy adventure!

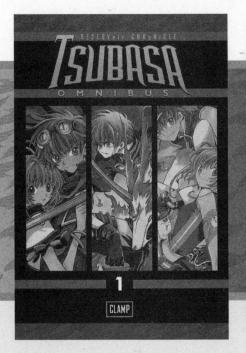

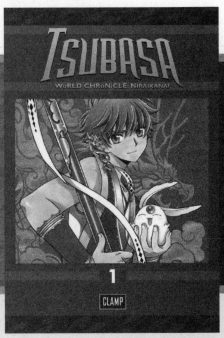

"[*Tsubasa*] takes readers on a fantastic ride that only gets more exhilarating with each successive chapter." —Anime News Network

In the Kingdom of Clow, an archaeological dig unleashes an incredible power, causing Princess Sakura to lose her memories. To save her, her childhood friend Syaoran must follow the orders of the Dimension Witch and travel alongside Kurogane, an unrivaled warrior; Fai, a powerful magician; and Mokona, a curiously strange creature, to retrieve Sakura's dispersed memories!

HKAC

A Kodansha Trade Paperback Original

Published in the United States by
Kodansha USA Publishing, LLC, New York.

Publication rights for this English edition arranged through
Kodansha Ltd., Tokyo.

First published in Japan in 2021 by Ichijinsha Inc., Tokyo as
Yakuza no oshigoto, volume 1.

ISBN 978-1-64651-801-2

Printed in the United States of America.

1st Printing

Translation: Max Greenway
Lettering: Nicole Roderick
Editing: Maggie Le
Kodansha Comics edition cover design by Phil Balsman

Publisher: Kiichiro Sugawara

Director of Publishing Services: Ben Applegate
Director of Publishing Operations: Dave Barrett
Publishing Services Managing Editors: Alanna Ruse, Madison Salters, with Grace Chen
Senior Production Manager: Angela Zurlo

KODANSHA.US

  **KODANSHA**